THE SCIENCE AND SUCCESS OF ENGELMANN'S DIRECT INSTRUCTION

Edited by Jean Stockard

Design and Marketing Editor: Christina Cox

Copy Editor: Tina Wells

Design: Beth Wood Design

Marketing Coordinator: Courtney Burkholder

The Science and Success of Engelmann's Direct Instruction

Edited by Jean Stockard

Copyright © 2014 by NIFDI Press
   A division of the National Institute for Direct Instruction
   805 Lincoln St.
   Eugene, Oregon 97401-2810
   USA

Printed in the United States of America

1 2 3 4 5 6

ISBN 978-1-939851-00-0

CONTENTS

FOREWORD

As a long-time school administrator and follower of what works in efforts to improve schools and raise student achievement, I have been captivated throughout my career by the ingenious creativity, fervent commitment, and ardent compassion for student learning manifested in the work of Siegfried Engelmann. It was nearly 40 years ago, as a beginning graduate student at the University of Oregon, that I met Engelmann and learned firsthand the power of combining logic, science, and vision that he has done throughout his career to empower student learning. Later, as first president of the Association for Direct Instruction and first editor of *The Direct Instruction News*, I had the privilege of working directly with Engelmann on early efforts to spread knowledge of his work to professional audiences on a wide scale. Engelmann has combined his training in philosophy, his research on the design of instruction, his strong belief that all students can learn if taught well, and his relentless commitment to the integrity of the teaching-learning process to enable more students to learn at higher levels. In doing so, he has made an incalculable difference in the lives of many thousands of students and their teachers.

This book captures the extraordinary accomplishments and brilliant career of one of America's most passionate and prolific educators and details the writings and program development constituting his body of work. For more than 50 years, "Ziggy," as he is affectionately called by friends and close colleagues, has been developing effective instructional programs for students at all levels and advocating for their broader use. *The Science and Success of Engelmann's Direct Instruction* provides clear insight into how Direct Instruction programs are developed (Chapter 1) and summarizes the research findings on their effectiveness (Chapter 2). It provides an intriguing account of the politics of educational program adoption and explores the inexplicable wide-scale "non-adoption" of this seemingly compelling approach to improving education (Chapter 3). Chapter 4 lays out the corpus of Engelmann's work, detailing the breadth and depth of his work across nearly five decades. The book also covers how Direct Instruction plays out at a systems level (Chapter 5) and how it has influenced and interacted with the development of a behavioral approach to education (Chapter 6). The final chapter speculates on the future of Direct Instruction (Chapter 7). A set of appendices to the book provides a comprehensive and well-done annotated bibliography of the instructional programs and other professional writings that Engelmann and his colleagues have published in a half century of extraordinary productivity. Also included in the appendices are the complete bibliographic citations of Engelmann's body of written work and a brief but fascinating overview of his career.

The book illustrates the broad scope of Direct Instruction, its wide-ranging applicability, and its extraordinary staying power in the increasingly high-stakes realm of educational accountability. Engelmann and his colleagues have developed programs across the educational curriculum—in beginning and intermediate level reading, in oral and written language, and in beginning and intermediate mathematics. Much of the text for the reading programs covers expository material in science, health, and social studies. Direct Instruction programs have been developed and widely applied for preschool through secondary school levels, and training routines have been developed for adult learners implementing the programs. The work of Engelmann and colleagues has been implemented broadly in compensatory education (Project Head Start, Project Follow Through, and Title I), in regular education (Reading First and other schoolwide implementations) and in special education settings in K–12. Finally, Direct Instruction programs have demonstrated unparalleled staying power, now approaching 50 years of application. The Direct Instruction approach incorporated findings from the 1960s and '70s work in teacher effectiveness and spawned research in educational psychology on teaching and learning from the '70s to the present. Today's wide-scale implementation of the response to intervention (RTI) model reflects the elements of Direct Instruction and illustrates the connectedness, formative influences and tremendous staying power of Engelmann's work across five decades. By any measure of influence, this record is truly extraordinary. It is for this reason that the journal *Remedial and Special Education* named Engelmann one of the 54 most influential people in the history of special education and that the Council of Scientific Society Presidents awarded him the 2002 Award of Achievement in Education Research.

What makes Direct Instruction unique? First, the design of Direct Instruction programs is based on principles of formal logic. Second, the approach is based on scientific research and on evidence-based principles of instructional design—a unique feature among educational instructional programs. Third, the programs are structured for explicit instructional delivery and program implementation to maximize student success and school improvement. Together, these features set Direct Instruction programs apart from all other curricular programs and instructional approaches in the educational marketplace. This is a defining feature of Engelmann's legacy.

But that's not all that's unique. Engelmann, himself, is unique. Now approaching his mid-80s and still as outspoken and vociferous as ever, he continues to go to his office each day—not to drink coffee and tell stories with old cronies—but to continue working passionately and relentlessly to develop the most highly effective instructional programs possible for an elite clientele—our nation's youth—both the underprivileged and under-performing children in our society whom he believes can learn well if only they are taught well–and the typically performing children whom he believes can achieve at higher levels if only they are taught and held to higher standards. This is his cause, and this has been his life. But this is only a glimpse of his story. The rest of the story unfolds in the pages of this book. For explanation, edification, and inspiration, I urge you to read on....

Stan Paine, PhD
National Distinguished Principal
Lead author, *Structuring Your Classroom for Academic Success*
Assistant Director of Administrator Licensure Program, University of Oregon

INTRODUCTION
Jean Stockard

This book is a tribute to the legacy and genius of Siegfried Engelmann and his decades of work in developing the Direct Instruction (DI) curricular programs. For almost a half century Engelmann has shown how all children can learn if they are taught effectively. The instructional programs he has developed reflect the most stringent requirements of the scientific world. They build on sound theoretical understandings of how effective instruction and learning occur, they involve painstaking attention to each detailed step of the instructional process, and they have been validated with rigorous tests of their efficacy. Engelmann's work has transformed the instructional experience of thousands of students and has also led to noted improvements in school behavioral climates and instructional practices. It clearly has the potential to solve the problem of low academic achievement that has plagued our nation for many years.

THE PROBLEM AND ITS SOLUTION

Reams of statistical data document problems with low achievement of students in the United States. For instance, the 2011 results from the National Assessment of Educational Progress (NAEP) showed that only about a third of all fourth graders could be classified as proficient in reading skills. Less than a fifth of African Americans, Hispanics, American Indians or Alaskan Natives reached this level (U.S. Department of Education, 2012a). Similar results appear in other subject areas and in the higher grades. International comparisons show that students in the United States are outperformed by those in many other countries. Even though U.S. expenditures on public education are at or above the international averages, American students' scores on international assessments of achievement are generally below the average of other nations (U.S. Department of Education, 2012b).

Educational achievement is strongly related to eventual educational attainment and many areas of adult well-being, such as occupational status, income, teenage childbearing, drug and alcohol abuse, social and psychological adjustment, and physical health and longevity. Thus, the data on low achievement in the United States translate into painful losses on many fronts. Individual students with lower levels of achievement are likely to have diminished opportunities and rewards throughout their lives. This harms not just them, but also their families and communities. On a national level the losses compound and can be seen in areas as diverse as a less skilled labor force and resultant economic losses to greater costs associated with social, psychological, and health services.

Over the last half century, hundreds, if not thousands, of books have addressed the problems of low academic achievement and failing schools. Just a sampling of titles from each decade illustrates how the concerns have pervaded public and scholarly discourse: *Equality of Educational Opportunity* (Coleman, 1966), *Crisis in the Classroom* (Silverman, 1970), *Illiterate America* (Kozol, 1985), *The Schools We Need and Why We don't Have Them* (Hirsch 1996), *So Much Reform, So Little Change* (Payne, 2008) and *Stop the School Bus: Getting Education Reform Back on Track* (Tirozzi, 2013). Each of these works, in its own way, documents the fact of low levels of achievement, the tremendous cost that it conveys, and the need for change.

Ironically, the answer to the problem has been available throughout virtually all of this time period. Starting in the mid-1960s, Zig Engelmann began his analysis of how children learn and the development of extraordinarily effective ways of teaching them. His work has been guided by two hallmark principles: 1) All children can learn when instruction is systematic, explicit, and efficient; 2) Poor achievement does not result from poor students, but from poor teaching. Working with preschool aged children from highly deprived backgrounds, he demonstrated these principles, teaching them to read and to do complex math problems before they reached traditional kindergarten age. He then expanded this work, developing instructional programs for reading and math, as well as other subjects such as spelling, language, and even music. His programs have targeted students at various age ranges, from preschoolers to adults with learning deficits.

All Direct Instruction programs embody the two guiding principles. The instruction is designed to be explicit, so that there is only one possible interpretation of the material presented. The sequencing of material is systematic, continually building on past learning and reinforcing previously learned material. Regularly scheduled testing ensures that students understand before moving on. As a result, the instruction is efficient, with students able to learn more in a shorter amount of time. The programs provide explicit guidelines for teachers, with clear directions on the wording that should be used to ensure that the material is presented in an explicit and efficient manner and in a way that continually motivates and reinforces students for their learning. All of the programs are developed through careful field testing and analysis.

Decades of research show that Engelmann's DI programs work. Effectiveness has been documented in widely different settings, including urban, rural, and suburban sites and in English speaking countries around the world. The positive results appear with students with different characteristics: middle class high achieving students and high risk students, general education students and special education students, schools with different racial-ethnic compositions, and preschoolers through adults. The positive results appear with different types of assessments, from state test scores to curriculum based measures to norm-referenced tests. They also appear with all types of research designs, from randomized control trials to various quasi-experimental group designs and single subject studies. The vast amount of data supporting the programs' efficacy is very unusual, not just in the field of education but in social science generally. Engelmann has clearly found the answer to low achievement and to the problems of our schools.

In what might be seen as a backhanded compliment, the term "explicit and systematic" instruction has been adopted and advocated by at least some within the educational establishment, including groups such as the National Reading Panel (2000). Instructional programs appear that claim to have these traits, and they are even called "direct instruction," using lower case rather than upper case initial letters. Yet research shows that none of these "little di" programs are as effective as Engelmann's Direct Instruction. It is not one or two characteristics of DI that make it effective, it is the totality of the approach – and especially the scientific nature of its development – that makes it effective. None of the little di programs use this systematic, scientific approach to development.

For almost 50 years the educational establishment has ignored the evidence of DI's effectiveness. In fact, this establishment has often actively worked to hide reports of DI's success from the public and policy makers. As a result, the promise and potential of Direct Instruction has still not been fulfilled.

Yet, despite this resistance from the mainstream educational establishment, Direct Instruction remains strong. It continues to be used by teachers and schools throughout the United States and other countries, helping many students achieve their full capacity. Research documenting its effectiveness continues to mount. More amazingly, Engelmann, the genius behind the developments, has continued to work into his 80s – to develop instructional programs, to help teachers teach and to guarantee that all students can learn.

THE CHAPTERS THAT FOLLOW

This book is a tribute to the success of Direct Instruction and, especially, to the genius and the resilience of Zig Engelmann. The first part of the book documents the extensive research embodied in the development of DI programs, the research that confirms their effectiveness, the unfavorable and short-sighted reactions of the education establishment to the work, and Engelmann's resilience and strength in continuing to develop programs, write essays and books, and promote learning and effective instruction for all students. The second part of the book examines the legacy of his work, including the guidance it gives for transforming schools to effective learning centers for all children and the ways in which it has influenced the tradition of behavioral management in schools, helping them to be safe for all children and places in which students can see themselves as competent and successful learners. The book ends with a look at the future, the potential for wider acceptance of Engelmann's developments, and the hope for truly solving the problems of achievement in America's schools.

The Scientific Basis of Direct Instruction

The first part of the book is titled "The Scientific Basis of Direct Instruction" and includes four chapters. In Chapter 1, "Research from the Inside," Engelmann describes how DI programs are developed and tested using extensive examples from his work. He notes how the development process involves logical analyses of subject matter, then testing ways to teach the material, and then revising and retesting. Taken as a whole, the process illustrates, in almost a classical manner, an inductive approach to research. Engelmann contrasts his method of curricular development with that used in less scientific approaches to the area. It is clear why these other approaches are less successful.

Chapter 2 is authored by Cristy Coughlin, who has conducted extensive reviews of the literature regarding the efficacy of Direct Instruction programs. She summarizes research findings on the effectiveness of DI, using numerous meta-analyses and literature reviews as the basis of the analysis. Unlike the inductive approach used in the development of programs, the efficacy studies use deductive reasoning, comparing the effectiveness of DI to that of other programs. All of the summary studies that Coughlin found document that Direct Instruction is more effective than other approaches.

Given the careful development of the programs documented in Chapter 1 and the strong evidence of their effectiveness discussed in Chapter 2, the failure of the educational establishment to fully embrace Direct Instruction is, at the least, baffling. The third chapter of this volume, written by Engelmann and Stockard and titled "Blinded to Evidence: How Educational Researchers Respond to Empirical Data," addresses this issue. Using insights from their individual experiences and scholarly traditions, the authors critically examine the response of the educational research community to empirical research such as that reviewed by Coughlin in Chapter 2. They contrast the educational establishment's actions to the traditional and widely accepted norms of scientific research and conclude that there is no rational or normative basis for their failure to endorse Direct Instruction.

The first part of the book ends with a chapter authored by Timothy Wood. In his chapter, "The Engelmann Corpus of Writings," Wood uses a thematic and historical approach to analyze Engelmann's writings from the mid-1960s to the mid-2010s. He explores Engelmann's writings related to theories of learning and instruction, curriculum development, educational reform and change, and criticisms of Direct Instruction and political roadblocks. The chapter bolsters others in this section by reinforcing understandings of the scientific basis of Engelmann's writings. It also shows the resilience and strength of Engelmann and his work, the continuities over time and, especially, the way in which he has persevered despite the "blindness" of the educational establishment.

Translating the Science to Schools

The second part of this book, "Translating the Science to Schools," examines the ways in which Direct Instruction has affected and transformed schools. Chapter 5, "Creating Successful Schools with Direct Instruction," is written by Kurt Engelmann. In this chapter K. Engelmann describes key elements of successful DI implementations, including a description of underlying principles, the ways in which these principles govern the actions of teachers and administrators, and challenges that can impede the success of DI implementations.

One of the long-lasting legacies of Siegfried Engelmann's work is the tradition of behavioral management and applied behavior analysis. In Chapter 6, "Direct Instruction and Behavior Support in Schools," Caitlin Rasplica examines the linkages of Direct Instruction and behavioral work within education. Taking a historical view she describes intersections in the developments of the fields and parallels in their specific designs. She shows how effective contemporary approaches to behavioral management for individual students, classrooms, and schools build on the insights and principles that are embodied in Engelmann's Direct Instruction programs as well as his analyses of effective instruction.

In the last chapter, "Debating DI's Future," Shepard Barbash examines the prospects for DI's survival and growth in a changing marketplace. Will teaching become a profession that is guided by scientific evidence? If so, then more and more teachers will use Direct Instruction. If not, then DI will remain unpopular and might even die out. Barbash makes the case for optimism and pessimism to show that both fates are possible. He argues that the best way to promote DI is to give everyone an honest report card on how schools are performing, hold educators accountable for their performance, and promote more competition among schools for students.

Engelmann's Writings: Bibliographies and Annotations

The book includes three appendices, all authored by Wood. They document Engelmann's extensive bibliographic record from his first published writings in the mid-1960s through the mid-2010s. Appendix A lists all the instructional programs that Engelmann has developed and includes a historical overview of the curriculum. Appendix B has a complete annotated bibliography of Engelmann's other writings, documenting the expansive content that is described in Chapter 4. Appendix C summarizes Engelmann's career by listing highlights of his work from the 1950s to the 2010s.

A LONG-TERM LEGACY

The authors of the chapters in this book represent multiple generations and multiple disciplines, bringing a variety of perspectives to their analyses of Engelmann's career and impact. As described more fully in their biographical sketches, none of the authors had undergraduate training in schools of education. Their educational backgrounds span the social sciences and humanities, from philosophy and history to psychology, geography and sociology. Some of the authors are in the first decade of their professional lives, some are mid-career, and others are Professors Emeriti. This diversity produces optimism regarding the future of Direct Instruction. Not only do those from a variety of backgrounds understand its importance to the society, this understanding goes beyond the generation that was involved with Direct Instruction's beginnings and extends to those who will be involved in the future.

This book is a tribute to the career of Siegfried Engelmann and the many ways in which the scientific basis of his work has impacted schools and students throughout the world. As documented in Chapter 4 and in the appendices, Engelmann has continued into his 80s to develop new programs and to write new articles, books, chapters, and blog entries on his website, Zigsite.com. Like geniuses from other disciplines, his work will no doubt continue to inspire and help others through generations to come. This volume should be seen as a celebration of all that Engelmann has accomplished to date, all that will appear in the coming years, and the impact of his work on future generations.

REFERENCES

Coleman, J.S. (1966). *Equality of educational opportunity.* Washington, DC: U.S. Department of Health, Education and Welfare. Office of Education.

Hirsch, E.D., Jr. (1996). *The schools we need and why we don't have them.* New York: Doubleday.

Kozol, J. (1985). *Illiterate America.* New York: Anchor Press.

National Reading Panel (2000). *Teaching children to read: An evidence-based assessment of the scientific research literature on reading and its implications for reading instruction* (NIH Publication No. 00-4769). Washington, D.C.: National Institutes of Health.

Payne, C.M. (2008). *So much reform, so little change: The persistence of failure in urban schools.* Cambridge: Harvard University Press.

Silberman, C.E. (1970). *Crisis in the classroom: The remaking of American education.* New York: Vintage Books.

Tirozzi, G.N. (2013). *Stop the school bus: Getting education reform back on track.* San Francisco: Jossey-Bass.

U.S. Department of Education (2012a). *National Center for Education Statistics: National assessment of educational progress reading assessments.* Washington, DC: Department of Education. (http://nces.ed.gov/nationsreportcard/naepdata/).

U.S. Department of Education (2012b). *Digest of education statistics.* Washington, DC: Department of Education. http://nces.ed.gov/programs/digest/d12/tables/dt12_143.asp.

PART I

THE SCIENTIFIC BASIS OF DIRECT INSTRUCTION

CHAPTER 1

Direct Instruction programs are generally described as "research based" and "extensively field tested." But it may be hard, from simply looking at the completed product, to see how this developmental research occurs. In this chapter Engelmann describes the research process used in program development. Using examples from various programs he shows the logical steps employed and describes how field tests are conducted. He also compares his methods to those used by others, clearly illustrating the importance of being research based in producing effective instructional materials.

RESEARCH FROM THE INSIDE
THE DEVELOPMENT AND TESTING OF DI PROGRAMS
Siegfried Engelmann

This chapter addresses the relationship between Direct Instruction program development and testing. Three characteristics of the testing process are discussed in detail: the qualitative nature of the work; the important role of theory and logic; and the extensive application of inductive reasoning, both for shaping and testing details of the programs. I begin with a brief history of the development of the programs and their scope.

SCOPE OF DIRECT INSTRUCTION PROGRAMS

Direct Instruction programs were created in response to inadequacies of available programs for teaching specific skills and content. The first Direct Instruction efforts were with disadvantaged preschool children in the Bereiter-Engelmann preschool, a laboratory school operated at the University of Illinois in the 1960s. The project's goal was to accelerate the intellectual development of these children in all "school-related" areas. Initially we tried several reading and math programs that were unsuccessful. We also observed that the children were deficient in language skills, but there was no language program that addressed the specific skills and content that needed work.

In response to these problems, we developed DISTAR programs (an acronym for Direct Instruction System for Teaching and Remediation), which were published by SRA. Initially, in the late 1960s, there were levels 1 and 2 of *DISTAR Reading* (1969), *DISTAR Language*, and *DISTAR Arithmetic*. (The titles, authors, and years of publication of all of the DI programs are given in Appendix A.)

In the next decades, these programs were revised, expanded into six-grade series, and given new names: *Reading Mastery* and *Connecting Math Concepts*. Two other DI series followed in the 1980s—*Reasoning and Writing* and *Spelling Mastery*. Several videodisc programs for math and science were published in the late 1980s. These included a series on *Chemistry and Energy*, another on *Elementary Earth Science* (1988), and several on math and algebra.

In addition to these series, there were programs for poor readers in Grades 4–12 (and adults)—*Corrective Reading Decoding* and *Corrective Reading Comprehension*. Both series have three levels. Other programs for high school students were designed to prepare them for exit tests—*Essentials for Algebra* and *Essentials for Writing*.

Most DI programs have been published by SRA. The videodisc programs, however, were produced by Systems Impact in the 1980s. Starting in the mid-1960s, DI programs for homeschoolers were published. The first three, published by Simon and Schuster, were *Give Your Child a Superior Mind* (1966), *Your Child Can Succeed! How to Get the Most Out of School for Your Child* (1975), and, in 1983, *Teach Your Child to Read in 100 Easy Lessons* (an abbreviated version of the first two levels of *Reading Mastery*). Computer-based programs, *Funnix Beginning Reading* and *Funnix Beginning Math*, are designed for parents, tutors, or teachers. A pair of print DI programs published by Sopris in 2010 are designed for teaching English to non-English speakers—*Direct Instruction Spoken English 1 and 2*.

LOGIC OF SCIENTIFIC PROGRAM DEVELOPMENT

All the DI programs were developed the same way, which is quite different from that of other developers. The development procedure incorporates logic and strategies for testing programs before they are published. The scheme incorporates procedures for obtaining empirical data on how students perform on the program being developed. A variation of the same scheme serves as a template for designing formal studies that focus on the technical details of program design. These studies have a character far different from studies that meet "gold standard" criteria, the currently popular term used to describe experiments that compare the effectiveness of different programs. (See Chapter 3 for additional discussion of this so-called gold standard in educational research.)

Qualitative Focus

Much of the salient information used in developing DI programs is qualitative, in contrast with "formal" research, which is quantitative. The most fundamental DI issues address what students don't know and what they learn. The documentation involves testing. The results of the tests serve as guideposts for either more testing or for teaching and then testing. Note, however, that the primary concern is with the qualitative implications the "trials" yield. We use numbers to determine whether we discovered something students don't know. We have some form of an operating rule that indicates, "If more than ___ students in this classroom fail the test, the content is something students do not know."

Beyond serving as an alert to problems, the numbers play a limited role. The primary focus is on three inferences:

• What don't students understand?

• What possibly broader misconceptions or lack of knowledge are implied?

• What efficient remedies are implied for both the narrowly conceived problem and broader misconceptions students have?

The procedures that are relevant to these issues identify what to teach and how to teach it. For example, working with very poor readers in middle school, we noted a trend in the mistakes they made. They made more frequent mistakes in reading beginning-reading words when the words appeared in connected text than when they occurred in lists of unrelated words. For example, students made more mistakes on these words in stories than in lists (*some, they, the, can, of, for*). We also noted that the mistakes were most frequently syntactically correct. For example, a student reads, "She walked *on* the street" instead of "*in* the street." We inferred a broader strategy that probably accounted for this tendency: Poor readers guess when they read "stories" or paragraphs. They tend not to guess as much when they read the same words presented as random words (in lists).

This conclusion seems obvious, but it doesn't suggest a specific mandate for what to teach. In other words: How could we use this information to provide better instruction?

The answer is limited by what we know about learning trends. A relevant fact is that the most effective way to change strong habitual behavior is to increase the rate at which students produce the new behavior. Note, however, that it takes hundreds of trials to change habitual responses. If students have used a guessing strategy since Grade 1, we would expect a gradual learning, not a sudden "aha" and a change of behavior. Furthermore, we don't have to speculate about how much practice is ultimately needed. We will be able to use student responses to our remedy as the guide for the amount of practice we need to provide.

Creating a Remedy

Before we test the remedy, we have to create it, and the central question at this point is simply, "How do we fix this problem?" There are different possible solutions. The one we used involved putting *random words in a story format*. We reasoned that this exposure would compel the learner to more closely associate the words that are read in lists with the words that occur in stories. This juxtaposition would make the point that these are the same words whether they occur randomly or in the context of syntactical constraints.

The specific story line that we used to achieve this melding of word types involved a talking dog named Chee. When Chee became frustrated, she spoke in unrelated words that the poor readers often confused. For example: "Chee got very mad and said, 'Of go for there to where who …'."

Students made frequent mistakes when they initially read Chee's responses. They often had to read the quote several times before getting it correct, and they showed physical signs of frustration. Their rate and accuracy in reading Chee utterances was far inferior to their performance in reading the same words in lists, but after reading the first Chee story, their rate-accuracy performance improved. The remedy was effective because it caused the students to be prepared to read random words as well as what they considered to be predictable words.

There is an indefinitely large number of possible ways to create specific instruction in response to any particular directive of the type "Teach _____." The information about guessing could generate hundreds of different concrete "teachings" that analytically address the issue. Some would be good, others impractical, and many poor. One good possibility is not to make up special stories but simply to show commonly confused words underlined in stories. Before reading a story, the teacher directs students to touch the underlined words and read them. When they read the story they make fewer mistakes on the underlined words, even though they are in a story context.

This solution may be as effective as the one we used. It addresses the problem and provides an uncomplicated and effective solution that can be applied to any story. We preferred the Chee approach because the responses start out the same as many other responses students make when reading stories: "She said, '…'…" and the targeted words are not signaled by underlining.

The point is that we don't predetermine everything we will teach and we don't use formal "research" procedures to compare alternatives. When developing programs, we address questions about two possible teaching solutions simply by judging which alternative we think will work best. However, if the exercises we design for teaching a specific discrimination or skill are not effective (as determined by observations of student responses), we change the instruction. Because we have data on students who have gone through the sequence we designed, we now have more information about what students don't know and what they confuse, so we are in a position to create a more refined solution. If the Chee stories hadn't worked, we would have tried something else, and the alternative would have been shaped by the specific mistakes students made.

In summary, the development of instruction involves some form of empirical "research," which has a strong emphasis on qualitative detail generated around issues of what students don't understand. The implication of the problem of misreading common words is the broad imperative: *Do something to reduce the errors on commonly used words in stories.* Our job is to transform that imperative into exercises that efficiently achieve the goal.

Needed Background Information

A version of this general directive (to reduce predictable errors) applies to everything learners don't know but "should" know. For instance, if learners don't know where to put periods in things they write, the general imperative is *Teach the learner where to put periods.* There is a complication, however, which is answered by the question, "What do students need to know before they can benefit from the remedy?"

Questions about what and how much to teach before introducing related teaching are governed by logic. If it is not possible to understand B without understanding A, and if students don't know either B or A, some form of A must be taught before B is taught. There is great latitude in how much is taught now and how much is taught later. So if students don't know what sentences are and therefore where to put periods, teaching students sentences would be logically prior to teaching how to punctuate them. If they are reliable in identifying declarative sentences, the rule for periods is simple: Put periods at the end of sentences.

The issue of how much to teach about sentences before teaching periods is not clearly implied by logic, which means 10 variations of what is taught could be effective. Any effective approach, however, must teach at least the minimum that students will need when they put periods at the end of the sentences. One simple way to determine what the *minimum* pre-teaching is would be to make up the items you plan to ask about periods and identify the minimum teaching needed to prepare students for those tasks.

Let's say you plan to present paragraphs with no periods and to present these tasks:

YOU ASK:	STUDENTS RESPOND:
Say the next group of words that are a sentence.	*She started to go home.*
What's the last word in the sentence?	*Home.*
So what do you write after the word **home**?	*A period.*

If students respond correctly to five or more tasks like the one above, they should be ready to put periods in sentences like the ones they practiced.

ANALYTIC INDUCTION

The logic that we use in developing programs is probably best described as *analytic induction*. In ideal (but not realistic) terms, we attempt to design programs that are consistent with a universal outcome: All properly prepared students who are taught will learn what they are taught.

Universal Predictions Are Refuted by an N of 1

Logically, if one properly prepared student goes through a well-designed sequence but doesn't learn what the sequence teaches, the universal prediction that all properly prepared students will learn is contradicted. There are two ways to resolve the discrepancy between expectation and outcome—change the sequence so it accommodates students like the one who failed or modify the assumed universal expectation to exclude students like the one who failed.

In actual practice, we wouldn't change the program in response to one student's failure. If a few students in a tryout fail to learn something, we examine their responses to determine if we can identify a common basis for the failure. In other words, we try to find a flaw in the program that accounts for this failure. We change the script, the examples, or whatever is logically required to correct the deficiency in the program.

Analytic induction was introduced to sociology by Znaniecki in the 1930s (Znaniecki, 1934) and was later energized in the 1950s by W. S. Robinson (1951). Analytic induction rejects *correlations* as a means of supporting hypotheses because correlations are probabilistic and, by definition, weak. Correlations state simply, "If C, then R" (if condition, then result within specific ranges of certainty). Analytic induction requires a far more robust relationship: "If *and only if* C, then R." This means that C doesn't cause outcomes other than the one hypothesized, and R is never observed as the effect of any cause but C.

Part of the difference between the logic of analytic induction and the current "gold standard" designs has to do with the minimum number of subjects needed to disprove a relationship (beyond that expressed by the null hypothesis). If the goal of the experiment is to *disprove* a universal statement, logically one subject is sufficient to contradict the universality of the statement. In other words, if one subject went through a program that violated what was deemed to be universally necessary to induce learning, and if that subject learned a targeted skill or concept, the "universal" statement would be categorically discredited and would have to be modified.

Statistically, more than one subject may be needed to buttress against the possibility that the outcome occurred by chance. A statistical requirement might be that performance of at least half of the subjects must contradict the outcome predicted by the universal assertion. If populations meet this standard, they provide prima facie evidence not only that the universal requirement is contradicted, but that the manner in which it is contradicted is probably at least as lawful as the universal assertion.

Refuting Piaget's Universal Assertions

I have conducted some formal research based on these assumptions of analytic induction. Several studies challenged Piaget's notion of development. I focused on Piaget because his developmental assumptions are part of current educational literacy, but his assumptions stand in strong opposition to the goal of making instruction scientific. For instance, his notion that students must first manipulate to gain understanding is accepted as truth by many, and manipulative activities for fifth graders are required by the Common Core State Standards (CCSS, 2012).

In the 1960s and 1970s, I conducted several studies in which children learned concepts like conservation of liquid amount through training that didn't provide any manipulating or even demonstrations of transferring contents of one glass to another (Engelmann, 1967). The fact that a large percentage of these children learned "conservation" skills provided overwhelming evidence that refuted Piaget's (1964) notion of what is essential for children to learn about conservation of liquid amounts.

In another study I provided training that violated conditions Piaget indicated were essential for children to learn concrete and formal operations. I believe that this study is important even though it involved only four students and no statistical scoring; but it indisputably contradicted Piaget's central assumptions about the relationship between learning and development. The test in the study involved conservation of volume, weight, speed, and specific gravity, using Piagetian tests administered by a Piagetian tester. The test of specific gravity with steel balls in water was augmented with a test of whether the balls would float in mercury. The four subjects were exactly six years old.

The instruction was explicitly designed to violate three of Piaget's central principles:

- Learning is subordinated to development and not vice versa.

- Logical structure cannot be obtained by external reinforcement.

- Logical structure is reached only through equilibration, by self regulation.

Part of Piaget's logical structure has to do with the order of learning. Conservation of volume (liquid amount) occurs first and the understanding of specific gravity occurs last (around the age of 14). So if a student passed the test of specific gravity but failed the test of conservation of volume, Piaget's assumptions about order of learning would be soundly contradicted.

The instruction lasted a total of three hours, provided for no equilibration, no manipulations, and no concrete instances of water transfer, weight change, or anything more concrete than rules. For example, children learned that if something floats in a medium, it is lighter than a piece of the medium the same size as the object. They applied the rule to verbal examples, not physical examples.

If an object floats in water, which is heavier, the object or a piece of medium the same size as the object?

The results were reported qualitatively. All four students passed the test of specific gravity with steel balls in water and in mercury. All passed the test of predicting what a whole candle and part of the candle would do in water. Children had learned the rule that if part of an object floats, the whole object floats. During the test one child first said that the candle would sink, but later when the tester was cutting the candle into two parts, she predicted that it would float. When asked why she changed her mind, the child pointed to a flake floating in the water and observed that when the tester was cutting the candle into two parts, that flake flew off. It was floating so the whole candle would float and both parts of it would float.

The children's performance clearly discredited Piaget's universal assertions because there was no subordination of what the children learned to development. The logical structure that permitted them to learn specific gravity was induced by external reinforcement, not through equilibration. The fact that some of the children failed tests of conservation, while passing tests involving specific gravity, further showed that the order of what is learned varies as a function of instruction. The fact that all these developmental aberrations were caused by three hours of instruction means that whatever Piaget has to say about development has limited implications for instruction.

The results of the experiment were not noted in any way by educators. Part of the reason is that educators don't understand the implications of analytic induction or the logic of universal statements. The field uses hundreds of half-truths in the form of universal assertions that have never been shaped by experimental demonstrations that challenge these assertions. Yet, all legitimate sciences have been shaped by demonstrations that refute universal assertions.

In education the current lore is that effective beginning-reading programs teach phonemic awareness, phonics, fluency, comprehension, and vocabulary (National Reading Panel, 2000). I could write a program that had provisions for all these categories and could guarantee that not one out of three students would learn to read well. The reason is simply that these categories are "true" only in the correlational sense, which means that they play a reasonable role in describing the big picture but cannot serve as criteria for developing effective instruction. Certainly the beginning-reading programs we develop have instruction in all these categories. In fact, the categories were identified through an analysis of DISTAR and presented in *Becoming a Nation of Readers* (Anderson, Hiebert, Scott, & Wilkinson, 1985). *These broad universal assertions, however, are inadequate to serve as guidelines for developing effective instruction.* Using the logic of analytic induction would reveal the technical provisions that would have to be made explicit before the assertions would be truly universal.

Contradicting "Norms" in Math

The instruction provided by the Bereiter-Engelmann preschool from 1964–1970 provided many demonstrations of disadvantaged preschoolers learning content and skills that went considerably beyond the range of what would be predicted by any developmental norms. For example, in math, the highest group of disadvantaged blacks who went through the program as 4- and 5-year-olds in 1964–1966 could perform the following operations:

- Count by ones, twos, threes, fours, fives, and tens.

- Work problems involving addition and subtraction with the unknowns in different positions: $3 + N = 8$, $3 + 8 = N$, $N + 3 = 5$, $9 - 5 = N$, $N - 2 = 7$, $12 - N = 5$.

- Work multiplication problems that had the unknown in different positions: $4 \times J = 28$, $7 \times 10 = T$. Note that some problems are solved by multiplying by the reciprocal of a fractional value.

- Work division problems: $20 \div 5$.

- Work fractions as division problems: $30/5 =$

- Solve problems in which the equal sign follows the first number: $N = 9 + 4$, $J = 9 - 4$.

- Work simple unit-analysis problems:

   R + T = J

   T =

   J =

   R =

The analysis used was based on two rules:

1. If you add, you end up with the big number. (The term that is alone on one side of the equal sign is the term you end up with.)

2. If you subtract, you start out with the big number.

- Children worked multiplication problems such as: $1/3 \times J = 4$ by multiplying by the reciprocal of the fractional value (3).

- They worked a variety of simple word problems with the unknown in different places:

   A girl wants to buy a cookie. The grocer tells her that 4 cookies cost 24 cents.

To work the problem, children specified the equation $4C = 24$, then worked it. (They understood that $4C = 4 \times C$.)

- They worked area problems, both those that gave the length of two sides, and those that specified one side and the total number of squares.

- They worked column-addition problems that involve carrying.

- Children identified fractions that were more than 1, equal to 1, and less than 1. They also identified fractions that equal whole numbers other than 1.

- Children worked division problems and understood that any fraction could be read as a division problem.

- Children could solve simple simultaneous equations and read and write various signs, including the dollar sign.

- The culmination of what they learned (see Box 1.1) was factoring expressions such as (4A + 12B + 2C) and arriving at the final equation: 2 (2A + 6B + 1C).

Box 1.1 How the Preschoolers Arrived at the Final Equation: 2 (2A + 6B + 1C)

The Bereiter-Engelmann preschoolers factored the following expression: (4A + 12B + 2C). Here is how they did it:

- Children would identify the common factor (2) then specify multiplying the expression by 2:

  2 (4A + 12B + 2C)

- They would observe that they changed the original value by multiplying and would have to divide to restore the original value. The result was

  2 (4A/2 +12B/2 + 2C/2)

- The children would indicate the division problem and answer for each fraction and create the final equation:

  2 (2A + 6B + 1C)

The two critical points about the preschool math curriculum are

1. It was not designed as a prototype for a school program but was designed to show something about the extent of the conceptual framework that could be induced in at-risk preschoolers through carefully crafted instruction.

2. It did not teach some things that are considered basic in traditional programs, only things that would demonstrate the preschoolers' capacity to learn abstract relationships. For instance, children were not taught any facts directly, simply counting operations that permitted them to perform finger operations to determine answers to specific questions. Children were reinforced for remembering facts, and some of them learned quite a few facts.

These preschool children did not work with manipulatives or follow any traditional guidelines about what could be learned by preschoolers. Their performance completely discredited such guidelines.

Any serious observation of what these children had learned should have been sufficient to raise serious questions about how these children were taught compared with how children were being taught in Head Start preschools. A 1966 video of the highest-performing children who completed the first Bereiter-Engelmann preschool appears on Zigsite.com (Engelmann, 1966). Look at the children's performance carefully and compare what the children do with what is currently assumed to be far beyond the ken of bright second-graders (such as understanding fractions that are more than 1 and fractions that are equal to whole numbers).

PROGRAM-REFERENCED TESTING

We don't consider the program we develop completed until we have data that come close to meeting the criterion that properly placed students learn everything the program teaches. We refer to this research as program-referenced testing, which is a special case of criterion-referenced testing. The referent is the instructional program. We are not concerned with norms at this point or with comparing the program we are developing with other programs. We simply pursue the answer to the question, "To what extent does the program teach everything it is designed to teach?"

Adoption Decisions and Program Referenced Testing

The question about how well programs teach what they are designed to teach should be the most basic one that underpins districts' decisions to adopt programs. Consider the context of program-referenced testing: A failed district selects program A and spends a considerable amount of resources installing it. The question, "Why did the district select this program rather than one of the many other alternatives?" reveals great discontinuity. *The district assumed that the adopted program would cause superior learning outcomes.* This is almost an axiomatic fact. What failed district would install a new program that didn't hold the promise of producing superior outcomes?

In typical scenarios over the past 50 years, districts install their adopted programs, but they never determine the extent to which the content of the program is being taught. Districts learn about the failure of the program from results of achievement tests that are very remote with respect to their content and format. The results certainly identify broad categories that were failed. But broadness has no place in providing specific instructional remedies. And even if the district were able to take information about broad categories and provide articulate instruction, the failure on the achievement test does not answer the primary question, which is: "To what extent did students learn everything taught in the adopted program?" The only data-based way to answer the question about exactly what the program taught *is to test everything the program taught.* Possibly, the students learned everything taught in the adopted program but failed the test because very little of the tested content was taught by the program.

The net result of not having data on what the program actually taught is that the district now must try to concoct a remedy, a plan B, without having necessary knowledge about the program that was adopted and installed. Clearly, the district needs information about the extent to which the adopted program met expectations of teaching everything it purported to teach.

Steps in DI Program Development and Program-Referenced Testing

DI programs are program-referenced tested as part of the program-development procedures. This testing and associated revisions of the material occurs before the program is published. There are three types of tests: a "teacher-student read," an empirical test of students who go through the field-test version of the program, and the test of students who go through a revised field-test program.

Before any material goes out to the field, we put it through a teacher-student read. Two adults do this read; one is familiar with DI. Ideally, that person plays the role of the student. The naïve adult usually plays the role of teacher and presents the script. All glitches are noted and addressed. The time required to present each exercise is recorded. We judge that this time is about two-thirds of the time that will be required when the program is taught to actual students.

Following the teacher-student read and changes to parts of the manuscript where problems are noted, we conduct an in-depth field test of the material. The ideal would be for teachers in four different classrooms to present the material to students. Two teachers would start at Lesson 1 and present the lessons. They indicate problems of weak responses or no response, wrong responses, awkward wording, and time for each exercise.

When these teachers reach Lesson 20, the second pair of teachers starts at Lesson 1. They go through a program that has been revised on the basis of problems encountered in the first field test try-out.

Note that the field-testing occurs as the program is being developed (rather than after the tryout version of the program is completed). The standard is that all students should learn everything the program teaches and learn it in a timely manner. Typically, not all students in the tryout are properly placed. If we have a group of 25 students who are going through a third-grade math program, 3–5 of the students are typically too low to be in the program. There are no options for removing these students and placing them in the appropriate level of the program (one designed for a lower grade). So for our purposes, we don't track the data for these students. We recognize that they will learn something, and, hopefully next year, they will repeat the level.

We try to identify tryout teachers who will follow the program faithfully and will not deviate from the script without noting such deviations. We are not interested in recruiting the best teachers, but average teachers. (If the best teachers did well using the tryout material, we would not have realistic information about average or lower-performing teachers.)

If teachers have never taught DI before, we provide brief training sessions (currently using Skype). We go over how teachers are to mark the manuscript to show where students made mistakes, show which parts had to be repeated, and record the time for each exercise.

We try to test the program as it is being developed because the timeline for completing the program may permit fewer than two years on program development. Also, we don't want our development to get so far ahead of the field that we are locked into material that may have to be changed if students or teachers have trouble with the early foundational skills.

We respond to all problems. We try to send out remedies to serious problems, such as students not learning a discrimination they will use, within no more than two days from the time we learn about the problem. We usually call teachers periodically and ask them about specific details.

Programs are revised quickly so that the teachers who are 20 lessons behind the original two teachers go through a corrected sequence. We recognize that we probably don't identify all the problems through a lesson-by-lesson analysis of teacher comments (and related student performance), so we provide safety nets—10-lesson tests. Each test evaluates every new skill that was taught in the preceding 10 lessons. For example, the test that follows Lesson 50 tests everything taught in Lessons 41–50. Teachers send us copies of students' tests. We examine the results carefully to identify problems that had not been reported. Often, we will send out specific remedies on the day that we receive the test results. After the second pair of tryout teachers has gone through the program, the sequence should be close to publishable form. We often feel that the material would benefit from another round of tryouts, but this is not usually a realistic option.

Benefits of Program-Referenced Testing

Following the testing (the tryouts), we can answer specific, teaching-related questions about anything that was taught in the program.

• Exactly what was taught?

• Which specific discriminations or skills had to be readjusted?

• With the readjusted instruction, what percentage of students passed the 10-lesson test segment that addressed those discriminations or skills?

Because the 10-lesson tests are part of the published program, districts have the potential to install a review process that documents whether students learn everything the program teaches. Because the pre-publication field-testing established that the students learned the material when it was presented properly, the 10-lesson tests and end-of-program cumulative test serve as powerful tools for institutionalizing practices that assure student mastery of the program content.

The design permits an analyst to draw *strong inferences* based on failures of students to learn the program content. The program has been shown to successfully teach everything the program presents. If test results of students who go through the published program show that students are not learning particular content, the problem would have to be either with the placement of students or the way teachers presented the material. The simplest way for the district to identify the problem would be to bring in a DI trainer to observe the teachers, identify what needs to be changed in their teaching, and provide the training.

This option is not available for programs that have not been program-referenced tested. The possible causes of student failure for these programs are not limited to improper teaching or student placement. Some students may fail to learn content because the program material has not been designed so all properly placed students are able to learn it.

Formative-Summative versus Program-Referenced Testing

Several people have suggested to me that the process we use in developing programs could be expressed as formative and summative evaluations. Both are referenced to the validity of the design or program. As the names imply, formative has something to do with the formation of a process or format. Formative validity is achieved by changing details of the work-in-progress so it obviates specific problems. Summative refers to something that is completed. Summative validity is achieved by judging whether the overall finished product is worth keeping.

The actual process of program development involves steps not covered by these labels. The general "rules" that the designers follow for creating the pre-publication material are articulated in *Rubric for Identifying Authentic DI Programs* (Engelmann & Colvin, 2006) and *Theory of Instruction: Principles and Applications* (Engelmann &

Carnine, 1991). If the authors apply these rules to the content as they develop it, the work is considered acceptable. The test is simply whether authors agree that the program seems to meet the instructional-design requirements.

This first phase of development is formative in the sense that it has to do with the creation of material, but it would be most appropriately identified as a "construct validity" phase. What is created is referenced to a construct or theoretical concept (Carmines & Zeller, 1991). Following this phase is the teacher-student read, which is best described as a low-grade efficacy trial. Following is the tryout with possibly four classrooms. This could be labeled a high-grade efficacy trial. Note that the teachers in this trial receive feedback that is not provided for teachers who use the published version of the program. The evaluation of both trials is formative because we use the data to try to fix whatever is wrong with the program. Throughout the development process, the evaluation criterion is very precise. "Does the program teach the students everything the program is designed to teach?" This question is translated into procedures that assure the identification of weak parts of the program, the construction and testing of remedies, and the retesting with other teachers and students to assure that the modified sequences are effective.

A cumulative test at the end of the program assesses all the major skills and operations students have been taught; therefore, this test would definitely have more of a summative function than the 10-lesson tests have. However, during the program-development process, the major goal would be formative by revealing some sequencing issues. If the cumulative-test results reveal that some students do not perform well on material taught and tested earlier in the program, the program is apparently weak in reviewing these skills and operations and should be revised to assure that examples occur more frequently as part of the students' independent work. Because it is likely that the review pattern of some skills would be modified on the basis of poor student performance on the cumulative test, the cumulative test would have a formative function for us, as well as a summative one.

Scriven (1967) observed that all assessments have a summative function, but only some have the additional capabilities of serving formative functions. One way to illustrate the relationship is to evaluate the parts of the program-referenced test. Did students perform acceptably on a particular part? The answer to this question is summative, a judgment about whether the instruction provided was worthy or not. If the answer is yes, the part meets our criterion for acceptability and we don't provide any formative changes. If the students did not perform acceptably on the part, we judge the part to be unacceptable and provide a formative remedy for the instruction that caused the unacceptable performance.

A standardized achievement test could provide the summative evaluation of the program, but the role of this test is deceptively unclear in determining the value of the program. If students perform well on the in-program tests but perform poorly on the achievement test, the students have apparently mastered the content that was taught. If decision makers are satisfied that this content is worthy, the program is highly valuable and should be retained.

In fact, the likelihood of students doing well in the program and performing poorly on the standardized test is low because the program would be designed to meet specific "standards," such as the Common Core State Standards. However, the cumulative test should be a far better judge of the program's worth than a remote achievement test that has multiple-choice items, forced choices, inadequate sampling of content, and other possible problems that may distort what students know and therefore distort judgments about the worth of the program.

If we measure the effectiveness of the program with a standardized achievement test, the formative function is problematic because the test does not clearly suggest the relationship between the instruction students received and the test items. If we have evidence that the students successfully went through a sequence that we judge to have covered the relevant skills and if students fail test items that were designed to evaluate these skills, a reasonable formative response would be to change the test. A more direct, but spurious, formative remedy is simply to teach to the test. This would involve changing the instruction so it focuses on items that are identical to or very similar to those appearing on the test. Of course this is cheating, but, unfortunately, low test scores serve as the basis for test-prep, and many districts provide extensive test-prep instruction that unquestionably involves cheating. This is not to say that the results of an achievement test are invalid, simply that they can't be used as a program-referenced test because it is not a test that measures precisely what students have been taught.

Remedies Generated by Program-Referenced Testing

The fact the DI programs are program-referenced tested and revised before publication means that patterns of student performance generate strong inferences about possible causes of student behavior. Identifying causes of student failure in material that has not been shaped by program-referenced testing is more difficult because there are more possible causes of failure.

There are three primary variables that affect student performance, and it is therefore logically complicated to figure out which variable or combination of variables caused the observed outcomes. The variables are

• the effectiveness of the program,

• the effectiveness of the teaching, and

• the placement of the students.

If a program has been designed so it is program-referenced tested, there are fewer causes of failure because the effectiveness of a program is not a possible cause of failure. The only possible causes have to do with the effectiveness of the teaching and the placement of students. If districts use instructional programs that have not been program-referenced tested before publication, student failure on test items implies combinations of all three variables–program, teaching, and student placement. There are eight possibilities (see Table 1.1). Of the eight, only one leads to success: the program effectively teaches everything it presents, the teaching is effective, and the students are properly placed (#8). The other seven possibilities result in student failure (#1–7). One possibility is that the students are improperly placed, and the program does not provide adequate instruction for the failed items. Another possibility is that the program is adequate and students are placed properly, but the teaching is weak. All possibilities are shown in Table 1.1.

Table 1.1 Possible Causes of Student Performance on Cumulative Test

Program	**Student Placement**	**Teaching**	**Outcome**
1. Poor	Good	Good	Failure
2. Good	Good	Poor	Failure
3. Good	Poor	Good	Failure
4. Poor	Poor	Good	Failure
5. Poor	Good	Poor	Failure
6. Good	Poor	Poor	Failure
7. Poor	Poor	Poor	Failure
8. Good	Good	Good	Success

A remedy for student performance won't work unless it targets the correct variable or combination of variables. The fact that a specific failure could be the effect of seven possible causes means that the appropriate remedy is identified by ruling out seven possibilities. This is rarely done. In fact, the three principal variables are not usually identified. Instead, various spurious causes of failure are identified and pursued with ineffective remedies. For example, a conclusion may be that students are "unmotivated" or "disinterested." Lack of motivation is often not the cause but the effect of the real causes. This false diagnosis leads to faulty instruction–high interest material, discussions that attempt to make concepts like the area of circles "more relevant and meaningful" to the students.

The teachers may be identified as the problem, and intensive in-service and more opportunities for teacher collaboration may follow, but chances are overwhelming that this response will not be effective because the district has no reliable data about whether the problems of student performance are caused by a poor program, poor teaching, poor placement of students, or some combination of the three variables.

Because DI programs have been shaped by program-referenced testing, there are only three possible causes of failure, not eight (Table 1.2):

- The teaching is inadequate;

- The placement is inappropriate;

- The teaching is inadequate and the placement is inappropriate.

Table 1.2 Possible Causes of Student Failure on Cumulative Test for DI Programs

Program	Student Placement	Teaching
1. Good	Good	Poor
2. Good	Poor	Good
3. Good	Poor	Poor

Identifying the specific causes of failure is therefore considerably more manageable when a DI program is used than it would be for a program that has not been shaped by program-referenced testing. The in-program 10-lesson tests and the cumulative test at the end of the program are tools designed for the teacher to identify specific problems. The remedies for poor performance are straightforward: present the specified remedies for each failed part of the test. The remedies require teachers to repeat specified parts of the program.

If a high percentage of students in a classroom fail several parts of a 10-lesson test, there is a problem with the teaching or student placement. The first step would be to assess the placement of the students. If the same students tend to fail all the problematic parts of the test, these students are probably misplaced and should be placed in a lower level of the program. The misplacement of students may be confirmed by looking at scores on the program's placement test or simply by observing the performance of the students on the next 10-lesson test. If the same students tend to make a large number of mistakes on both tests, they are probably misplaced.

The simplest way to evaluate whether the teaching is a problem is for a trainer or coach to observe the lessons. If the teacher is mechanically sound and the teacher teaches students to mastery without spending excessive time repeating parts of the lesson, the teaching can be ruled out as a possible cause of the poor student performance. If the teacher simply rattles off the words in the script without responding to student mistakes, the teaching is a problem. The remedy is for a coach or trainer to teach proper reinforcement and correction procedures. These procedures are difficult for most teachers to learn.

There are a lot of additional details that are used to shape remedies, but the process is manageable because the programs provide an implicit promise of success. Although the programs are not perfect, if the placement and teaching are adequate, students will master everything the programs teach. Furthermore, if students master everything that is taught, they will probably perform well on tests, even those that may not be perfectly congruent with what students have been taught.

REFERENCES

Anderson, R., Hiebert, E., Scott, J., & Wilkinson, I. (1985). *Becoming a nation of readers: The report of the commission on reading.* Washington, DC: National Institute of Education.

Carmines, E. G., & Zeller, R. A. (1991). *Reliability and validity assessment.* Newbury Park, CA: Sage Publications.

Common Core State Standards (2012). *Measurement and data grade 5, 5a.* Retrieved from http://www.corestandards.org/Math/Content/5/MD.

Engelmann, S. (1966). *Kindergartners showing off their math skills [video].* Retrieved from http://zigsite.com/video/zig_math_video.html

Engelmann, S. (1967). *Teaching formal operations to preschool children.* Ontario Journal of Educational Research, 9(3) 193–207.

Engelmann, S., & Carnine, D. (1991). *Theory of instruction: Principles and applications.* Eugene, OR: ADI Press. (Originally published 1982 by Irvington Publishers.)

Engelmann, S., & Colvin, G. (2006). *Rubric for identifying authentic direct instruction programs.* Eugene, OR: Engelmann Foundation. Retrieved from: http://zigsite.com/PDFs/rubric.pdf

Engelmann, S., & Engelmann, T. (1966). *Give your child a superior mind: A program for the preschool child.* New York: Simon & Schuster.

Engelmann, S., & Engelmann, T. (1975). *Your child can succeed! How to get the most out of school for your child.* New York: Simon & Schuster.

Engelmann, S., Haddox, P., & Bruner, E. (1983). *Teach your child to read in 100 easy lessons.* New York: Simon & Schuster.

National Governors Association Center for Best Practices & Council of Chief State School Officers. (2010). *Common Core State Standards for Mathematics.* Washington, DC: Authors.

National Reading Panel. (2000). Report of the National Reading Panel. *Teaching children to read: An evidence-based assessment of the scientific research literature on reading and its implications for reading instruction* (NIH Publication No. 00-4769). Washington, DC: U.S. Government Printing Office.

Piaget, J. (1964). Development and learning. In R. E. Ripple and V.N. Rockcastle (Eds.), *Piaget rediscovered.* Ithica, NY: Cornell University Press.

Robinson, W. S. (1951). The logical structure of analytic induction. *American Sociological Review,* 16, 812–818.

Scriven, M. (1967). The methodology of evaluation. In R. W. Tyler, R. M. Gagne, & M. Scriven (Eds.), *Perspectives of curriculum evaluation,* 39–83. Chicago, IL: Rand McNally.

Znaniecki, F. (1934). *The method of sociology.* New York: Farrar & Rinehart.

CHAPTER 2

Hundreds of studies have examined the effectiveness of Direct Instruction programs, and several authors have systematically examined and summarized this literature. In this chapter Cristy Coughlin reviews these summaries, looking at the results of both meta-analyses and systematic literature reviews. Along the way she discusses the importance of these reviews and their relationship to educational policy.

OUTCOMES OF ENGELMANN'S DIRECT INSTRUCTION
RESEARCH SYNTHESES

Cristy Coughlin

Research on the effectiveness of Engelmann's Direct Instruction (DI) programs has spanned close to half a century, offering a broad demonstration of its impact on a wide variety of populations, within different settings, and across numerous subject areas. The earliest research begins with Engelmann's studies in the 1960s. These early studies provided the initial empirical support for the effectiveness of DI teaching strategies as well as the framework for continued DI program development and testing as discussed in Chapter 1 of this book. In 1968, and extending eight years onward, Project Follow Through provided one of the most significant demonstrations of the effectiveness of Direct Instruction programs. By comparing effects of various instructional models implemented across 170 communities in the United States, Project Follow Through was the largest educational experiment the country has undertaken. While the intent of the project was to identify educational interventions that worked, the results of Project Follow Through failed to affect policy on a large scale. There was no push by the federal government to adopt those interventions that were shown to be most effective, including Direct Instruction, which was the most effective of all the models examined (Engelmann, 2007).

Despite the lack of progress in the policy realm, research on DI program effectiveness continued. In the 1970s and 1980s, many studies were conducted to test the effectiveness of DI programs with different populations, especially with special education students and students in disadvantaged communities. This line of research extended into the 1990s, 2000s, and 2010s as researchers sought to broaden the scope of studies. Recently, researchers have prioritized larger-scale studies that examined Direct Instruction implementation in entire schools and districts, and additional outcomes, including longitudinal impact and sustainability, have been identified as important areas of interest.

Ideally, we would hope that educational policy and practice are based on such rich and broad sources of empirical evidence of effectiveness. Yet, adoption and dissemination of educational interventions and curricula have been historically driven by theories on how children learn, the political climate of schools and districts, contemporary educational philosophies, and the popularity of faddish approaches. Though unsupported by substantial evidence, schools have been quick to implement a program before it is evident that the program will likely impart change in their students' achievement. However, due to recent educational reform efforts and the enactment of federal policies, a shift toward identifying and promoting the use of evidence-based or research-validated practices and programs in schools has taken place. Legislation such as the No Child Left Behind (NCLB) Act and reauthorization in 2004 of the Individuals with Disabilities Education Act (IDEA) has served as a catalyst for these efforts. Today, schools are held more accountable for student achievement than ever before.

To guide decision-making at the national, state, and local levels, educators and policymakers need to make sense of the evidence regarding the relative effectiveness of instructional practices. Given the backdrop of limited funding and hundreds of curricula claiming to be research-based, making sense of the evidence on program effectiveness can be an arduous duty to undertake. Because it is infeasible to conduct another experiment with the same magnitude as Project Follow Through, syntheses of available research are typically used to guide conclusions about the effectiveness of practices. Since Direct Instruction programs are characterized by a long history, wide implementation, and extensive research, the effectiveness of DI curricula can be scrutinized through the lens of rigorous research syntheses.

The purpose of this chapter is to serve as a tertiary review of the enormous amount of literature on Direct Instruction's effectiveness, summarizing and discussing the results of several oft-cited research syntheses. First, an overview of the role and fundamental features of all research syntheses is provided. Then, different approaches used to integrate research findings are presented, discussing the procedural variations between these methodologies that have the potential to impact outcomes and conclusions. Drawing from these considerations, DI research syntheses are then compared, with results summarized by subject area, population, and focus of implementation. Finally, based on this broad examination of the DI literature base, conclusions, implications, and directions for future research are highlighted.

THE ROLE OF RESEARCH SYNTHESES

Research syntheses are one method of integrating the empirical evidence on educational interventions' effects, making findings and conclusions more understandable and accessible to a wider audience. The medical field has embraced the use of research syntheses to inform practice, going so far as to establish a consortium of researchers assigned with the task of analyzing the cumulative evidence existing in hundreds of areas within medicine and public health (Cochrane Collaboration, 2008).

Similarly, the American Psychological Association organized the Presidential Task Force on Evidence-Based Practice in 2005 to undertake the "integration of the best available research with clinical expertise in the context of patient characteristics, culture, and preferences" (APA, 2006, p. 273). The field of education has sought to create expert panels to achieve similar goals by distinguishing effective educational interventions from those that are less effective, including, for example, the National Reading Panel and the National Mathematics Advisory Panel. Relying on the use of various types of research syntheses, these organizations are crucial to the identification and dissemination of research-validated practices.

Types of Research Syntheses: Systematic Reviews and Meta-Analyses

While every research synthesis intends to review and integrate the cumulative findings of individual studies within the same topic area, there are different approaches a researcher can take to achieve this goal. Two types of syntheses are commonly used: systematic reviews and meta-analyses. In brief, a systematic review forms the foundation of any synthesis, with meta-analyses going one step further to add a quantitative element to the summarization of results.

Systematic Reviews

A *systematic review* is a broad term used here to describe a literature review seeking to collect and examine all primary research conducted in a given area in an explicit and standardized manner. To conduct a systematic review, researchers proceed though a sequence of steps, much like the stages that characterize primary research studies, generally including the following: establishing a research question, searching the literature, gathering information from studies, evaluating the quality of studies, and analyzing the outcomes (Cooper, 2010). Conducting a systematic review of literature requires researchers to apply the same level of rigor as when conducting primary research studies. This involves researchers applying techniques to minimize the difference in results obtained from retrieved studies and those studies that were not found. This is accomplished by consistently applying specific criteria to determine which studies will be included and excluded from the review, regardless of whether or not results support the researchers' hypotheses. Systematic reviews are widely used in the medical fields to guide decisions and policy-making about evidence-based treatments, integrating the results of randomized trials of healthcare interventions and treatments.

There have been several systematic reviews of the Direct Instruction research base, synthesizing research on the effectiveness of *Reading Mastery* (Schieffer, Marchand-Martella, Martella, Simonsen, & Waldron-Soler, 2002), *Corrective Reading* (Przychodzin-Havis et al., 2005), DI math programs (Przychodzin, Marchand-Martella,

Martella, & Azim, 2004), and DI spelling programs (Simonsen & Gunter, 2001). In addition, syntheses that examine the effectiveness of using DI with special education populations (Kinder, Kubina, & Marchand-Martella, 2005) or as a school reform model (American Institutes for Research, 1999) have been conducted. The results of each of these reviews are summarized in later sections of this chapter.

Meta-Analyses

Like systematic reviews, a *meta-analysis* necessitates a thorough, comprehensive review of all of the research completed within a specific topic area and calls for a systematic approach to coding and evaluating the results of this research. Utilized in conjunction with systematic reviews, meta-analysis involves quantitatively integrating the results of numerous studies. Shifting away from the use of statistical significance for judging program effects, typical of primary research studies, the magnitude and direction of results are emphasized by utilizing an effect size estimate.

Meta-analysis is uniquely useful for interpreting a research base with the following attributes: 1) when the effect of an intervention has been examined across a broad range of settings, populations, and methodologies; 2) when contradictory findings may exist; and 3) when it is desirable to explore hypothesized mediators and moderators of effects (Rosenthal, 1984). As Kavale (2001) points out, "meta-analytic renderings of research domains move the decision process beyond the false assumption that a single study, no matter how 'perfect,' can provide the basis for sound decision" (p. 262). Therefore by quantitatively analyzing the *cumulative* results of a series of individual studies, more confident conclusions can be drawn from syntheses of research (Cowan, 2004).

Typically, individual study findings and subsequent judgments of intervention effectiveness are based on whether results are statistically significant. Statistical significance suggests that the obtained results are not likely to have occurred by chance alone and that differences between groups are unlikely to be a product of sampling error. Whether the difference is statistically significant or not largely relies on sample size. The larger the sample size, the more likely it is that differences will approach the level of statistical significance. When the intent is to integrate results from multiple studies, and because sample size can vary so much within a literature base—which is very true for studies on Direct Instruction programs, with samples ranging from under 10 students up to more than 30,000 students—relying on statistical significance to judge effects is biased against those studies with fewer participants. Additionally, statistical significance provides little insight into the magnitude or importance of a program's effect.

Because studies use different measures and dependent variables, meta-analyses typically use effect sizes as a common metric to compare results across studies. Transforming raw values into effect sizes allows researchers to standardize results. Effect sizes represent the size of the effect in terms of standard deviation units, making it possible to compare variables measured on different scales. Rather than interpreting results in terms of statistical significance, effect sizes convey whether results have practical significance—meaning that the effect of the intervention had a real, important impact on children's learning. Cohen's *d*, which is the standardized difference between two means, is often calculated to estimate effect size. Cohen (1988) established guidelines for interpreting the magnitude of these effect size estimates, so that values of 0.20 are considered *small*, 0.50 are *medium*, and 0.80 are *large*. Within the field of education, an effect size of 0.25 is generally considered educationally significant (Tallmadge, 1977). Still, some research syntheses attempt to synthesize results based on statistical significance, utilizing simple polling or vote-counting, where the number of statistically significant differences reported across all studies included in the synthesis is tallied. Most of the systematic reviews discussed in this chapter employ this vote-counting approach of quantitatively synthesizing results, whereas the meta-analyses included in this review use effect size estimates to capture program effects.

Stages of Research Syntheses and Procedural Variations

Researchers have developed several specific models for conducting research syntheses (e.g., Jackson, 1980; Cooper, 2010), all of which generally follow basic steps that mirror the progression of activities in primary research studies. As Cooper (2010) points out, every decision made along each step of the research synthesis process has a potential impact on the study's conclusions, and variations in methodological decisions can result in contrasting conclusions from different researchers. To exemplify this influence, we can examine some of the procedural variations identified by Cooper (2010) and Shadish, Cook, and Campbell (2002) and the accompanying stages where decisions that affect these variations might take place.

First, at the initial stage of conducting a research synthesis, a research question is formulated, and variables and relationships of interest are identified and defined. The greater the extent to which these definitions vary across syntheses, the more likely differences in conclusions will result. For example, a researcher who defines Direct Instruction as "a set of effective teaching practices" would draw very different conclusions from a researcher who defines Direct Instruction as "any program developed and authored by Siegfried Engelmann."

Once a research question is fully defined, a comprehensive literature search follows, wherein a researcher will seek to locate as many relevant studies as possible. At this stage of the synthesis, a researcher's selection of which search terms to use and what sources to reference can result in a different set of studies synthesized, therefore potentially leading to different conclusions. One synthesis which, for example, utilizes a thorough search through databases containing dissertation studies and other unpublished work, and another synthesis, which restricts inclusions to studies only published in peer-reviewed journals, would result in conclusions drawn from two different bodies of literature.

After all relevant studies are obtained, necessary information is extracted from each study as trained individuals classify and report study features and findings. When obtaining information from studies, the intent is to retrieve data relevant to the research question, including any features that are hypothesized to influence outcomes (i.e., mediators and moderators of an effect). It is therefore necessary for researchers to thoughtfully select which characteristics will be coded. They must remember that if too little information is retrieved, there exists the possibility that important influences on cumulative effects will be missed. On the other hand, it is necessary to classify variables into categories that are as parsimonious as possible.

The impact of variation in study characteristics selected for coding, how these characteristics are conceptualized and distinguished, and differences in training for individuals responsible for coding studies may influence cumulative conclusions drawn from the synthesis. Even if the exact same set of studies were retrieved when the literature base was searched, small differences in the way that participants in these studies were described in the coding scheme could affect outcomes. For example, with one synthesis capturing disability status in many categories and the other collapsing students with disabilities into one category, the first synthesis might capture an important influence on outcomes and the second synthesis might miss variations in this influential factor altogether.

After studies are collected and coded, the researcher must apply exclusion criteria, separating studies that will be analyzed within the synthesis from those that don't meet requirements for inclusion. In meta-analyses, researchers will typically adhere to some criteria for study design and methodology when excluding studies, so that the type of methodology employed in a study is congruent with the larger research question of the synthesis. For example, if the question of interest is whether Curriculum X is more effective than Curriculum Y, then it is logical for a researcher to only be interested in findings from studies with a comparison group. This would then exclude studies that only examine change in achievement before and after implementation of Curriculum X, without comparing these changes to students who had received instruction with a different curriculum. Other exclusionary criteria that may be applied at this stage of the synthesis might be related to sample characteristics (e.g., excluding studies of students in a certain age group if the research question is only interested in effects on elementary-aged students), details about the implementation of the intervention (e.g., only including studies that report data on fidelity of implementation), or accessibility of necessary quantitative information (e.g., studies that report requisite means and standard deviations to calculate effect sizes).

Finally, when comparing and contrasting results across studies, a researcher has to make decisions about which procedures to use when analyzing and integrating cumulative findings and how to interpret and discuss the importance of these findings. As noted earlier, authors of research syntheses on Direct Instruction programs have used effect size estimates, vote-counting of statistical significance, and simple tallying of positive findings to quantitatively integrate results. These different approaches are not just a matter of preference, but are designed to capture distinct aspects of the literature base, namely, the average magnitude of a program's effects, the likelihood of differences between experimental and comparison groups being attributed to chance alone, and the proportion of studies reporting generally positive findings for the experimental group. Application and interpretation of these various techniques will likely prompt divergences in the collective conclusions made.

These procedural variations are only a snapshot of the range of decisions that a researcher makes when conducting a research synthesis. When reflecting on conclusions asserted from a synthesis of research, it is important to consider that these conclusions are a product of accumulating variations and that each decision made by the researcher has contributed to the researcher's overall interpretation of findings amassed. If conclusions across syntheses conflict, a review of the procedural decisions made by authors of both syntheses may provide insight about factors that may have contributed to these differences, bringing to light decisions that may be questionable and areas where further investigation may be warranted.

Within the Direct Instruction literature base, systematic reviews and meta-analyses have been repeatedly used to integrate and make sense of the hundreds of studies conducted. Conclusions drawn from these syntheses have been generally very consistent, with systematic reviews and meta-analyses resulting in very similar conclusions about the positive effects of DI programs. The following sections will summarize these conclusions, discussing results as they correspond to various populations, settings, and subject areas studied, and exploring the procedural variations that may have led to discrepancies from one synthesis to another. Table 2.1 also displays summaries of these syntheses.

Table 2.1 Research Syntheses Reviewed

Adams and Engelmann (1996)

Type of synthesis	Meta-analysis
Area of review	General education, special education, reading, math, language, spelling
Number of studies reviewed	34
Purpose	To compare the effectiveness of Direct Instruction with other interventions
Inclusion/exclusion criteria, design	Experimental and quasi-experimental designs that included a comparison group and pretest-posttest scores
Inclusion/exclusion criteria, publication type	Published and unpublished studies through 1996
Inclusion/exclusion criteria, sample of participants	No restrictions identified
Findings (Average Effect Sizes)	Overall effect size: +0.87
	General education: +0.82
	Special education: +0.90
	Reading: +0.69
	Math: +1.11
	Language: +0.49
	Spelling: +1.33

American Institutes for Research (1999)

Type of synthesis	Systematic review
Area of review	General education
Number of studies reviewed	18 studies involving Direct Instruction, extracted from a total of 130 studies selected that compare the impact of 24 school reform models

Table 2.1 Research Syntheses Reviewed (continued)

Purpose	To compare the impact of different school reform models on student achievement
Inclusion/Exclusion criteria, design	Experimental and quasi-experimental designs with a comparison group; one-group pretest-posttest, single-subject, and case study designs
Inclusion/Exclusion criteria, publication type	Published and unpublished studies through 1999
Inclusion/Exclusion criteria, sample of participants	No restrictions identified
Findings	Direct Instruction was identified as 1 of 3 approaches to reach the highest standard, "strong evidence of positive effects on student achievement."

Borman, Hewes, Overman, & Brown (2003)

Type of synthesis	Meta-analysis
Area of review	General education
Number of studies reviewed	49 studies involving Direct Instruction, extracted from a total of 232 studies selected that compare the impact of 29 school reform models
Purpose	To synthesize the research on whole-school reform models
Inclusion/exclusion criteria, design	Experimental and quasi-experimental designs that included a comparison group; one-group pretest-posttest designs
Inclusion/exclusion criteria, publication type	Published and unpublished studies through 2001
Inclusion/exclusion criteria, sample of participants	Only included students from the school's regular education program
Findings	All design types: Average effect size = +0.21. Designs that incorporated a comparison group (i.e., excluding one group pretest-posttest designs): Average effect size = +0.15

Table 2.1 Research Syntheses Reviewed (continued)

	Direct Instruction was classified as 1 of 3 whole-school reform models that demonstrated "strongest evidence of effectiveness."

Kinder, Kubina, & Marchand-Martella (2005)

Type of synthesis	Systematic review
Area of review	Special education
Number of studies reviewed	45 studies: 37 with high incidence disability population, 8 with low incidence disability population
Purpose	To synthesize research literature that examines effects of DI programs on students with disabilities and those in special education settings
Inclusion/exclusion criteria, design	Experimental and quasi-experimental designs with a comparison group; one-group pretest-posttest, single-subject, and case study designs
Inclusion/exclusion criteria, publication type	Published studies that appeared in peer-reviewed education journals through 2005
Inclusion/exclusion criteria, sample of participants	Only included studies of students with disabilities
Findings	Overall: 90% of studies examined noted positive effects for Direct Instruction programs
	Reading: program effectiveness was well-supported by studies
	Math, spelling, writing, and language: limited number of studies were identified, further research recommended.

Przychodzin, Marchand-Martella, & Azim (2004)

Type of synthesis	Systematic review
Area of review	Mathematics

Table 2.1 Research Syntheses Reviewed (continued)

Number of studies reviewed	11 primary studies, plus Adams & Engelmann's meta-analysis findings in the area of math
Purpose	To synthesize research literature that examines effects of DI mathematics programs
Inclusion/exclusion criteria, design	Experimental and quasi-experimental designs with a comparison group; one-group pretest-posttest and single-subject designs
Inclusion/exclusion criteria, publication type	Studies published in peer-reviewed journals between 1990 and 2004
Inclusion/exclusion criteria, sample of participants	No restrictions identified
Findings	10 out of 11 primary studies reviewed noted positive effects for Direct Instruction programs

Przychodzin-Havis et al. (2005)

Type of synthesis	Systematic review
Area of review	Reading
Number of studies reviewed	28
Purpose	To synthesize research literature that examines effects of *Corrective Reading*
Inclusion/exclusion criteria, design	Experimental and quasi-experimental designs with a comparison group; one-group pretest-posttest and single-subject designs
Inclusion/exclusion criteria, publication type	Published studies through 2005
Inclusion/exclusion criteria, sample of participants	No restrictions identified
Findings	93% of studies reviewed "found positive results for students who were taught using *Corrective Reading*" and that "only one study noted greater effects with another intervention over *Corrective Reading*."

Table 2.1 Research Syntheses Reviewed (continued)

Schieffer, Marchand-Martella, Martella, Simonsen, & Waldron-Soler (2002)

Type of synthesis	Systematic review
Area of review	Reading
Number of studies reviewed	21
Purpose	To examine the effectiveness of *Reading Mastery/DISTAR*
Inclusion/exclusion criteria, design	Experimental and quasi-experimental designs with a comparison group
Inclusion/exclusion criteria, publication type	Studies published in peer-reviewed journals through 2002
Inclusion/exclusion criteria, sample of participants	No restrictions identified
Findings	67% of studies favored *Reading Mastery/DISTAR* Reading.
	19% of studies reported no significant differences.
	14% of studies favored comparison reading programs.

Simonsen & Gunter (2001)

Type of synthesis	Systematic review
Area of review	Spelling
Number of studies reviewed	18
Purpose	To review research related to empirically validated methodologies of spelling instruction and examine research that compares DI spelling programs to other spelling programs
Inclusion/exclusion criteria, design	No restrictions identified
Inclusion/exclusion criteria, publication type	Studies published through 2001
Inclusion/exclusion criteria, sample of participants	No restrictions identified

Table 2.1 Research Syntheses Reviewed (continued)

Findings	Studies comparing DI spelling programs to other programs consistently reported better performance for those students instructed with *Spelling Mastery* or *Corrective Spelling Through Morphographs*.
	Studies examining pre-post gains on spelling performance reported positive results.

White (1988)

Type of synthesis	Meta-analysis
Area of review	Special education, reading, math, language
Number of studies reviewed	25
Purpose	To synthesize research literature that compares the effectiveness of Direct Instruction with comparison interventions, for students with disabilities
Inclusion/Exclusion criteria, design	Experimental and quasi-experimental designs that included a comparison group, comparison group had to be comparable to experimental group at the start of intervention implementation
Inclusion/Exclusion criteria, publication type	Published and unpublished studies through 1986
Inclusion/Exclusion criteria, sample of participants	Only included students with disabilities
Findings (Average Effect Sizes)	Overall: +0.84
	Reading: +0.85
	Decoding: +0.64
	Comprehension: +0.54
	Math: +0.50
	Language: +1.21
	High incidence disabilities: +0.80
	Low incidence disabilities: +1.01

DIRECT INSTRUCTION IN SPECIAL EDUCATION

Arguably the most extensively researched population within the DI literature base, there have been hundreds of studies published that have involved students with disabilities and students in special education settings. This can largely be attributed to the alignment of DI programs with the diverse needs of students comprising this population. With the reauthorization of the Individuals with Disabilities Education Act (IDEA) in 2004, schools are now required to provide specially designed instruction to students eligible to receive special education services. This specially designed instruction refers to the adaptation of content or delivery of instruction to meet the unique needs of students eligible for special education services. These modifications might include adjusting the pace of instruction to ensure student mastery of concepts taught, matching instructional level to student skill level, identifying and prioritizing the most important concepts to teach, providing ample opportunity for student responding and teacher feedback, among others (Carnine, Silbert, Kame'enui, & Tarver, 2004).

Packaged together, these effective teaching practices, along with careful attention to the design of instruction and organizational structure of material, provide the framework for all DI programs. Students are taught concepts and ideas that can be best generalized and applied to the widest possible range of examples that a student might encounter. Examples and nonexamples are carefully selected and material is sequenced so that minimal confusion and a high rate of student success in acquiring new concepts and information are demonstrated. Relatively fast pacing, choral responding of students, teacher signaling, and scripted presentation contribute to rapid student progress through lessons. Because these features of DI curricula are inherent in the structured program design, their applicability to students with special needs is obvious, and, when implemented in the context of special education, research has demonstrated that student achievement is consistently accelerated.

Three research syntheses have sought to integrate individual studies that have examined the impact of DI programs on special education. The following sections summarize these syntheses.

Meta-Analyses: Special Education

Two meta-analyses of studies of DI with special education students have been published, one in the 1980s and one in the 1990s.

Adams and Engelmann (1996)

In the most extensive meta-analysis conducted on the Direct Instruction literature to date, Adams and Engelmann (1996) synthesized findings from 34 research studies that compared the effectiveness of DI programs with other types of interventions. Included in their meta-analysis were studies that examined DI within a variety of subject areas with participation from both general education and special education students. For studies that included students with disabilities or took place within special education settings, Adams and Engelmann reported an average effect size of 0.90. This value indicates that, on average, special education students receiving instruction with DI curricula scored nine tenths of a standard deviation higher than students in the comparison group. As noted before, Cohen's (1988) guidelines for inter-preting the relative magnitude of an effect size estimate can be used as one method for referencing effect sizes reported in this meta-analysis. The mean effect size estimate identified in this meta-analysis, 0.90, exceeds Cohen's benchmark of a *large* effect size of 0.80.

White (1988)

Almost a decade earlier than Adams and Engelmann's 1996 synthesis, White (1988) conducted the first meta-analysis of DI research, focusing only on its effects within special education populations. Based on 25 studies that examined the effec-tiveness of Direct Instruction compared to the effectiveness of other interventions for students with disabilities, White calculated an average effect size of 0.84. Only about half of the 25 studies that were included in White's meta-analysis were also synthesized in the Adams and Engelmann meta-analysis; however, the mean effect sizes reported in these two syntheses were quite similar. Interestingly, despite the span of eight years lapsed between these two meta-analyses and differences in exclusionary criteria for determining eligibility of studies, the cumulative conclusion about the average effect of DI programs on special education students based on White's synthesis differed by only .06 from the average effect size calculated from the body of literature retrieved by Adams and Engelmann. To further put these effect sizes in context, we can refer to Forness, Kavale, Blum, and Lloyd (1997) who report the results of a "mega-analysis" of meta-analyses within the field of special education and related services. Forness et al. reviewed 18 meta-analyses that integrated the effectiveness of various strate-gies, approaches, and programs in special education instruction, referencing White (1988) to obtain effect size information for Direct Instruction. Of the 18 interventions reviewed, DI's average effect size of 0.84 was the fourth highest reported, and was clas-sified by Forness et al. as one of seven recommended interventions shown to be most effective with special education populations.

Systematic Review: Special Education

In addition to the 1996 and 1988 meta-analyses, a more recent systematic review conducted by Kinder et al. (2005) provides an overview of the overwhelmingly positive effects produced when DI programs are used with special education populations. The authors discuss the research base related to students with high-incidence and low-incidence disabilities separately, describing a total of 45 studies across student disability categories: 37 with high incidence and 8 with low incidence disabilities. In order to be eligible for review, studies had to appear in peer-reviewed educational journals. This resulted in exclusion of unpublished studies and those considered as gray literature, including dissertations, technical reports, and conference presentations. Experimental and quasi-experimental comparison designs and studies employing case studies, one-group pretest-posttest designs, and single-subject methodology were included. The criteria for study design were less stringent in this review than in the 1988 and 1996 meta-analyses, resulting in a group of studies with less methodological rigor.

Rather than illustrating the magnitude of an intervention's impact by calculating effect sizes, Kinder et al. provide a narrative review of characteristics and findings of the studies selected through their systematic search of the literature base. From the 37 studies examining the impact of DI programs on students with *high-incidence* disabilities, only 8% reported better performance by students who received instruction from non-DI methods than students receiving DI programs. Across these studies, where the majority of students were identified with learning disabilities and of elementary or middle school age, Direct Instruction programs were reported to be effective in increasing skills in areas of reading and spelling. Math and writing program effectiveness was supported with fewer studies, and results obtained from language studies were inconclusive, with most studies showing few significant differences in posttest scores between students receiving DI programs and those receiving instruction through other methods and curricula. Seven of the 8 studies investigating DI outcomes of students with *low incidence* disabilities did not include a comparison group, so general conclusions about the comparative effectiveness of DI programs vs. alternative approaches within this sub-sample were not possible. Still, all 8 of these studies reported improved performance for students instructed with DI curricula. The majority of students included in these studies were identified with intellectual disabilities, and all but one of these studies examined the effectiveness of Direct Instruction reading or language programs.

Summary of Research on Direct Instruction and Special Education

Based on the results of these three syntheses, it is apparent that DI programs have resulted in positive outcomes for special education students. The results and conclusions drawn from these syntheses are remarkably consistent despite their procedural variations, which included differences in quantitative estimates of effect (i.e., statistical significance, effect size, or general positive results), inclusion criteria for study design, and literature search procedures used. For students with disabilities, IDEA's reauthorization requires that schools provide specially designed instruction, a mandate that can be supported though the use of Direct Instruction curricula. Further, research on DI program effectiveness addresses the legislative call for schools to use evidence-based or scientifically validated instructional practices in special education. While these attributes of the DI literature base are advantageous in application with special education populations, they also have broader utility and the potential to positively impact the learning of typically performing students. General education applications will be the focus of the next section.

DIRECT INSTRUCTION IN GENERAL EDUCATION

While there is ample evidence to the contrary, a widely held misconception is that DI programs are *only* appropriate for low-achieving and special education students. This misconception may have stemmed from the consideration of DI as a "basic skills" model in Project Follow Through. Further, because DI programs have been shown time and again to accelerate the learning of lower-performing students who have presumably fallen behind in other programs, the programs are often exclusively used with remedial and special education populations (Adams & Engelmann, 1996). Yet, when examining the research base on the effectiveness of DI programs in general education settings, it is apparent that this misconception lacks empirical support. In fact, research syntheses summarizing the effects of implementation of Direct Instruction within general education settings and as a whole-school reform model provide convincing evidence to the contrary, suggesting that DI can also meaningfully impact the learning of typically developing students.

Meta-Analyses: General Education

Two meta-analyses have examined the impact of Direct Instruction on students in general education.

Borman, Hewes, Overman, and Brown (2003)

In a meta-analysis of research on 29 comprehensive school reform (CSR) models, Borman et al. (2003) investigated the extent to which each of these models was supported by scientifically based research, considering the quality and quantity of supporting research as well as the statistical significance and positivity of findings. Studies employing an experimental or quasi-experimental design in which a comparison could be used to calculate an effect were eligible for review. In addition, one-group pretest-posttest designs were considered, which ended up characterizing the methodology used to obtain almost half of the outcomes analyzed. Each of the 29 CSR models was classified into one of four categories: *strongest evidence of effectiveness, highly promising evidence of effectiveness, promising evidence of effectiveness,* and *greatest need for additional research.* The Direct Instruction model was represented by 49 of the 232 studies, involving over 40,000 students. The 49 individual DI studies were the largest number of studies included in the meta-analysis for any one CSR model. An average effect size of 0.21 was calculated across these 49 studies, which included studies with all types of research designs. An average effect size of 0.15 was computed based on studies that employed some form of control group (i.e., excluding one-group pretest-posttest designs).

The DI model was one of three CSR models to be classified in the *strongest evidence of effectiveness* category. To be classified under the *strongest evidence of effectiveness* category, the Direct Instruction model had to be represented by 10 or more studies, a criterion used to indicate generalizability to the population of schools likely to implement CSR models. Additionally, the model had to demonstrate statistically significant and positive effects on student achievement in studies using comparison groups against which to reference gains, including at least 5 third-party studies not conducted by the model's developer.

Adams and Engelmann (1996)

The findings of the Borman et al. (2003) meta-analysis serve to inform the field of education about the relative effects of recent school reform efforts, but also reiterate conclusions of earlier syntheses of research. In Adams and Engelmann's 1996 meta-analysis, the mean effect size associated with studies involving students receiving instruction in the general education setting was 0.82, exceeding conventional guidelines for defining a *large* effect. This larger estimate differs quite a bit from the estimate of 0.21 reported in Borman et al. (2003), which is likely attributed to the slightly different focus of these two meta-analyses (comparing DI with other school reform models vs. comparing DI with other instructional approaches), but may also result from variation in inclusion/exclusion criteria used in each meta-analysis to select its study sample.

Systematic Review: General Education

To further explore the impact of Direct Instruction in general education, a systematic review, conducted by an organization interested in identifying the most effective whole-school instructional approaches, provides us with a narrative understanding of the evidence in this area. Given the task of reviewing the evidence base behind school reform models, the American Institutes for Research (AIR; 1999) synthesized research evidence on 24 reform models in order to draw conclusions about which models were most effective at improving student learning. Ratings were given to each model based on the amount of rigorous research conducted and the strength of results reported in that research. These ratings prompted the AIR to identify Direct Instruction as one of only three approaches to reach the highest standard, having "strong evidence of positive effects on student achievement" (AIR, 1999, p. 4). To achieve this superior rating, the research base on each model had to include at least 4 rigorous studies that demonstrated positive effects on student achievement, with at least 3 of these studies reporting statistically significant differences in favor of the model of interest.

Summary of Research on Direct Instruction in General Education

The effectiveness of Direct Instruction as a school reform model and with typically achieving students has been demonstrated over the last several decades. Studies conducted since the 1980s have shown that DI programs are, in fact, very effective when used with average- and high-achieving students (e.g., Ashworth, 1999; Gersten, Becker, Heiry, & White, 1984; Ginn, Keel, & Fredrick, 2002; Robinson & Hesse, 1981; Sexton, 1989; Tarver & Jung, 1995; Vitale & Joseph, 2008), and numerous studies have supported the implementation of DI schoolwide (e.g., Borman et al., 2003; Carlson & Francis, 2002; Cross, Rebarber, & Wilson, 2002; MacIver & Kemper, 2002; O'Brien & Ware, 2002). The results from these primary studies, in conjunction with the meta-analytic findings and systematic review conclusions discussed here, help to refute the notion that DI is only useful within the realm of special education.

Considering the possibility of differential intervention effects across varied populations (e.g., special education vs. general education) is important in order to understand situations and environments that are most conducive for positive effects of implementation. Similarly, differences in outcomes by subject area (e.g., reading vs. math) are important to consider, and can be especially helpful in informing policymakers' and educators' decisions about curriculum adoption. Meta-analyses have provided effect sizes that account for DI's cumulative success in the subject areas of reading, language, and math, as well as other subjects, and several systematic reviews have complemented these analyses. These reviews are summarized in the next sections.

DIRECT INSTRUCTION IN READING

Compared to other subject areas, DI reading programs have received the most research attention, documenting positive effects on a wide variety of students and evidencing alignment with empirical research on reading instruction. The National Reading Panel (NRP, 2000) report outlines conclusions that were made about effective reading instruction, based on an extensive review of research evidence from thousands of empirical studies in the area of reading (National Institute of Child Health and Human Development, 2000). Components consistently shown to result in gains in reading achievement were discussed, and recommendations for teaching reading were included. Salient features of Direct Instruction reading programs were among the recommendations provided, including an emphasis on the importance of explicit instruction in phonemic awareness and phonics, ample opportunity for guided reading practice, and corrective feedback (National Institute of Child Health and Human Development, 2000). These recommendations reinforce the notion that DI curricula are based on empirical research on how best to teach children to read.

In contrast with the NRP report, research syntheses on Direct Instruction effectiveness are less concerned about identifying which independent instructional features are closely linked to student achievement. Rather, these syntheses seek to explore the magnitude of effects demonstrated when these features are packaged and sequenced into a comprehensive program for teaching reading. Along with reading-specific meta-analytic findings, we can turn to systematic reviews of DI reading program research to gather a better understanding of the evidence behind using Direct Instruction to teach reading.

Meta-Analyses: Reading

Two of the meta-analyses of Direct Instruction previously discussed (Adams and Engelmann, 1996; and White, 1988) reported results that pertain specifically to reading outcomes. Adams and Engelmann's meta-analysis included participants representing both general education and special education populations and found an average effect size of 0.69 for reading outcomes., This indicates that after instruction with *Reading Mastery, Corrective Reading*, and other DI reading programs, students scored, on average, 0.69 of a standard deviation higher than students whose reading instruction was based on some other approach.

White (1988) limited his meta-analysis to students in special education settings and reported an average effect size of 0.85 across 13 studies involving DI reading programs. This meta-analysis also examined the impact of instruction on specific reading skills. Effect sizes of 0.64 and 0.54 were reported for decoding and comprehension outcomes, respectively.

Systematic Reviews: Reading

While the meta-analyses described above provide a quantitative representation of the impact of the Direct Instruction approach on reading outcomes, they do not discuss findings specific to the various DI reading curricula. Two systematic reviews have examined specific programs, one synthesizing the evidence base behind *Reading Mastery/DISTAR Reading* and the second addressing research on *Corrective Reading*.

Schieffer, Marchand-Martella, Martella, Simonsen, and Waldron-Soler (2002) conducted a systematic review of research on effects of *Reading Mastery/DISTAR Reading*, employing a polling or "vote counting" of statistical significance and mean score differences. They included a total of 21 studies that compared implementation of *Reading Mastery and DISTAR Reading* to other reading approaches. The authors reported the percentage of studies that favored the use of DI programs based on statistically significant differences between DI and comparison programs on measures of reading achievement. They found that 67% of the studies in their sample favored *Reading Mastery/DISTAR Reading*, 19% of studies reported no significant differences, and 14% favored comparison reading programs.

To synthesize the research on *Corrective Reading*, Przychodzin-Havis et al. (2005) simply tallied the number of studies that reported positive findings from using *Corrective Reading*. This review examined 28 studies that represented a myriad of experimental designs, including studies that compared DI to other approaches as well as studies that only investigated differences from pretest to posttest with one group of students receiving instruction with *Corrective Reading*. Przychodzin-Havis et al. concluded that 93% of studies reviewed "found positive results for students who were taught using *Corrective Reading*" and that "only one study [out of 28] noted greater effects with another intervention over *Corrective Reading*" (p. 62).

Summary of Research on Direct Instruction in Reading

Most of the research on Direct Instruction has focused on evaluating reading outcomes and the effectiveness of DI reading programs, leading to a large research base from which to synthesize. While this research has examined effects of DI reading curricula implemented in a variety of contexts, there are still areas that would benefit from more research. One of the greatest contributions of the research syntheses mentioned in this section is the descriptive discussion of study characteristics. This discussion identifies the experimental designs, populations, settings, and type of dependent measures that comprise the range of research included in each synthesis. For example, studies on *Corrective Reading* examined by Przychodzin-Havis et al., were most likely to employ a pre-experimental design (e.g., one-group pretest-posttest design), involve elementary and/or middle school students, and take place in special education settings. This information is useful for researchers by identifying areas for future investigation and for educators by exemplifying the conditions under which Direct Instruction programs have been effective.

Although Engelmann has produced Direct Instruction programs for numerous subject areas (see Chapter 4 and Appendix A for examples), research on the efficacy of DI programs has tended to prioritize reading. Yet the literature provides numerous demonstrations of the impact of DI in the areas of math, language, and spelling. The cumulative evidence within these subject areas is summarized in the next sections.

DIRECT INSTRUCTION IN MATHEMATICS

Much like in the area of reading, there has been a recent push by the federal government to identify effective practices and instructional programs in the area of mathematics. In 2001, the National Center for Education Statistics revealed that only 26% of the nation's 4th grade students, 27% of 8th grade students, and 17% of 12th grade students were considered to score at the proficient level in math. Compared to other countries, the mathematics performance of American children ranked in the bottom half of 41 participating countries (Gonzales et al., 2008). As a result of these startling statistics, the National Mathematics Advisory Panel (NMAP; 2008), modeled after the National Reading Panel, and the National Council of Teachers of Mathematics (NCTM; 2000) have worked over recent years to provide recommendations to educators and policymakers about how mathematics should be taught in schools across the country, developing content standards and identifying curricula that are best aligned with these standards and most effective at improving math achievement. The structure and content taught in DI math programs, which include *DISTAR Arithmetic* (the original DI mathematics program implemented as part of the DI model in Project Follow Through), *Corrective Mathematics, Connecting Math Concepts* and, the most recent addition, *Funnix*, are in accordance with recommendations put forth by NCTM and NMAP, including the call for scientific validation of curriculum impact on student outcomes (Przychodzin et al., 2004). The data on the effectiveness of DI mathematics programs have been summarized with both meta-analyses and a systematic review.

Effect size estimates specific to mathematics have been calculated in two meta-analyses. Based on 33 comparisons of math achievement scores across studies included in their meta-analysis, Adams and Engelmann (1996) reported an average effect size of 1.11 in favor of Direct Instruction programs, with most of these comparisons involving general education students. Well above Cohen's *large* benchmark (0.80), an effect size of 1.11 indicates that, on average, students receiving their math instruction with a DI program score over one standard deviation higher than students who received instruction with a comparison curriculum. For special education students, White (1988) reported an average effect size of 0.50, based on four studies. This value is lower than that reported by Adams and Engelmann, but still indicates a *medium* effect.

A systematic review of mathematics studies was conducted by Przychodzin, Marchand-Martella, and Azim (2004), who reviewed results of 11 primary studies as well as the results of Adams and Engelmann's meta-analytic findings in the area of math. Eight of these studies exclusively examined the effectiveness of DI math curricula on general education students and 3 studies involved students with disabilities. Overall, only one of the 11 studies in this review reported better gains made by the comparison group. That single study (Young, Baker, & Martin, 1990) compared instruction with *DISTAR Arithmetic* to an adaptation of the DI program, incorporating modifications based on discrimination learning theory. The Young et al. study found that the adaptation resulted in greater gains of a small sample of students with moderate intellectual disabilities when assessing effects with a single-subject design.

The research on DI math programs has typically involved students in general education. Because only a handful of studies have investigated effects of DI math programs with students with disabilities (even though most reported promising results) future research would be helpful to strengthen confidence in overall conclusions about effectiveness with this population.

DIRECT INSTRUCTION IN LANGUAGE

The area of language was a focus of earlier research on Direct Instruction programs, and results from Project Follow Through in the area of language illustrate the initial evidence supporting the effectiveness of DI language programs (Engelmann, 2007). When results of the DI model were compared to results of the other Follow Through models, effect sizes for language were very large, with scores of students who participated in the DI model averaging one standard deviation higher than the average score of students in all other Follow Through models (Engelmann, 2007). Further, students receiving the DI model demonstrated statistically significantly higher performance on all language measures when compared to every other model (Bereiter & Kurland, 1981–1982). DI language programs continue to be studied, and meta-analyses conducted since Follow Through offer insight into cumulative effects of these programs.

Based on their analysis of 39 comparisons derived from 34 studies of DI language programs, Adams and Engelmann (1996) reported an average effect size of 0.49. This indicates that, on average, students in these studies scored one half of a standard deviation higher than comparison students—an educationally significant difference. As Adams and Engelmann included studies involving both general education and special education students, this effect size is representative of both populations. White's (1988) meta-analysis, which included 3 studies of DI language programs with only special education students, resulted in an average effect size of 1.21.

Given the range of results from these syntheses, it is difficult to reach conclusions about the relative effects of DI language programs on general education and special education populations. Because of the limited sample size in White's meta-analysis and the fact that Adams and Engelmann calculated the effect size for language programs by combining studies involving special education and general education populations, it is not possible to discern which populations benefit most from Direct Instruction in language. However, these syntheses suggest that DI programs, on average, produce an educationally significant impact on language skills of both typically developing students and students with disabilities.

DIRECT INSTRUCTION IN SPELLING

Though most of the research on Direct Instruction program effectiveness has focused on the areas of reading followed by math and language, research syntheses have also sought to review research on DI programs in spelling. Often, DI spelling programs are researched in conjunction with other DI programs as part of whole-school implementation of the Direct Instruction model (e.g., Cross, Rebarber, & Wilson, 2002; Grossen, 2004). Adams and Engelmann's (1996) findings in the area of spelling and a systematic review of DI spelling research begin to tell a story about the cumulative evidence around Direct Instruction spelling programs.

Adams and Engelmann (1996) calculated an effect size of 1.33 in the area of spelling. This estimate was based on only 3 studies, with 1 study specifically evaluating DI spelling program effectiveness, another study reporting spelling results from Project Follow Through, and the final study including spelling as an outcome measure for DI reading program implementation.

Conducted about five years after Adams and Engelmann's meta-analysis, Simonsen and Gunter's (2001) systematic review provided an analysis of a larger sample of spelling-related studies. Extracting results from a total of 18 studies, Simonsen and Gunter synthesized findings from a review of research on effective spelling instruction. The review concluded that combining components of Direct Instruction delivery, such as systematic error correction and sequenced lessons, with phonemic (i.e., letter-sound correspondence), whole word (i.e., explicit instruction and practice in spelling irregular words), and morphographic approaches (i.e., combining spelling of small units of meanings or morphographs) typically resulted in meaningful gains in spelling performance. Simonsen and Gunter's review also specifically examined the effects of DI spelling programs, *Spelling Mastery* and *Corrective Spelling Through Morphographs*. Based on 4 studies that employed a comparison group design, DI spelling programs consistently demonstrated better outcomes than comparison strategies. Further, another 4 studies that examined spelling gains following instruction with DI programs reported positive results for students in general education, elementary and middle school, and for students experiencing difficulties in the area of spelling. As the authors of these research syntheses assert, while results of these studies of DI spelling programs are promising and demonstrate positive outcomes, much more research is warranted. Additional demonstrations of impact, use with a wider variety of students, and more rigorous design methodology would help to improve the quality of the research base on DI spelling programs.

SUMMARY AND DISCUSSION

Direct Instruction has the advantage of a long history of research on its effectiveness and widespread implementation in schools. Because of this history, an enormous literature base has been amassed, capturing effects on a wide variety of students, including students in the general education setting and students with disabilities. Further, study outcomes across different subject areas allow closer examination of the effectiveness of DI programs in reading, math, language, and spelling. The research syntheses discussed in this chapter and summarized in Table 2.1 help us to make sense of this extensive evidence base. Despite the range of procedural variations that have inherently influenced the cumulative findings of these syntheses, there has been remarkable consistency in conclusions about the effectiveness of Direct Instruction programs, with all of the reviews concluding that DI programs are more effective than other programs and that the effects are well beyond the levels traditionally used to denote educationally important effects.

While it is hopeful that this evidence will inform future policy and reform efforts, further research within the field of Direct Instruction is necessary. Additional studies, especially in the areas of math, spelling, and language, are needed, and studies that employ more rigorous methodology, such as randomized control trials, would continue to reinforce the DI research base. Moreover, evaluations on a larger scale, at the whole-school or district level, are important to better understand the systemic features linked to improved outcomes. These features have the potential to improve practice, support scaling-up efforts, and increase sustainability of large-scale implementations. Similarly, more research is warranted to examine the relationship between fidelity to implementation guidelines and student outcomes.

As the movement toward identification and dissemination of scientifically validated or evidence-based educational interventions continues to gain momentum, educators and policymakers will be required to make sense of the research that exists on the effectiveness of a spectrum of programs and curricula. Research syntheses prove to be a valuable resource in guiding decision-making at the national, state, and local level, as much more confident conclusions can be drawn from examining the cumulative results of studies than from considering the idiosyncratic findings of individual studies alone. As consumers of these syntheses, it is crucial for educators and policymakers to consider the implications of procedural variations in synthesis methodology. Because research syntheses are intended to help make sense of large bodies of research, it is important for persons responsible for disseminating the conclusions drawn from the syntheses to clearly identify what these conclusions represent, how to interpret them in practice, and what limitations exist–continuously keeping in mind the intent of the synthesis in the first place.

REFERENCES

Adams G., & Engelmann, S. (1996). *Research on Direct Instruction: 25 years beyond DISTAR*. Seattle, WA: Educational Achievement Systems.

American Psychological Association's Presidential Task Force on Evidence-Based Practice. (2006). Evidence-based practice in psychology. *American Psychologist, 61,* 271–283.

Ashworth, D. R. (1999). Effects of Direct Instruction and basal reading instruction programs on the reading achievement of second graders. *Reading Improvement, 26*(4), 150–156.

Bereiter, C., & Kurland, M. (1981–1982). A constructive look at Follow Through results. *Interchange, 12,* 1–22.

Borman, G. D., Hewes, G. M., Overman, L. T., & Brown, S. (2003). Comprehensive school reform and achievement: A meta-analysis. *Review of Educational Research, 73*(2), 125–230.

Carlson, C. D., & Francis, D. J. (2002). Increasing the reading achievement of at-risk children through Direct Instruction: Evaluation of the Rodeo Institute for Teacher Excellence (RITE). *Journal of Education for Students Placed at Risk, 7*(2), pp. 141–166.

Carnine, D., Silbert, J., Kame'enui, E., & Tarver, S. (2004). *Direct Instruction reading* (4th ed.). Upper Saddle River, NJ: Pearson.

Cochrane Collaboration. (2008). *The Cochrane Library: Independent high-quality evidence for health care decision making.* Retrieved December 31, 2010 from http://www.thecochranelibrary.com

Cohen, J. (1988). *Statistical power analysis for the behavioral sciences* (2nd ed.). Hillsdale, NJ: Erlbaum.

Cooper H. (2010). *Research synthesis and meta-analysis.* Thousand Oaks, CA: Sage.

Cowan, P. A. (2004). Advancing evidence-based practice through meta-analysis. *Nephrology Nursing Journal, 31*(3), 343–347.

Cross, R. W., Rebarber, T., & Wilson, S. F. (2002). Student gains in a privately managed network of charter schools using Direct Instruction. *Journal of Direct Instruction, 2*(1), 3–21.

Engelmann, S. (2007). *Teaching needy kids in our backwards system.* Eugene, OR: ADI Press.

Forness, S. R., Kavale, K. A., Blum, I. M., & Lloyd, J. W. (1997). Mega-analysis of meta-analysis: What works in special education. *Teaching Exceptional Children, 19*(6), 4–9.

Gersten, R. M., Becker, W. C., Heiry, T. J., & White, W. A. T. (1984). Entry IQ and yearly academic growth of children in Direct Instruction programs: A longitudinal study of low SES children. *Educational Evaluation and Policy Analysis, 6*(2), 109–121.

Ginn, P. V., Keel, M. C., & Fredrick, L. D. (2002). Using *Reasoning and Writing* with gifted fifth grade students. *Journal of Direct Instruction, 2*(1), 41–47.

Gonzales, P., Williams, T., Jocelyn, L., Roey, S., Kastberg, D., & Brenwald, S. (2008). Highlights from TIMSS 2007: *Mathematics and science achievement of U.S. fourth- and eighth-grade students in an international context (NCES 2009-001 revised).* Washington, DC: National Center for Education Statistics, Institute of Education Sciences, U.S. Department of Education.

Grossen, B. (2004). Success of a Direct Instruction model at a secondary level school with high-risk students. *Reading & Writing Quarterly, 20,* 161–178.

Jackson, G. B. (1980). Methods for integrative reviews. *Review of Educational Research, 50,* 438–460.

Kavale, K. A. (2001). Decision making in special education: The function of meta-analysis. *Exceptionality, 9*(4), 245–268.

Kinder, D., Kubina, R., & Marchand-Martella, N. E. (2005). Special education and Direct Instruction: An effective combination. *Journal of Direct Instruction, 5*(1), 1–36.

MacIver, M. A., & Kemper, E. (2002). The impact of Direct Instruction on elementary students' reading achievement in an urban school district. *Journal of Education for Students Placed at Risk, 7,*(2) 197–220.

National Center for Education Statistics. (2001). *The nation's report card: Mathematics highlights 2000.* Washington, DC: U.S. Department of Education/Office of Educational Research and Improvement.

National Council of Teachers of Mathematics (NCTM). (2000). *Executive summary: Principles and standards for school mathematics.* Retrieved December 15, 2010 from http://www.nctm.org/uploadedFiles/Math_Standards/12752_exec_pssm.pdf\

National Institute of Child Health and Human Development. (2000). *Report of the National Reading Panel. Teaching children to read: An evidence-based assessment of the scientific research literature on reading and its implications for reading instruction: Reports of the subgroups* (NIH Publication No. 00-4754). Washington, DC: U.S. Government Printing Office.

National Mathematics Advisory Panel (NMAP). (2008). *Foundations for success: The final report of the National Mathematics Advisory Panel.* Washington, DC: U.S. Department of Education. Retrieved December 15, 2010 from http://www2.ed.gov/about/bdscomm/list/mathpanel/report/final-report.pdf

O'Brien, D. M., & Ware, A. M. (2002). Implementing research-based reading programs in the Fort Worth Independent school district. *Journal of Education for Students Placed at Risk, 7,* 167–195.

Przychodzin, A. M., Marchand-Martella, N. E., Martella, R. C., & Azim, D. (2004). Direct Instruction mathematics programs: An overview and research summary. *Journal of Direct Instruction, 4*(1), 53–84.

Przychodzin-Havis, A. M., Marchand-Martella, N. E., Martella, R. C., Miller, D. A., Warner, L., Leonard, B., et al. (2005). An analysis of *Corrective Reading* research. *Journal of Direct Instruction, 5*(1), 37–65.

Robinson, J. W., & Hesse, K. D. (1981). A morphemically based spelling program's effect on spelling skills and spelling performance of seventh grade students. *Journal of Educational Research, 75*(1), 56–62.

Rosenthal, R. (1984). *Meta-analytic procedures for social research.* Newbury Park, CA: Sage.

Schieffer, C., Marchand-Martella, N. E., Martella, R. C., Simonsen, F. L., & Waldron-Soler, K. M. (2002). An analysis of the *Reading Mastery* program: Effective components and research review. *Journal of Direct Instruction, 2*(2), 87–119.

Sexton, C. W. (1989). Effectiveness of the *DISTAR Reading I* program in developing first graders' language skills. *Journal of Educational Research, 82*(5), 289–293.

Shadish, W., Cook, T., & Campbell, D. (2002) *Experimental and quasi-experimental designs for generalized causal inference.* Boston: Houghton Mifflin.

Simonsen, F., & Gunter, L. (2001). Best practices in spelling instruction: A research summary. *Journal of Direct Instruction, 1*(2), 97–105.

Tallmadge, G. K. (1977). *The Joint Dissemination Review Panel Ideabook.* Washington, DC: National Institute of Education and U.S. Office of Education.

Tarver, S. G., & Jung, J. S. (1995). A comparison of mathematics achievement and mathematics attitudes of first and second graders instructed with either a discovery-learning mathematics curriculum or a Direct Instruction curriculum. *Effective School Practices, 14*(1), 49–57.

U.S. Department of Education. (2002). *No Child Left Behind: A desktop reference.* Washington, DC: Office of Elementary and Secondary Education.

Vitale, M. R., & Joseph, B. L. (2008). Broadening the institutional value of Direct Instruction implemented in a low-SES elementary school: Implications for scale-up and school reform. *Journal of Direct Instruction, 8*(1), 1–18

White, W. A. T. (1988). A meta-analysis of the effects of Direct Instruction in special education. *Education and Treatment of Children, 11*(4), 364–374.

Young, M., Baker, J., & Martin, M. (1990). Teaching basic number skills to students with a moderate intellectual disability. *Education and Training in Mental Retardation, 25,* 83–93.

CHAPTER 3

The previous two chapters have documented the ways in which DI programs are research-based and validated. In Chapter 1, Engelmann described how the systematic development of DI programs incorporates logical reasoning and ongoing research. Chapter 2 summarized the large amount of empirical research that has documented the efficacy of DI programs and how students make much stronger gains with these curricula than with other programs. Yet the educational community continues to ignore this work, to the detriment of millions of children and their readiness to participate as educated citizens of our society. In this chapter Engelmann and Stockard reflect on this failure. Drawing on their individual research backgrounds, they describe several instances in which educational researchers have ignored the empirical evidence, discuss how this contradicts scientific traditions and logic, and examine how it harms students and the society as a whole.

BLINDED TO EVIDENCE
HOW EDUCATIONAL RESEARCHERS
RESPOND TO EMPIRICAL DATA
Siegfried Engelmann and Jean Stockard

Both of us have spent decades involved in research, albeit in different academic fields and using different methodological approaches and theoretical traditions. Despite the differences in our academic backgrounds and experiences, our conclusions regarding educational research are very similar. This chapter describes our views and, particularly, the ways in which we have seen educational researchers misconstrue and ignore the empirical data related to Direct Instruction. This chapter has three parts. The first, Is the "Gold Standard" Really Gold?, authored by Engelmann, describes the educational research establishment's current fascination with so-called "gold standard" research and the ways in which political, professional, or personal bias overrides the research evidence. The second part, A Social Scientist's View of Educational Research, authored by Stockard, delineates norms that are common to science, describes the ways in which the DI corpus of research conforms to these norms, and presents two very costly examples of educational researchers ignoring these norms and the empirical results. In the conclusion, we reflect on possible reasons for these actions and the costs to students and society.

IS THE "GOLD STANDARD" REALLY GOLD?
S. Engelmann

Much has been made in recent years of a "gold standard" in research, urging the educational community to focus almost exclusively on randomized control trials, supposedly emulating medical research. In reality, when well-conducted studies fail to support favored scenarios or when they support programs that are not in favor, the data are ignored. The first section below, Gold Standard Failure, describes such instances. The second section, Quest for Pristine Internal Validity of Educational Studies, questions the worth of this "gold standard" approach and demonstrates why it is futile.

GOLD STANDARD FAILURE

Our view of the literature is certainly influenced by our perspective about developing and field-testing instructional programs and by the various "low probability" demonstrations that we have conducted, described in Chapter 1. From this viewpoint, it seems that those who screen and evaluate studies that compare specific instructional approaches set criteria that mimic medical research in a highly selective manner. For instance, medical research endorses a gold standard largely for efficacy studies (tightly controlled lab experiments), but education endorses it for all studies. The centerpiece of the medical gold standard is random assignment of subjects. However, there's also the requirement of blind or double-blind conditions, which means that neither the subjects nor those who analyze the data know whether a given subject is in the experimental group or is receiving a placebo.

The double-blind criterion is not easily satisfied in educational experiments that compare programs. Certainly studies that may be completed in two weeks could be conducted in a "lab" setting. There may also be hope of conducting some educational double-blind, "gold standard" experiments; however, it is unlikely studies involving year-long programs can meet the double-blind requirements. Imagine students in a school who don't know that they are in a program quite different from the program students in the grade above them went through the last year. Consider the improbability of a teacher who doesn't know that this year's program is not the one the school used last year.

Possibly duplicity in how results are used provides the greatest difference between medical and educational research. If a gold-standard medical study provides conclusive evidence that something works, it is promoted; if the study provides evidence that something does not work, the ineffective process is publicly rejected. In contrast, if a gold-standard educational study provides conclusive evidence that a favored program worked, there would be a strong effort to publicize this fact; however, if the study showed that a favored approach failed, there would be no attempts to publicize or to caution use of the approach that caused the unfavorable outcomes. Also, differential treatment occurs if an unfavored approach has evidence of effectiveness. If studies of an unfavored approach do not meet gold standards but have been reported in respected journals, the evidence is rejected.

There are four large studies that support these assertions:

1. The national evaluation of Project Follow Through (Kennedy, 1978; Stebbins, St. Pierre, Proper, Anderson, & Cerva, 1977);

2. The Rodeo Institute for Teacher Excellence (RITE) studies in Dallas (Carlson & Francis, 2003);

3. The state of Tennessee's Student/Teacher Achievement Ratio (Project STAR) study on class size (Word et al., 1990, 1994); and

4. Chicago's Striving Reader Initiative (Metis Associates, 2011).

Tale of Two Successful Unfavored (and Unpublicized) Approaches

The reactions of the educational establishment to two very large and successful implementations of Direct Instruction–Project Follow Through and the Rodeo Institute work–illustrate how highly successful, but unfavored, approaches are ignored and unpublicized.

Project Follow Through

The evaluation of Project Follow Through (the largest educational research study ever conducted) compared the performance of 22 different approaches to teaching at-risk students in Grades K through 3. Direct Instruction was the only approach in which students had positive gains in all of the outcomes measured, both academic and affective, and the DI model produced the highest scores on all these outcomes (Bereiter & Kurland, 1981–82; Stebbins et al., 1977; Watkins, 1997). Long-term follow-up studies documented lasting impacts of the program, as students in the DI program maintained higher levels of achievement through the high school years and were more likely to finish high school and go on to college (Meyer, 1984). There is no scientific basis for rejecting Follow Through outcomes; yet, the study was ignored at its completion and has been rejected by the What Works Clearinghouse (WWC) on the grounds that it is too old to be valid (WWC, 2007).

Rodeo Institute for Teacher Excellence (RITE)

More recently, the Rodeo Institute for Teacher Excellence (RITE) funded an extensive implementation of Direct Instruction reading programs for at-risk students in the primary grades. RITE also conducted evaluations of the programs that involved over 9,300 students and 277 teachers. Again, the results were overwhelmingly positive (Carlson & Francis, 2003). The study has been rejected by the WWC, and the intervention has received no recognition as a highly successful effort (WWC, 2007). RITE and the Follow Through studies involved an "unpopular" program (Direct Instruction), and the studies were rejected.

Tale of Two Unsuccessful Favored Approaches

The state of Tennessee's Student/Teacher Achievement Ratio (STAR) study of class size (Word et al., 1990, 1994) and the Chicago Striving Reader Initiative involve approaches that are in accord with currently popular views about causes of academic problems and the solutions. Both these studies were "gold standard" in that both used random assignment of subjects. Yet educators have drawn conclusions from these studies that are not supported by the evidence.

Project STAR

The STAR study involved reducing the number of students in regular classrooms to 23. The total number of students in the study was 1,650, over a four-year period. The study used random assignment of classrooms in the same school, with half the classes smaller than the others. Students in the smaller classes had achievement scores that were higher than those in the larger classes. However, the associated effect sizes, an average of 0.21 (Mosteller, 1995, p. 121), were only a fraction of those found in Project Follow Through's 1.40 average (Adams & Engelmann, 1996, p. 52; Bereiter & Kurland, 1981–82) and below the level typically used to denote "educational importance," 0.25 (Tallmadge, 1977).

Despite the poor STAR results, the findings were widely publicized. An article on the STAR project that appeared in *The Future of Children* ended with these confident remarks:

> Because a controlled education experiment ... of this quality, magnitude, and duration is a rarity, it is important that both educators and policymakers have access to its statistical information and understand its implications. Thought should be given by both public and private organizations to making sure that this information is preserved and well documented and that access to it is encouraged. The ... statewide controlled experiment is a valuable device for assessing educational interventions and, thereby, improving school systems. (Mosteller, 1995, p. 127)

The book *Evidence Matters: Randomized Trials in Education Research* (Mosteller & Boruch, 2002) featured only one educational study, STAR. California was convinced by the unqualified endorsements of the STAR project and reduced class size at the state level. Around the same time Mosteller's article (quoted above) was published, however, California was looking at disappointing data on the performance of its students. The 1994 National Assessment of Educational Progress (NAEP) assessment showed that only 18% of California's students were rated proficient or advanced in reading. California's national ranking on NAEP was second from last in reading (NAEP, 1996). There were obviously flaws in the design of the STAR study, but these were not identified before the fact. The biggest lesson that came from STAR is that random assignment cannot compensate for poor internal validity.

The Striving Reader Initiative

Smaller class size received (and continues to receive) considerable press (Krueger & Whitmore, 2001; Mosteller, 1995). In contrast, a colossal five-year study in Chicago, the Striving Reader Initiative, was a gold-standard showcase for a considerable number of variables endorsed by the literature. The study was initiated in 2007 when Arnie Duncan (who later became Secretary of Education) was CEO of Chicago Public Schools. This study has received virtually no press. The probable reason is that the initial reports show not only that it didn't do as well as expected, but that it produced no apparent positive results.

The Striving Reader Initiative was designed to remedy reading failure of students in Grades 6–8. The project had random assignment of 31 treatment schools and 32 control schools. The initiative involved a three-tier intervention model that featured a full-school, 90-minute, daily immersion in reading comprehension and a focus on subject areas. The experimental schools initiated longer school days, after-school activities, more adults in the classroom, smaller class size, small-group differentiated instruction, staff development, teacher collaboration, counseling, high interest reading material, and frequent assessments.

The year four report issued in 2011 is over 180 pages and contains many tables (Metis Associates, 2011). Although the experimental schools were judged to be well implemented, results of the first year assessment showed no significant differences for any grade or any of the subgroups. After two years there were no differences. After three years, "results indicate that there was no detectable overall impact of the program on Tier 2 and 3 students" (p. 120). In addition, "there was no overall treatment effect for all students in the ITT sample at the end of the fourth project year ..." (p. 156).

Over the four years, only one of the 24 subgroups obtained a statistically significant outcome in favor of the experimental group. That achievement occurred in the fourth year; however, the p value was 0.048 (which would not be considered significant if the significance criterion was 0.01 rather than 0.05). More than one outcome would have been significant by chance alone (5 per hundred measures at the 0.05 level). Also, the effect size was 0.174, far below what is required for generally recognized educationally important effects (0.25; Tallmadge, 1977). Finally, the normal curve equivalent (NCE) scores for both groups were far below the mean of sixth graders and differed by less than 2 points (Control: 36.513 and Treatment: 38.333). If students had performed at grade level, they would have had scores in the 60s, which means both controls and experimental students were years below the norm for sixth graders. These are obviously not the results Arnie Duncan and others anticipated.

The fact that the results are not publicized, however, suggests that the system is deeply prejudiced and unscientific in its orientation. The Chicago study represents a milestone for educational studies with its large numbers of students and gold-standard experimental design. The results should therefore be unquestionably valid. Why wouldn't it follow that the field should embrace the results and conclude that either there is no way to remedy the underachievement of these striving students or that the way Chicago approached the problem has been documented to be the wrong way?

Those seem to be the only conclusions, and they seem to be highly relevant to the instruction for Striving Readers. Shouldn't teachers and administrators know that the Chicago approach was inert? Shouldn't the specific instructional material and practices used in this effort be recognized as being ineffective or at least questionable? In a broader sense, shouldn't those who proposed this apparently naïve intervention be recognized as lacking credibility?

The ultimate question may be: If no conclusions are to be drawn from a study that fails to show significant results, wouldn't it have been wiser to design an intervention that did not meet the gold standard? In that way, there would be a modest reason for not publicizing the results.

Bias

In summary, there seems to be an overriding bias in recognizing the worth of the four large studies. Follow Through, the RITE study, and the Striving Reader Initiative had results that were not consonant with current prejudices about instruction. The results were ignored or actively suppressed. The STAR project had outcomes consistent with the current prejudices about instruction and the results were embraced and continue to be embraced, even after the California results strongly contradicted the STAR conclusions (NAEP, 1996) and despite weak outcomes. For instance, a Center for Public Education report on class size and student achievement (CPE, n.d., para. 6) concluded, "The most influential contemporary evidence that smaller classes lead to improved achievement is Tennessee's Project STAR."

QUEST FOR PRISTINE INTERNAL VALIDITY OF EDUCATIONAL STUDIES

The STAR study had very obvious problems of internal validity that were not on a handy list of possibilities. Because the study used random assignment of classrooms in the same school, two teachers teaching the fourth grade discover that one has a smaller class. The other teacher understandably asks, "Why does that teacher have less work than I have?" One possible response is for the slighted teacher not to work as hard. Scores in that classroom go down compared to the other classroom, and a spurious difference is created. The probability of investigators knowing everything to control is apparently slim, but even obvious details are not controlled well in many studies.

Medical research recognizes that the greatest cause of poor internal validity in effectiveness studies is that patients don't provide accurate statements about whether they took the medication as scheduled (Glintborg, Hillestrom, Olsen, Dalhoff, & Poulsen, 2007). Parallel problems occur in educational studies. Studies often have inadequate provisions for documenting whether teachers are providing the instruction scheduled. Teacher reports of having started on time, ending on time, and teaching the material according to particular procedures are potential causes of distortions.

Are results distorted that much by not using random assignments? With the Chicago Striving Reader study, there would be no difference in any results if matched-pairs rather than random assignment were used to create the groups.

Unlike most medical trials, studies that evaluate instructional programs do not articulately describe the treatments. Studies that evaluate an experimental drug reveal an extreme difference between instructional and medical research. The drug, its schedule, and related information about dos and don'ts can be summarized succinctly. In contrast, a description of the schedule and related information for an instructional program would require many pages and would describe contingencies that have no clear parallel in trials that evaluate drugs. The reason is that an instructional treatment is the product of three variables—program, teaching, and placement of students. (See Chapter 1, Tables 1.1 and 1.2.) Unless all are controlled, serious distortions may occur.

This is not to say that nothing is revealed from studies that have flaws. The better program should produce better results. So if the numbers are large enough, the more effective programs should produce solid evidence of causing superior student performance. The caution is that the results are based on a correlation, so they don't imply what someone needs to do to cause positive outcomes in a particular classroom.

Large numbers of studies seem to be the key for evaluating any approach, but DI is the *only* approach that has large numbers of older studies that document its effectiveness. Unfortunately the DI studies that have large numbers are judged by the WWC to be invalid. Medical studies are not stricken from the record if they are more than 20 years old; however, the WWC rejects studies older than 20 years. This provision affects only one approach—DI (Stockard, 2010).

Should DI "replicate" these studies to provide more current findings?

No.

The field should follow the lead of medical research and recognize reasonably well-designed studies whether or not the results are recent or consistent with current prejudices. Furthermore, the field should encourage research that challenges the various universal assertions that appear in the literature.

A purging based on analytic induction, the logical approach described in detail in Chapter 1, would disclose the technical nature of the causes of learning that will otherwise remain hidden in correlational half truths that dominate much of current educational literacy. The ultimate goal would be the institutionalization of practices that guarantee continued use of programs that stand up to mandated program-referenced testing (also described in detail in Chapter 1). The beneficiaries would not only be students, but also teachers and administrators who engineer scientific instruction.

A SOCIAL SCIENTIST'S VIEW OF EDUCATION RESEARCH

Jean Stockard

In the following discussion, many of the points made by Engelmann in the first part of this chapter are echoed from a different perspective, that of a social scientist reflecting on educational research from outside the discipline. In the first section, key normative elements of science common to the social, biological, and physical sciences are described. The second section details ways in which the Direct Instruction tradition of program development and research conforms to each of these elements and how the DI tradition's adherence to these norms contrasts sharply with the vast majority of educational research. The third section describes two of the most egregious examples of ways in which the educational research community has violated basic rules of science and misrepresented research results.

NORMATIVE TRADITIONS OF SCIENCE

In introductory classes to the field, and in more in-depth courses required of majors, undergraduate students in the social sciences study the methodological proce-dures and norms that have guided the disciplines for generations. While the subject matter of the social sciences is, of course, different and, many would argue, more complex than the biological and physical sciences, the normative traditions are similar, if not identical (Kemeny, 1969; Nagel, 1961). The discussion below focuses on four key norms of science.

1. Science Is Theory Based

Science is guided by theoretical speculations about how the world works. These speculations form the basis of all scientific work, from a chemist theorizing about the way in which chemical compounds will interact, to economists speculating about how changes in monetary policy affect inflation rates, or sociologists hypothesizing about relationships between changes in the demographic composition of communities and rates of lethal violence. No matter what the topic of study, scientists are guided by theoretical understandings regarding their areas of interest, generally building on theoretical traditions in their own and/or other fields. This theoretical work is both inductive and deductive in nature.

Good scientists use both inductive and deductive approaches. They compare their theoretical speculations with the data, revise these speculations when empirical results indicate that they should, test developing hypotheses, and then, as needed, revise their theories. As a field of study matures, the speculations become conceptual models and explanatory theoretical systems. Parsimonious theoretical explanations, those which use the fewest underlying assumptions or variables, are seen as the most elegant and the ultimate goal (Cohen, 1989; Einstein, 1934; Kaplan, 1964; Kemeny, 1969).

2. Science Is Cumulative in Nature

We use the findings of past work to guide our future work. Using the Popperian notion of falsification, hypotheses that are proven false are discarded, and those that receive support (or technically have not yet been falsified) are retained (Cohen, 1989; Popper, 1962). We continue to test hypotheses, but expand our analyses to see if results hold under varying conditions.

A variety of terms have been used to describe this cumulative process. One is the notion of a cumulative research program, or a phased model of research, involving the gradual development of understandings and causal inferences, typically moving from rather small and highly focused controlled experimental designs to tests with more varied settings, subjects, and outcomes and employing a range of methods and techniques (Cohen, 1989; Huitt, Monetti, & Hummel, 2009). Another is the "grounded theory of generalized causal inference" described by Shadish, Cook, and Campbell (2002), which involves the systematic comparison of results from a variety of settings, samples, and research approaches. The third and perhaps most commonly cited in the current literature is the meta-analytic tradition, discussed in Chapter 2 of this volume, which uses quantitative techniques to summarize large sets of research results (Bornstein, Hedges, Higgins, & Rothstein, 2009; Wolf, 1986). Despite the differing terms, all of the approaches are based on the notion that scientific understandings are cumulative in nature, building on multiple tests of hypotheses. As Cook and Campbell, authors of the most widely cited works on research design, put it,

> We stress the need for *many* tests to determine whether a causal proposition has or has not withstood falsification; such determinations cannot be made on one or two failures to achieve predicted results. (1979, p. 31, emphasis in original)

3. Good Science Is Flexible

The best social science theories and the most reliable accumulations of results are based on data derived through multiple methods, in a wide range of settings, using both inductive and deductive reasoning, employing qualitative and quantitative analyses, and adjusting the research design to the conditions.

> Among scientists, belief in the experiment as the *only* means to settle disputes about causation is gone, though it is still the preferred method in many circumstances. Gone, too, is the belief that the power experimental methods often displayed in the laboratory would transfer easily to applications in field settings. (Shadish, Cook, & Campbell, 2002, p. 30, emphasis in original)

Note that this call for multiple methods and approaches that match the needs of the situation is in complete agreement with Engelmann's conclusions regarding the utility of the so-called "gold standard" approach for educational research discussed in the first part of this chapter.

4. Good Science Is Honest and Open

In the social sciences we have strong traditions of blind peer review, with scholars who do not know the identity of the authors reviewing and critiquing all material before publication. We also have strong norms regarding the sharing of data so that others can check our results, perhaps with different analytic strategies. Replication is encouraged, for only through multiple tests can we be assured that results are valid. In fact, without such openness and honesty none of the other scientific norms actually matters.

DIRECT INSTRUCTION AND NORMATIVE SCIENCE

The Direct Instruction corpus of work is a classic example of each of the elements of normative science.

1. Strong Theoretical Base

First, DI has a strong theoretical base. As detailed in Chapter 4 and Appendix B, Engelmann and his colleagues have written extensively on the theory of learning that underlies the development of the DI instructional programs with works such as *Conceptual Learning* (Engelmann, 1969), *Theory of Instruction* (Engelmann & Carnine, 1991), and *Inferred Functions of Performance and Learning* (Engelmann & Steely, 2004).

While the theoretical writings are intellectually connected with the long-established and classical tradition of the logical empiricists (see Engelmann and Carnine, 2010), Engelmann and Carnine's Theory of Instruction (1991) stands by itself as a fully articulated analysis of how children learn and can be effectively taught. Each element of the theory was carefully tested as it was developed, illustrating the interplay of inductive and deductive analyses mentioned above.

2. Cumulative in Nature

Second, the work is cumulative in nature. In fact, the Direct Instruction literature can be seen as a classic example of the phased model of research with the gradual expansion of focus and methodologies. The development of curricular programs grew from the initial work with preschoolers through the elementary grades and to programs for those in the upper grades and adults. The academic subjects involved moved from reading and mathematics to science and social studies (see Appendices A and C).

Detailed guidelines for behavioral management and implementation of the programs have been developed, as discussed in Chapters 5 and 6 of this volume. The curriculum has been developed through lengthy and detailed experiments with different populations of students and in different settings, using the methods described in Chapter 1. Extensive work has validated the principles of learning and instruction that provide the theoretical base. Field-testing with large and varied populations of students and teachers has examined the extent of the programs' effectiveness across many different settings (Engelmann, 2007; Engelmann & Carnine, 1991; Huitt, Monetti, & Hummel, 2009). Perhaps most important, evidence of the efficacy of the curriculum has continued to expand over the years with, as described in Chapter 2, highly consistent results.

3. Varied Approaches

Third, research related to Direct Instruction has taken many different forms and approaches, embodying the flexibility that is the hallmark of a mature science. While there are dozens of randomized control trials testing the efficacy of the DI programs, there are also many field-based studies employing large samples as well as so-called "single subject designs" looking at more unique and specialized populations. Scholars have examined the impact of Direct Instruction with many different groups, from gifted students to those with severe disabilities. They have employed quantitative and qualitative methods; and they have looked at not just impacts on achievement, but at impacts on perceptions of self-confidence and self-efficacy of students and teachers as well as ways in which the programs can best be implemented. The result is a strong cumulative body of work that embodies consistent documentation of the ways in which DI programs promote high achievement among students with a wide variety of demographic characteristics, in many different settings, and at all ability levels.

4. Honest and Open

Finally, the body of DI research conforms to the norm of honest and open research. The work has appeared in peer-reviewed journals around the world, having been checked and cross-checked by independent researchers. In the context of a meta-analysis project, Borman, Hewes, Overman, and Brown (2003) documented the extent of these differences and commented on the relatively large amount of work on DI conducted by researchers not affiliated with the programs' development. Borman and colleagues (2003) identified 49 studies of DI compared to a median of only 4 studies for the other 28 models they examined.

THE EDUCATIONAL RESEARCH COMMUNITY AND DIRECT INSTRUCTION

Even though Direct Instruction research conforms closely to the norms of science and the cumulated body of work is strong and consistent, the educational research community has, for many years, ignored and actively resisted these findings. Two egregious examples are examined below. Many could have been chosen, but these were selected because they involve the expenditure of vast amounts of money with the full endorsement of the federal government. Their beginnings are separated by almost four decades but show disturbing parallels of what could be seen as purposeful manipulation of research results to hide the ways in which DI programs promote strong student learning.

Project Follow Through

Project Follow Through has been called the largest educational experiment that was ever conducted. Beginning in 1967, as an element of President Johnson's War on Poverty, it continued until the summer of 1995, with a total price tag of about one billion dollars (Grossen, 1996). The project was built on the assumption that low levels of educational achievement were a major factor in the perpetuation of poverty from one generation to another. More than 20 different educational models, including Direct Instruction, were implemented in 170 high poverty communities throughout the country as a way to test the relative efficacy of each approach. Carefully designed assessment procedures were developed by two independent evaluation agencies to determine which of the models would be most successful in developing students' achievement and their self-esteem. Assessments included comparisons to "control" schools with similar characteristics as well as comparisons to national norms.

The results of the evaluation were clear cut. Direct Instruction was the clear winner. It was the only approach that resulted in students having positive changes in all of the measured outcomes. Some of the programs even had negative results, with students having worse outcomes at the end of the intervention (see Adams, 1996; Becker & Engelmann, 1996; Bereiter & Kurland, 1981–82; Grossen, 1996; Watkins, 1997).

In a world in which the norms of science are valued and honored, one would expect that these findings, based on such a well-designed and extensive experiment, would lead the educational research community to embrace Direct Instruction. In fact, however, just the opposite occurred. Most of the other programs in the experiment were programs favored by the educational establishment, such as those discussed in the first part of this chapter. To a large extent, many of these programs are still popular today, albeit sometimes having slightly altered names, such as "whole language" to describe the "language experience" approach and "developmentally appropriate" instead of "Open Education" (Grossen, 1996, p. 9).

In a series of maneuvers that are almost impossible to believe but which are, in fact, well documented, the educational research community changed the research question. While originally interested in which program produced the most favorable results, the question morphed into asking, "What was the aggregate result of the programs?" In other words, the results of all the different models were simply lumped together (House, Glass, McLean, & Walker, 1978). Given that 20 of the 22 models had negative or null results, the new conclusion was that the programs had no effect. Educational researchers wrote extensive critiques of the Follow Through design, criticizing the use of quantitative analyses and comparisons and suggesting that an ethnographic and case-study descriptive approach would be more appropriate (see Grossen, 1996, p. 7). Even though the evidence–from the original rules of the game–was overwhelming, the educational research community chose to ignore the evidence and alter the rules so that this would seem legitimate.

What Works Clearinghouse

Over three decades after Follow Through began, the U.S. Department of Education established the What Works Clearinghouse (WWC). The stated purpose of the WWC is to be "a central and trusted source of scientific evidence for what works in education ...to provide accurate information on education research" (WWC, 2013a). Like Project Follow Through, the WWC has been extraordinarily expensive, with costs of well over 75 million dollars in its first 10 years of existence (U.S. General Accountability Office, 2010, p. 25). Yet, like Follow Through, the WWC has failed to live up to its promise, presenting very misleading reports to the public, analyses that denigrate strong programs, such as Direct Instruction, and promote far weaker ones. Many of the problems stem from the criteria that the WWC uses to choose studies for review as well as outright errors and misinterpretations of the studies that are accepted.

Criteria for WWC Acceptance

While the conclusion of the Follow Through project incorporated criticism of quantitative research and experimental designs, the What Works Clearinghouse, somewhat ironically, made an about-face. It strongly promotes randomized control trials, seeing these as the "gold standard" discussed in the first half of this chapter and virtually dismisses almost all other research designs. Studies that are accepted for the WWC review must typically meet a long list of methodological criteria, such as pretest scores within given ranges for each group, extensive data on attrition of subjects, and publication within the last two decades (WWC, 2013b).

Not surprisingly, very few studies have met the WWC criteria. The U.S. General Accountability Office (U.S. GAO) reports that less than 10% of all studies examined pass their requirements (U.S. GAO, 2010, p. 13). The acceptance rate for studies of DI is even lower. Of the more than 200 studies of Direct Instruction that the WWC claimed to have examined by mid 2013, only 10 (5%) were found to meet their criteria either fully or in part.

As described more extensively in other writings (e.g., Stockard, 2010, 2012, 2013a; Stockard & Wood, 2012), the elements of the DI literature that reflect its maturity and should, given the norms regarding the cumulative nature of science, add weight to judgments of its merit instead appear to have worked against its acceptance by the WWC. For instance, the automatic exclusion of studies conducted more than 20 years ago effectively discards the large number of randomized control trials that were at the basis of the early development of the programs. To date the WWC officials have refused to provide any scientific basis for this decision. While they have claimed that this policy ensures that results will be valid for today's students, they have provided no evidence to suggest that the way in which students learn has altered over time (Stockard, 2008). The preference for small, tightly restricted, randomized control trials effectively excludes most field-based studies of larger populations and those that use advanced statistical methods for controls. Such larger, field-based trials (like the RITE work analyzed by Carlson and Francis, 2003, and discussed earlier in this chapter) are especially important for ensuring external validity and have been much more common in the DI literature as the field has matured.

Having such strict criteria for studies to be reviewed would be important if this made a difference in the results. In other words, if the criteria affected results of studies such that those that met the criteria had more accurate estimates of a program's efficacy, one could argue that it would be important to maintain these "standards." Given the large number of studies of Direct Instruction, it is possible to test this hypothesis, and I did so with a sample of works that examined the use of *Reading Mastery* with students with learning difficulties. The extent to which the studies met the WWC's criteria varied, with some meeting most of them and some meeting very few. (None met all the criteria, and all met at least one criterion.) In an extensive statistical analysis, I found that none of the criteria had a significant relationship to estimates of the effect of DI. In other words, whether or not the criteria were met, or whether a few or many of the criteria were met, the estimates of the effect of *Reading Mastery* on students' achievement remained unchanged–positive and significant, similar to the effects reported in Chapter 2, and well beyond the levels usually seen as educationally important (Stockard, 2013a).

WWC Errors in Interpretations

Given that the WWC's reports are based on only a small fraction of the extant literature it is crucial that decisions regarding the inclusion or exclusion of studies, as well as the interpretation of those that are accepted, be as accurate as possible. In other words, because their reports are based on a very small fraction of the extant literature it is crucial that such reports be accurate. However, in other writings I have documented numerous errors (see Stockard, 2008, 2010, 2012, and 2013a; Stockard & Wood, 2013). These involve errors in decisions regarding the exclusion of studies, such as the decision to exclude RITE's large scale evaluation discussed by Engelmann in the first part of this chapter. The WWC claimed that the inclusion of teacher training and instruction in behavior management, both key elements of DI programs, introduced confounds to the study and made it invalid.

I have also found serious errors in decisions regarding studies that were included in their reviews, documenting serious problems in 4 of the 10 studies of DI programs that the WWC had accepted for review by 2013. For example two studies accepted for a review of *Corrective Reading* used only selected elements of the program and the authors explicitly stated that their analysis should not be used to evaluate its efficacy. Analyses of study results that were accepted for review have been far from error free, with summary reports that sometimes distort and misrepresent the findings of the authors. For instance, an article that compared two highly similar Direct Instruction reading programs (*Reading Mastery* and *Horizons*) found that both produced achievement gains that were significantly greater than national norms would expect and that the impact of the two programs was similar. The WWC chose to ignore the comparison to the national norms and instead focused on the lack of difference between the two programs, concluding that there was no evidence that *Reading Mastery* was effective. (See Stockard, 2008, 2013a, and Stockard & Wood, 2012, for more extensive discussion.) To date, the WWC has refused to admit to any of these documented errors and has concluded only that some DI programs have "potentially positive" effects, a conclusion in stark contrast to the cumulated weight of scholarly research, such as the material summarized in Chapter 2.

The errors in the WWC procedures have extended to misrepresenting results for weak programs and providing positive ratings when the research evidence indicates that a different conclusion would be appropriate. For instance, the WWC has given high rankings to the Reading Recovery program, a short-term tutoring intervention. One of the studies used to justify this rating compared the standard Reading Recovery program to a "modified" program that included explicit instruction in phonological skills. Students in both the unmodified Reading Recovery program and the modified program (including instruction in phonologically based elements) eventually caught up with the other children, but the students in the modified program were able to discontinue tutoring much earlier. The standard Reading Recovery program was found to be 37% less efficient than the program that included instruction in phonics. In addition, students in the modified program continued to have higher levels of achievement and higher rates of learning at the end of the school year. The authors provide an extensive discussion and additional analyses that demonstrate the fallacy involved in Reading Recovery's assumptions about the ways in which word recognition skills develop. They clearly conclude that Reading Recovery is not an efficient method for teaching children to read and that phonological training is superior.

The WWC chose to ignore any results regarding the comparison group that received phonological training and had superior achievement, "because it was a modified version of the standard program" (Stockard, 2008, pp. 13-14). In correspondence explaining their decision they noted that the results with the other comparison groups were mentioned in a technical appendix of the WWC report, implying that such information could be available for those who were interested. Of course, the chance of a parent or school official accessing a technical appendix to find information that contradicts the inaccurate information given in the major pages of the web site is extremely remote, and most users of the website would reach the erroneous conclusion that the Reading Recovery program was effective. (See Stockard, 2008, for a fuller discussion and copies of correspondence with the WWC.)

Violating the Norms of Science

Although several decades separate the beginnings of Project Follow Through and the What Works Clearinghouse, the parallels in the ways in which they have violated the norms of science are striking and, to a social scientist, chilling. It could be suggested that, in its original conceptualization and design, Project Follow Through conformed to three of the four key norms of science described earlier:

1. Follow Through was based on the theoretical assumption that higher educational achievement was a key element to combatting generations of poverty.

2. Follow Through incorporated the notion of cumulating evidence by testing programs in multiple sites and over a period of years.

3. Follow Through could be seen as incorporating flexibility through its use of community and parental involvement and many different educational approaches.

Unfortunately, Project Follow Through failed to meet the most important scientific norm of honesty and openness:

4. Follow Through changed the research question and altered the presentation of the results to disguise the clear superiority of Direct Instruction.

The WWC lauds itself as "a central and trusted source of scientific evidence" (WWC, 2013), however, it fails to conform to all four key norms of science.

1. To date, the WWC has provided no theoretical basis for their approach, although the methodological literature, such as that cited above, could provide a great deal of guidance for such endeavors.

2. The very restrictive approach the WWC has taken to the literature, with an arbitrary cut-off date of studies to be reviewed and stringent criteria regarding the design of acceptable studies, has made a full examination of the cumulative literature virtually impossible.

3. The WWC acceptance protocols fly in the face of the flexibility advocated by the classic methodological tradition.

4. Finally, and most disturbing, the evidence suggests that, like the ultimate purveyors of the Follow Through results, the WWC has violated the scientific norms of honesty and openness. Violations of this norm appear in the inclusion and exclusion decisions, as well as the summaries of studies described above.

Other problems noted in analyses of the WWC work include failures to inform users of the ways in which their findings conflict with the established literature (e.g., the ways in which their conclusions regarding Direct Instruction contradict the meta-analytic findings described in Chapter 2), having no external peer review process, and failing to be transparent in procedures and processes, even though, as a federally funded program, it is required to do so. Finally, when errors occur, the WWC has failed to post public retractions and corrections of erroneous reports, allowing misrepresentations to remain in the public eye.

CONCLUSION

In the sections above we have given several examples of the ways in which the educational community, and particularly educational researchers, have ignored empirical evidence. In contrast to scientific norms that call for flexibility in approaches and building a strong cumulative tradition of research, the current fad in educational research involves the so-called "gold standard" approach of randomized control trials conducted under severely restricted conditions. We assert that this approach is inappropriate for most work in education and produces results that are neither internally nor externally valid (Stockard, 2013a, b). Even more disturbing than the current preoccupation with one narrow approach to research is the concerted pattern of those in power of misconstruing research results. For less favored programs, such as Direct Instruction, strong and positive results are hidden or misrepresented. In contrast, for favored programs, such as "whole language" and "constructivist" approaches, much smaller positive results are publicized and promoted and negative and null results are hidden or misrepresented.

While our analysis has focused to a large extent on issues related to logic and scientific design, we should not lose sight of the ultimate purpose of educational research—helping students. What could have been averted if the evidence from project Follow Through had been given the political attention that had been promised? What could happen if the What Works Clearinghouse presented an honest and complete compilation of the research evidence?

Two longitudinal studies of the impact of Direct Instruction provide indications of the potential. Linda Meyer (1984) looked at the long-term impact of Project Follow Through, comparing the rates of high school graduation and college acceptance of students in a Direct Instruction Follow Through program at the start of their schooling career to the rates of students in the comparison group in a nearby school with very similar demographic characteristics. The Follow Through students were over one and a half times as likely to graduate from high school and twice as likely to apply to and be accepted at college. More recently, Stockard, Carnine, Rasplica, Paine, and Chaparro (2014) looked at the high school experiences of students with varying exposure to Direct Instruction in their elementary years. Those with more exposure were significantly more likely to be prepared for higher education: more than twice as likely to take advanced college preparatory mathematics classes; more than twice as likely to take advanced placement and/or college entrance exams, such as the SAT or ACT; and ranked significantly higher in their high school class.

Reams of evidence in the social sciences document the importance of educational attainment in promoting higher incomes and occupational status, lower crime rates, greater family stability, and better health. In fact, this finding was the impetus for starting the Follow Through program. The results of the Meyer (1984) and Stockard et al. (2014) studies, separated by almost three decades, show that the potential is great. If the results of Project Follow Through had changed the course of education, as originally envisioned, the adult fates of millions of young people, and the face of the nation, would be substantially different.

Given the dramatic nature of this potential impact, one must ask why the educational research community has so vociferously resisted the accumulated data and research results. The discussions above suggest that they have not just ignored the evidence but have, in direct violation of the norms of science, actively manipulated their presentation of findings to hide the efficacy of Direct Instruction programs from the public. One could suggest that these actions reflect, either intentionally or unintentionally, attempts to maintain the privilege and power of educational researchers as well as those with vested interests in ineffective curricular programs. By promulgating the fiction that no educational approach is especially effective, they conclude that much more work is needed to develop effective curricula. In other words, they create a justification for their continued employment and for the continued expenditure of millions of dollars in the educational research enterprise. They also justify the continued use of ineffective programs for students throughout the nation, enriching the coffers of authors and publishers of these ineffective programs.

The research community, individual researchers, publishing firms, and authors of these ineffective approaches continue to garner grants, prestige, and money. In the meantime, generations of students have been, and continue to be, denied access to highly effective curricula. The nation has lost the potential contribution of generations of talented young people. The gap between the powerful and the less powerful remains and, in fact, in recent years has widened. The reasoning behind this process may or may not be consciously self-serving. But, in the end, the motive doesn't matter because the result is the same. The educational research community, and the publishing empires to which it is connected, continue to enrich themselves. The vast majority of students they purport to serve continue to lose.

Both of us, as authors, have approached this issue from our own perspective: Engelmann as the author of the Direct Instruction programs and a participant in education for many years, Stockard from a career as a social scientist. Yet, we agree on the bottom line. The educational research community appears to have willfully ignored the research evidence. They have done this for many years and in direct contradiction to logic and to the norms of the scientific community. The big losers are the students and the society as a whole, as the strong evidence regarding the effectiveness of Direct Instruction is degraded and ignored and ineffective programs are promoted. The bias of educational researchers trumps the research evidence, and students and the society are the losers.

REFERENCES

Adams, G. L. (1996). Project Follow-Through: In-depth and beyond. *Effective School Practices, 15*(1), 43–55.

Adams, G. L., & Engelmann, S. (1996). *Research on Direct Instruction: 25 years beyond DISTAR*. Seattle, WA: Educational Achievement Systems.

Becker, W. C., & Engelmann, S. (1996). Sponsor findings from Project Follow-Through, *Effective School Practices, 15*(1), 33–42

Bereiter, C., & Kurland, M. (1981–82). A constructive look at Follow Through results, *Interchange, 12*, 1–22.

Borman, G. D., Hewes, G. M., Overman, L. T., & Brown, S. (2003). Comprehensive school reform and achievement: A meta-analysis. *Review of Educational Research, 73*(2), 125–230.

Bornstein, M., Hedges, L. V., Higgins, J. P. T., & Rothstein, H. R. (2009). *Introduction to meta-analysis*. New York: Wiley.

Center for Public Education (CPE). (n.d.). *Class size and student achievement: Research review*. Alexandria, VA: Author. Retrieved from http://www.centerforpubliceducation.org/Main-Menu/Organizing-a-school/Class-size-and-student-achievement-At-a-glance/Class-size-and-student-achievement-Research-review.html

Carlson, C. D., & Francis, D. J. (2003). Increasing the reading achievement of at-risk children through direct instruction: Evaluation of the Rodeo Institute for Teacher Excellence (RITE). *Journal of Education for*

Students Placed At Risk, 7(2), 141–166.

Cohen, B. P. (1989). *Developing sociological knowledge: Theory and method* (2nd ed.). Chicago: Nelson-Hall.

Cook, T. D., & Campbell, D. T. (1979). *Quasi-experimentation: Design and analysis issues for field settings.* Chicago: Rand McNally.

Glintborg, B., Hillestrom, P., Olsen, L., Dalhoff, K., & Poulsen, H. (2007). Are patients reliable when self-reporting medication use? Validation of structured drug interviews and home visits by analysis and prescription data in acutely hospitalized patients. *Journal of Clinical Pharmacology, 47*(11), 1440–1449.

Grossen, B. (1996). The story behind Project Follow-Through. *Effective School Practices, 15*(1), 4–9.

Einstein, A. (1934). *Essays in Science: The authorized translation from the volume originally published as: "Mein Weltbild."* New York: Philosopical Library. (Republished in 2011 ebook format, New York: Philosophical Library/Open Road).

Engelmann, S. (1969). *Conceptual learning.* San Rafael, CA: Dimensions Publishing Company.

Engelmann, S. (2007). *Teaching needy kids in our backward system.* Eugene, OR: ADI Press.

Engelmann, S., & Carnine, D. (1991). *Theory of Instruction: Principles and Applications.* Eugene, OR: ADI Press. (Originally published 1982, New York: Irvington Publishing).

Engelmann, S., & Carnine, D. (2010). *Could John Stuart Mill have saved our schools?* Verona, WI: Full Court Press.

Engelmann, S., & Steely, D. (2004). *Inferred functions of performance and learning.* Mahwah, NJ: Lawrence Erlbaum.

House, E., Glass, G., McLean, L., & Walker, D. (1978). No simple answer: Critique of the FT evaluation. *Harvard Educational Review, 48*(2), 128–160.

Huitt, W. G., Monetti, D. M., & Hummel, J. H. (2009). Direct approach to instruction. In C. Reigeluth & A. Carr-Chellman (Eds.), Instructional-design theories and models: (Vol. III) *Building a common knowledge base* (pp. 73–98). Mahwah, NJ: Lawrence Erlbaum.

Kaplan, A. (1964). *The conduct of inquiry: Methodology for behavioral science.* Scranton, PA: Chandler.

Kemeny, J. G. (1969). *A philosopher looks at science.* Princeton, NJ: D. Van Nostrand.

Kennedy, M. M. (1978). *Findings from the Follow Through planned variation study.* U.S. Office of Education. Retrieved from https://www.msu.edu/~mkennedy/publications/docs/Federal Programs/Follow Through/ Kennedy 78 FT findings.pdf

Krueger, A. B., & Whitmore, D. M. (2001). The effect of attending a small class in the early grades on college-test taking and middle school test results: Evidence from Project STAR. *Economic Journal, 111*, 1–28.

Metis Associates. (2011). *Chicago Public Schools Striving Readers Initiative: Year four evaluation report.* New York: Author. Retrieved from http://www2.ed.gov/programs/strivingreaders/chicagoeval32011.pdf

Meyer, L. A. (1984). Long-term academic effects of the Direct Instruction Project Follow Through. *Elementary School Journal. 84*, 380–394.

Mosteller, F. (1995). The Tennessee study of class size in the early school grades. *The Future of Children, 5*(2), 113–127.

Mosteller, F., & Boruch, R. (Eds.). (2002). *Evidence matters: Randomized trials in education research.* Washington, DC: Brookings Press.

Nagel, E. (1961). *The structure of science: Problems in the logic of scientific explanation.* New York: Harcort, Brace, & World.

National Assessment of Educational Progress (NAEP). (1996). *NAEP 1994 reading report card for the nation and the states.* Washington, DC: National Center for Education Statistics, U.S. Department of Education.

Popper, K. R. (1962). *Conjectures and refutations: The growth of scientific knowledge.* New York: Basic Books.

Shadish, W. R., Cook, T.D., & Campbell, D. T. (2002). *Experimental and quasi-experimental designs for generalized causal inference.* Boston: Houghton Mifflin.

Stebbins, L. B., St. Pierre, R. G., Proper, E. C., Anderson, R. B., & Cerva,T. R. (1977). *Education as experimentation: A planned variation model* (Vol IV-A). Cambridge, MA: Abt Associates. Retrieved from: http://www.eric.ed.gov/ERIC- WebPortal/search/detailmini. jsp?_nfpb=true&_&ERICExtSearch_Search-Value_0=ED148490&ERICExtSearch_SearchType_0=no&accno=ED148490

Stockard, J. (2008). *The What Works Clearinghouse beginning reading reports and rating of reading mastery: An evaluation and comment,* NIFDI Technical Report 2008-4. Eugene, OR: National Institute for Direct Instruction.

Stockard, J. (2010). An analysis of the fidelity implementation policies of the What Works Clearinghouse. *Current Issues in Education, 13*(4).

Stockard, J. (2012). *A Summary of concerns regarding the What Works Clearinghouse.* Eugene, OR: National Institute for Direct Instruction.

Stockard, J. (2013a). *Examining the What Works Clearinghouse and its reviews of Direct Instruction programs.* NIFDI Technical Report 2013-1. Eugene, OR: National Institute for Direct Instruction.

Stockard, J. (2013b). Merging the accountability and scientific research requirements of the No Child Left Behind Act: Using cohort control groups. *Quality and Quantity: International Journal of Methodology, 47*(2013), pp. 2225–2257.

Stockard, J., Carnine, L., Rasplica, C., Paine, S., & Chaparro, E. (2014). *The long term impacts of Direct Instruction.* Eugene, OR: National Institute for Direct Instruction.

Stockard, J., & Wood, T. (2012). *Reading Mastery and learning disabled students: A comment on the What Works Clearinghouse Review.* NIFDI Technical Report 2012-2. Eugene, OR: National Institute for Direct Instruction.

Stockard, J. & Wood, T.W. (2013). *The What Works Clearinghouse review process: An analysis of errors in two recent reports.* NIFDI Technical Report 2013-4. Eugene, OR: National Institute for Direct Instruction.

Tallmadge, G. K. (1977). *The Joint Dissemination Review Panel ideabook.* Washington, DC: National Institute of Education and U.S. Office of Education.

U.S.Government Accountability Office. (2010). *Department of Education: Improved dissemination and timely product release would enhance the usefulness of the What Works Clearinghouse (GAO-10-644).* Washington, DC: Author.

Watkins, C. L. (1997). *Project Follow Through: A case study of contingencies influencing instructional practices of the educational establishment.* Cambridge, MA: Cambridge Center for Behavioral Studies._

What Works Clearinghouse. (2007). *Beginning reading topic report.* Washington, DC: U.S. Department of Education. Retrieved from: http://bit.ly/rHCevF

What Works Clearinghouse. (2013). About Us. Washington, DC: U.S. Department of education. Retrieved from http://ies.ed.gov/ncee/wwc/aboutus.aspx.

What Works Clearinghouse. (2013). *Procedures and standards handbook* (Version 3.0). Washington, DC: U.S. Department of Education. Retrieved from: http://ies.ed.gov/ncee/wwc/documentsum.aspx?sid=19

Wolf, F. M. (1986). *Meta-analysis: Quantitative methods for research synthesis.* Thousand Oaks, CA: Sage.

Word, E., Johnston, J., Pate Bain, H., Fulton, D. B., Boyd Zaharias, J., Lintz, M. N., et al. (1990). *Student-teacher achievement ratio (STAR): Tennessee's K–3 class-size study.* Nashville, TN: Tennessee State Department of Education.

Word, E., Johnston, J., Pate Bain, H., Fulton, D. B., Boyd Zaharias, J., Lintz, M. N., et al. (1994). *The state of Tennessee's student/teacher achievement ratio (STAR) project: Technical report 1985–1990.* Nashville: Tennessee State Department of Education. Retrieved from: http://d64.e2services.net/class/STARsummary.pdf

CHAPTER 4

Engelmann has been writing books, articles, and curricular programs since the mid-1960s. Bibliographic citations and abstracts of these materials, developed by Timothy Wood, are in the appendices of this book. Chapter 4, also by Wood, analyzes this vast corpus of material. Based on his reading of this material as well as interviews with Engelmann, Wood identifies key thematic elements of Engelmann's writings and describes the context of Engelmann's career in which the various elements appeared and re-appeared.

THE ENGELMANN CORPUS OF WRITINGS
Timothy W. Wood

This chapter discusses the development of Engelmann's career in education, specifically examining the progression of his publications: academic programs, scholarly articles, and books. His writing career spans nearly fifty years, covering a variety of topics centered on the education system in the United States. Engelmann's contribution to the field of education is remarkable in terms of scope and size. The following tracks the progression of his writing in terms of topic, writing style and thematic trends.

In preparation for this publication and in order to establish a better understanding of the motivation for and goals of his publications, I conducted an interview with Engelmann over two days in February of 2013. Our discussion of his career and the progression of his writing style and scope supplemented my analysis of all of his publications. I have included quotes from the interview in the discussion below, retaining his direct and colorful speaking style.

This chapter includes five major sections, focusing on four central themes of Engelmann's publications, all of which have been prominent and reoccurring through his career. The five sections cover Engelmann's theoretical understanding of learning and instruction, his development of effective curricular material that embody these principles, his promotion of reform and change in education, responses to criticisms and roadblocks, and current directions in his work. Each section examines his motivations for the publications and how he adapted his approach to specific issues over time. Some of Engelmann's publications span more than one of these unifying themes and have been accounted for in multiple sections to fully understand their intention. Additionally I have provided background and insight into his career before working in the field of education. To provide greater information on Engelmann's publications, including his scholarly articles, books, programs, and general musings on education, an annotated bibliography has been included in Appendix A and Appendix B. Appendix C provides an overview of his career.

THEORETICAL UNDERSTANDING OF LEARNING AND INSTRUCTION

Never one to follow the beaten path in education, Siegfried Engelmann's professional career began as a self-employed investment counselor (1955–1960) before moving to the posts of creative director, vice-president, and various other positions in different advertising agencies. While working for these agencies Engelmann began analyzing techniques for marketing to children in order to determine what type of input was necessary to induce retention. His work on these marketing strategies led him to begin developing his own techniques for teaching children, initially using his own three sons as participants and developing the basis for what would become the Direct Instruction programs and techniques.

During these early experiments Engelmann realized the relation between what his sons learned and how he instructed them. He filmed his teaching sessions with his sons to demonstrate how his teaching techniques were successful with young children and how they could acquire advanced skills earlier than previously expected. The work with his sons led to a position as a Research Associate for the Institute for Research on Exceptional Children in Champaign, Illinois (1964–1966), working with Carl Bereiter. It was here that the two developed the Bereiter-Engelmann preschool in 1964 to help disadvantaged students succeed. It was through his work in the preschool that Engelmann developed and tested his theory of instruction, showing that all children can learn when properly taught and challenging other theories and approaches.

All Children Can Learn with Proper Instruction

Engelmann experienced a relatively easy transition into the formal field of education. Reflecting on this transition Engelmann remarked,

When I got into education, the first thing that struck me was it's all logical, it's all totally logical. It's not logical in the sense of deductions, but from an inductive standpoint it's absolutely logical. I was fortunate enough to work with real young kids who didn't know anything so whatever I taught them, they learned. The obverse was if they screwed up, I screwed up, because I did something wrong.

It was these early experiences that allowed Engelmann to establish a greater understanding of how a child's mind worked and interpreted information. During these interactions Engelmann further developed his understanding of the critical relation between how he instructed the children in terms of wording, set of examples, sequencing of examples, and what they learned. He applied a scientific approach to understanding instruction by analyzing all the relevant variables to determine their role and influence on the act of instruction. Engelmann concluded that instruction needed to be as clear as possible to avoid any confusion by the students. By providing clear and explicit instruction the students will learn more efficiently. Furthermore students' acquisition of knowledge depended on appropriate instruction, and, if the child failed to learn, it was the result of improper instruction. With this understanding of how children learned, Engelmann began further developing his theories of instruction, which would result in the first Direct Instruction programs and accompanying techniques.

Engelmann's earliest publications in the 1960s covered his research on instruction for disadvantaged children. He discussed his experiments of teaching techniques for at-risk children and his first-hand observations of how they received and interpreted instruction. He specifically sought to determine how children learn, how to instruct them most efficiently and effectively, and how appropriate instruction differs for children of different backgrounds and skills. Engelmann utilized a scientific method to analyze each variable of instruction to determine the most efficient and effective instructional approach. Through these experiments he determined that, in comparison to their more affluent peers, disadvantaged students had a deficit in language skills, which hindered their learning rate.

This lack of language skills made the acquisition of reading skills more difficult, so Engelmann began focusing on developing language and reading skills in tandem. This research solidified Engelmann's theory that students' acquisition of knowledge and development of skills depends on the teacher's appropriate instruction, which needs to be adjusted based on the child's skill level. A teacher must recognize and understand the students' skills and what type of instruction they need to progress and acquire new skills in the most efficient and effective manner so they become confident and successful students. He concluded that the success of students depends on the use of appropriate academic curriculum, the proper placement of students into classrooms in terms of their skill level, and adequate instruction from teachers.

The Bereiter-Engelmann preschool provided Engelmann an opportunity to assist the children in learning critical skills to succeed in school, but also to determine the most effective and efficient methods of instruction for disadvantaged students. Engelmann's work at the preschool strengthened his understanding of the most effective ways to organize and orient preschools to heighten children's skills and prepare them for their future education. His observations and analysis led to the conclusion that the present organization of preschool education was problematic for all children and that a restructuring could lead to the greater success of all children in the present and in their future academic careers. *Engelmann had developed a theory of instruction based on a scientific approach to understanding how children learn.*

By viewing humans as inherently logical, Engelmann devised an instructional approach built around providing clear and concise instruction to avoid any confusion on the meaning or interpretation of information. Engelmann's approach was designed to heighten effectiveness and efficiency. When students misinterpret instructional lessons, teachers must repeat or expand lessons to provide greater clarity, thus taking more time to teach the material. If, however, the instruction is clear and concise, misinterpretation is unlikely to occur and learning can happen more quickly and efficiently. Additionally Engelmann promoted teaching to mastery so students would have a firm understanding of the information taught and be prepared to progress in their program. Teaching to mastery increases efficiency because it ensures all students have the necessary skills to advance, and they will not need additional review to progress. Furthermore if students learn to mastery they develop confidence in their ability to learn, making them more likely to continue their educational pursuits and to succeed. Engelmann continued to write about the theory of instruction and learning throughout his career, producing extensive books and articles. These works delineated the logic of the theory, included empirical tests of the theory, contrasted the approach to that of others and showed its relationship to classical philosophical writings. Table 4-1 includes examples of these writings.

Table 4.1 Selected Engelmann Publications on Theory of Instruction

Engelmann, S. (1969). *Conceptual learning.* San Rafael, CA: Dimensions Publishing Company.

Becker, W. C., & Engelmann, S. (1978). Systems for basic instruction: Theory and applications. In A. C. Catania & T. A. Brigham (Eds.), *Handbook of applied behavior analysis: Social and instructional processes* (pp. 325-377). New York: Irvington.

Engelmann, S., & Carnine, D. (1982). *Theory of Instruction: Principles and Applications.* New York: Irvington. (Reprinted 1991, Eugene, OR: ADI Press)

Engelmann, S. (1997). Theory of mastery and acceleration. In J. W. Lloyd, E. J. Kame'enui, & D. Chard (Eds.), *Issues in educating students with disabilities* (pp. 177-195). Mahwah, NJ: Lawrence Erlbaum.

Engelmann, S. (2002). *Models and expectations.* Eugene, OR: National Institute for Direct Instruction, 1-22.

Engelmann, S., & Steely, D. (2004). *Inferred functions of performance and learning.* Mahwah, NJ: Lawrence Erlbaum.

Engelmann, S., & Carnine, D. (2010). *Could John Stuart Mill have saved our schools?* Verona, WI: Full Court Press.

Engelmann's theory of instruction challenged prominent views of the capabilities of children to learn by stressing the dependence of children's learning on the teacher's instruction. He believed the root of children's failure to learn was in the teacher's instruction, not the students' skills, perceived capabilities, or age. This view sharply contrasted with Jean Piaget's psychological theories on how children learn. While working at the Bereiter-Engelmann preschool, Engelmann began what would become a long fight to disprove Jean Piaget's theories.

Refuting Piaget's Theories

Beginning in the mid-1960s Engelmann started writing a series of articles on Jean Piaget's theories of child development and his own theories on how children learn (Table 4.2). Piaget's theories were well accepted in education, but Engelmann felt that they misrepresented children's capabilities. Engelmann's primary motivation behind his articles on Piaget was to disprove Piaget's theories because they were well accepted in the field of psychology and Engelmann believed them to be detrimental to children learning all that they could and the promotion of Direct Instruction. Piaget claimed that children could be taught skills and concepts such as analytic induction and the conservation of water only after reaching a certain age. Demonstrating that a child could learn these skills before this age would disprove his universal theories.

Table 4.2 Selected Engelmann Publications on Piaget's Theories

Engelmann, S. (1967). Teaching formal operations to preschool advantaged and disadvantaged children. *Ontario Journal of Educational Research, 9*(3), 193–207.

Engelmann, S. (1967). Cognitive structures related to the principles of conservation. In D. W. Brison & E. V. Sullivan (Eds.), *Recent research on the acquisition of conservation of substance* (pp. 25–51). Toronto, Ontario, Canada: Ontario Institute for Studies in Education.

Engelmann, S. E. (1971). Does the Piagetian approach imply instruction? In D. R. Green, M. P. Ford, & G. B. Flamer (Eds.), *Measurement and Piaget (pp. 118-126). New York: McGraw-Hill.*

Engelmann, S. (1982). Piaget and instruction. *ADI News, 2*(1), 1, 6.

As described in Chapter 1 of this volume, Engelmann was indeed successful in showing how children could learn these skills before the age Piaget believed was necessary. But his articles on these findings went relatively unnoticed and Piaget's theories remained widely accepted as valid despite their serious flaws and lack of empirical evidence. Over the years Engelmann continued to write numerous articles criticizing Piaget's theories while explaining how he observed children's learning process and detailing his theories of instruction. Engelmann conducted multiple experiments that demonstrated how Piaget's theories were wrong about every conclusion he made. His focus on this topic for a prolonged period of time was intended to educate the fields of psychology and education on how children learn and to provide empirical evidence for his conclusions.

Engelmann believed the flaws in Piaget's theories were the result of not understanding the process of instruction and how skills are learned. Discussing Piaget's theories Engelmann said,

> *Basically everything [Piaget] had [was] wrong because he didn't have, he didn't know, he didn't understand instruction and what it takes to induce this stuff or how little it often takes to induce it... He thinks in terms of these correlations. He designs what he considers essential on the basis of what's correlated with what, rather than what causes it.*

Engelmann believed Piaget's theories were misguided and damaging to children's potential and future because children are able to learn critical skills earlier than Piaget determined and progress at a faster rate. For this reason, he said Piaget "is not a friend of kids."

Problems with Other Programs

In addition to his analyses of Piaget, Engelmann wrote multiple articles on the problems with various academic programs, highlighting their faults or shortcomings (Table 4.3). He sought to thoroughly explain why these programs failed and why the organization and execution of Direct Instruction programs succeeded, highlighting the key role of explicit and systematic structuring of the curriculum and appropriate placement of students. Engelmann still recognizes problems in the programs used for disadvantaged students today, stating,

> *[The schools] are systematically killing low-performing kids. They're loving them so much they are killing them, and they are doing that by placing them over their heads.*

By placing students in classes that are teaching skills for which the students are not prepared, they will be unable to acquire new skills as fast as more affluent students and will continue to fall behind them. Eventually, by progressively falling further behind, the students will cease learning, as the information is too complex and advanced for them to interpret and master. This situation is one example of unintended consequences in the world of education Engelmann has written about extensively and sought to rectify. Decision makers in education believe their choices are thoughtful and philosophically sound, but often fail to understand how children learn best and the importance of the relationship between the program used, adequate teaching, and proper placement of the student.

Table 4.3 Selected Engelmann Writings on Problems with Other Programs

Engelmann, S. (1970). The effectiveness of Direct Instruction on IQ performance and achievement in reading and arithmetic. In J. Hellmuth (Ed.), *Disadvantaged child Vol. 3* (pp. 339–361). New York: Brunner/Mazel.

Engelmann, S., & Steely, D. (1980). *Implementation of basal reading in grades 4–6: Final report.* Chicago: Science Research Associates.

Engelmann, Z. (1982). A study of 4th–6th grade basal reading series: How much do they teach? *ADI News, 1*(3), 1, 4–5, 19. (Reprinted in 1989 in *ADI News, 8*(4), 17-23.)

Engelmann, S. (1983). Engelmann compares traditional basals with SRA's new *Reading Mastery 3 & 4. ADI News, 2*(3), 28–31.

Engelmann, S., & Meyer, L. A. (1984). *Reading comprehension instruction in grades 4, 5, and 6: Program characteristics, teacher perceptions, teacher behaviors, and student performance.* Paper presented at the 68th Annual Meeting of the American Educational Research Association (New Orleans, LA, April 23-27, 1984). Chicago: Science Research Associates.

Crawford, D., Engelmann, K. E., & Engelmann, S. (2008). Direct Instruction. In E. M. Anderman & L. H. Anderman (Eds.), *Psychology of classroom learning: An encyclopedia* (pp. 326-330). New York: Macmillan.

Summary

Engelmann developed a sound and comprehensive theory of learning and instruction and thoroughly combatted Piaget's well accepted theories on learning while simultaneously promoting the Direct Instruction programs he designed, specifically their success with at-risk children. The programs were designed to maximize efficiency and effectiveness in order to accelerate the learning of disadvantaged students to allow them to compete with their more affluent peers on a level playing field. Engelmann had determined learning and academic success depended on three major factors: the program used, the adequacy of the teaching, and the proper placement of the student in the program, based on their skill level. Furthermore the success of the child relies on the selection of a program, which should be chosen based on data demonstrating the program's effectiveness, not just good intentions. Success is not dependent on the student's current learning capability, but the instruction provided to them. Failure can always be attributed to one of these three factors.

Engelmann used a scientific approach to determine the best form of instruction and promoted a reliance on data for empirical evidence of the validity of a program. The determination and dedication of Engelmann and his colleagues to help children succeed in a supportive environment is evident in the vast amount of writing on education and learning they produced in the following decades, including many curricular programs.

DEVELOPING EFFECTIVE CURRICULAR MATERIALS THAT EMBODY THESE PRINCIPLES

Engelmann's earliest publications involved drawing attention to the struggles of disadvantaged students in schools and the most effective approach to teach them. Following the creation of the Bereiter-Engelmann preschool and the development of the DISTAR instructional programs Engelmann began reporting on the success of these programs and the theories behind them. Engelmann not only promoted his programs with these articles, but also legitimized them by showing their strong success in comparison to other curricula. While promoting Direct Instruction programs he also demonstrated how a theory of instruction could solve the problems in education he was writing about. Engelmann has frequently stressed the importance of relying on data to determine the effectiveness of a program, which is why he frequently refers to the expansive data set accumulated on DISTAR during Project Follow Through.

Project Follow Through

Project Follow Through was the largest and most expensive experiment in education when it was devised in the 1960s. The experiment was funded by the U.S. federal government and designed to determine the most successful academic program for teaching at-risk children. Direct Instruction was one of the participating programs and was shown to be the most successful program tested by far.

Initially the final goal of the Follow Through project was to implement the most successful program nationwide, but when the first formal evaluation of the project occurred in April of 1977 the director of the project had changed and determined the project had a different intention: determining the aggregate success of the project rather than the success of the individual models. Despite data showing Direct Instruction to be the most effective model by far, the director and other organizations such as the Ford Foundation determined it not to be consistently effective and therefore should not be implemented nationwide. The difference in effectiveness was primarily due to varying levels of implementation fidelity. School districts with higher levels of implementation fidelity reported greater levels of success with their students.

Project Follow Through provided a wealth of data on the effectiveness of Direct Instruction programs with a variety of students, which Engelmann and colleagues analyzed at great length in the following decades. Despite the success of the Direct Instruction programs with students and teachers, the overall failure of the government to implement the most effective program left its mark on Engelmann's and others' opinions on the education system as a whole. Reflecting on his experience in working with Project Follow Through, Engelmann commented,

> *After a while in this field everybody quits, and they quit because they can't take it any more and nothing has changed. Things are no better now than they were then. There are a lot of people I'm working with now who are real veterans and they have stuck through everything but are thinking of quitting and sometimes I even get the idea [that] you can't win. We are a century from where we need to be. We are going to have to redo philosophy to get things in place before they ever catch on to what is going on and what can be done, but it doesn't matter how many times you show it or what you show. They are not going to do anything about it.*

Disheartened by the results of Project Follow Through, Engelmann had to reevaluate the development and promotion of Direct Instruction and the best way to continue helping students succeed. He continues to focus on the development and implementation of Direct Instruction rather than taking the political route to create greater awareness of the problems in education and the existence of an effective program that could fix these problems. However, Engelmann sees the same problems he observed in Project Follow Through active today in school systems,

> *Everything they do is wrong because they don't understand any of it. I mean how to use time, how to schedule things, how to teach them, how to follow up, or how to place kids. It is just as ugly now as it was then. It just has different words and different rationales, but it has gone nowhere.*

Expansion of DI to a Broader Range of Students

Like his struggle to disprove Piaget and discredit his universal theories, Engelmann responded to roadblocks by moving forward and continuing to make a meaningful difference in education, adapting along the way to advance and promote his philosophy of education. Following the decision of Project Follow Through's director not to implement Direct Instruction nationwide, Engelmann continued to support Direct Instruction programs and techniques by demonstrating their effectiveness with a broader range of students. He showed how Direct Instruction was not only effective with disadvantaged students, but could also be used successfully with middle-class students, above-average students, and severely handicapped students.

Discussing the challenges of using Direct Instruction with a wider range of students Engelmann stated,

> *Direct Instruction is not like magic, it is a series of procedures that you provide for efficient teaching to any of these groups.*

Engelmann's studies with these other students (Table 4.4) demonstrated the effectiveness of his theories of instruction and that the theories are not only applicable to disadvantaged children, but to all learners. Furthermore it showed how learning is the culmination of proper placement of the student, adequate instruction, and the use of effective programs. All three elements are essential to the success of the student and must be coordinated together to be effective. It is an application of scientific practices to assess the problem and control the variables to determine the most effective solution for the given situation.

Table 4.4 Selected Publications on the Expansion of Direct Instruction

Engelmann, S., & Rosov, R. (1975). Tactual hearing experiment with deaf and hearing subjects. *Exceptional Children, 41*(40), 243–253.

Williams, P., Granzin, A., Engelmann, S., & Becker, W. C. (1979). Teaching language to the truly naïve learner: An analog study using a tactual vocoder. *Journal of Special Education Technology, 2,* 5–15.

Becker, W. C., Engelmann, S., Carnine, D. W., & Maggs, A. (1982). Direct Instruction technology: Making learning happen. In P. Karoly & J. Steffen (Eds.), *Improving children's competence: Advances in child behavior analysis and therapy,* (Vol. 1, pp. 151-206). Lexington, MA: D. C. Heath & Company.

Engelmann, S., & Carnine, D. (1982). Direct Instruction outcomes with middle-class second graders. *ADI News, 1*(2), 4–5. (Reprinted in 1989 in *ADI News, 8*(2), 2–5.)

Singer, G., Close, D., Colvin, G., & Engelmann, S. (1983). DI for severely handicapped learners. *ADI News, 2*(4), 3–4.

Hofmeister, A. M., Engelmann, S., & Carnine, D. (1985). *Designing videodisc-based courseware for the high school.* Paper presented at the annual meeting of the American Educational Research Association (Chicago, IL, March 31-April 4, 1985).

Engelmann, S., & Carnine, D. (1989). Supporting teachers and students in math and science education through videodisc courses. *Educational Technology, 29*(8), 46–50.

Williams, P., & Engelmann, S. (1989). Teaching absolute pitch. *ADI News, 9*(1), 23–26.

Engelmann, S. (2012). Middle-Class Follow Through students. Available from http://zigsite.com/PDFs/FTMiddleClass3.pdf.

The expansion of Direct Instruction programs also involved the incorporation of new forms of technology to provide additional aids to teachers and to attempt to teach difficult tasks and unfamiliar skills. Motivated by the potential of videodisc technology Engelmann and his colleagues began developing Direct Instruction based videodisc programs in the late 1970s and conducted experiments on their effectiveness. The development of videodisc technology would provide teachers with an additional aid to their instruction, but also a greater likelihood of adequate teaching. He and his colleagues continued to revise these videodisc programs throughout the years, expanding the programs to include more subjects and be applicable to larger audiences. The continued use of technology as an aid to instruction led to the development of programs utilizing more recent technology such as DVDs and handheld computer devices such as iPads. The use of technology served a dual purpose of providing an additional aid to the teacher and providing a tool that could be used by a wider range of students and teachers, which heightens students' ability to learn.

Beginning in the mid-1970s Engelmann and colleagues conducted extensive research on the development and use of tactual vocoders to teach deaf and hard-of-hearing students to recognize words delivered through the devices. The vocoders served as a teaching aid to help the students develop proper speech by feeling the different vibrations for each sound in a word. Similar to his earlier work with disadvantaged children, Engelmann's work with deaf and hard-of-hearing students provided increased focus on an underserved population in the field of education.

Engelmann's experiments also included students without hearing difficulties, which aided his understanding of unfamiliar learning. Continuing on this path, Engelmann began to conduct research on teaching unfamiliar skills. He believed the study of unfamiliar learning was necessary to better understand how children learn:

> *... what does it mean if a kid requires hundreds of repetitions to learn something? You learn how to interpret that and you also learn systematically how you can move them from here to there.*

By examining the process of unfamiliar learning, Engelmann gained a greater understanding of the process of learning and the importance of learning to mastery. By understanding how children learn unfamiliar tasks or problems it becomes easier to teach them difficult skills such as distinguishing musical notes.

PROMOTING REFORM AND CHANGE IN EDUCATION

Apart from the development and promotion of Direct Instruction programs and accompanying instructional theories Engelmann sought to fix the problems of the entire school system. After observing the failure of students across the country, Engelmann determined the root of failure in the education of children to be the school system as a whole, consisting of the teachers, the colleges that train them, administrators, the programs they select, and education researchers who do not support the most effective programs. Engelmann argued that the lack of connection and poor communication between these components resulted in the failure of students. All of the components need to have strong communication and be devoted to the success of all students. Teachers are not always trained in the most efficient and effective practices, administrators don't always have firsthand experience working with students and do not always choose programs based on data of proven success, and some researchers will promote inferior programs. Engelmann has written extensively of this problem beginning with proposals on how to restructure school systems and later on how the failure of the school system is a form of academic child abuse (Table 4.5).

Table 4.5 Selected Engelmann Publications on School Reform

Bereiter, C., & Engelmann, S. (1966). *Teaching disadvantaged children in the preschool.* Englewood Cliffs, NJ: Prentice-Hall.

Engelmann, S. (1969) *Preventing failure in the primary grades.* Chicago: Science Research Associates. (Reprinted in 1997 by ADI Press.)

Engelmann, S. (1982). Advocacy for children. Available from http://zigsite.com/Advocacy-Children.html.

Engelmann, S. (1987). Educational guidelines: Who is kidding whom? *ADI News, 6*(4), 2–3.

Engelmann, S. (1991). Change schools through revolution, not evolution. *Journal of Behavioral Education, 1*(3), 295-304.

Engelmann, S. (1992). *War against the schools' academic child abuse.* Portland, OR: Halcyon House.

Engelmann's first publications in this area discussed the need to restructure preschools to become academically oriented to better prepare children for entering elementary school. He then moved on to examining the education system as a whole and the need for a philosophy of education that would clarify the role of the schools, teachers, administrators, programs, and tests. Following these articles Engelmann wrote about the lack of advocacy for students and how the current school systems were harmful and their treatment of children should be viewed as academic child abuse. As problems in the school system remained relatively unchanged, Engelmann's focus on the problems increased and his language used to describe the situation became stronger, as evident in his 1992 publication *War Against the Schools' Academic Child Abuse.* As the problems progressed over time Engelmann felt it was necessary to heighten awareness on the issues to hopefully resolve them. He determined the lack of advocacy was detrimental to society and the situation needed to be viewed as a form of war. Accompanying his analysis of the school system Engelmann provided detailed guidelines for a restructuring that would allow for educational equality among all students.

In 2000 Engelmann launched Zigsite.com, a website designed to give greater exposure to DI by addressing important issues in education, while also trying to humanize Direct Instruction. Zigsite was designed to act as a separate entity from the National Institute for Direct Instruction's website, focusing on issues in education and not acting as a marketplace for DI programs or implementation support. The content of the website is wide-ranging but captures all the elements of his work with wit and style. For instance, beginning in 2008, Engelmann has written a series of fictional dialogues between Socrates and participants in the world of education, in which they discuss prominent issues in the field. Following the work of Plato, Engelmann constructed dialogues in a question-answer format to analyze important issues such as bussing, No Child Left Behind, and teacher training. The dialogue is designed to decipher a problem by ruling out competing possibilities until the truth becomes evident. The site also provides an outlet to share personal experiences in education, such as his early videos working with disadvantaged children in the 1960s.

RESPONDING TO CRITICISMS AND ROADBLOCKS

Engelmann's research and theories on instruction were not well received in the academic circles of education and psychology despite their demonstrated success. Engelmann and his colleagues had to overcome a widespread belief that rigorous and/ or demanding programs would be harmful to children, causing extreme anxiety, fear of school, and robot-like conformity. While Engelmann's work on Piaget received little response from the educational establishment, the curricular programs he and his colleagues developed often confronted harsh criticism and backlash from experts in various fields. These early criticisms significantly damaged the promotion and implementation of Direct Instruction. Still disturbed over the criticisms by these experts Engelmann commented

> *In my opinion, guys like Labov, who was a renowned sociolinguist and one of the most severe critics ... is an evil person. What he wrote prevented thousands, maybe millions, of kids from being taught properly, simply because he claimed DI was somehow prejudiced against the kids. ... Sociolinguists are way off base even trying to discuss this matter because the issue is the performance of kids. Sociolinguistics is limited to discussing the structure of language, which has nothing to do with the performance of anybody.*

Beginning with his criticisms of Piaget's theories on learning, Engelmann continued to draw attention to poor systems of instruction and ineffective teaching techniques while simultaneously defending his programs against unfounded criticisms, such as that by Labov (Table 4.6). In some instances Engelmann's responses to criticisms were intended to provide a new perspective on the issues discussed in order to have a greater understanding of the roots of the problems and how they can be solved. In others he felt it was necessary to respond to maintain the integrity of Direct Instruction and protect it from outlandish claims and misinterpretation of data, which could be popularized if not directly confronted. Engelmann's later responses to criticisms were posted to his website, Zigsite.com.

Despite the criticisms Engelmann and colleagues persevered to advance Direct Instruction and their programs, revising the programs along the way to achieve their goal of helping all children succeed. In review of his career of promoting Direct Instruction Engelmann stated,

> *We have never won a battle, never. We have never come out on top and yet in terms of data we have always come out on top. I mean we have demonstrated everything we have talked about fairly lavishly with data.*

Engelmann's determination and dedication to help children succeed in a supportive environment is evident in the vast amount of writing on education and learning he produced. While positive reviews were often overwhelmed by the criticisms, Engelmann and his colleagues were not deterred and continued their work, having faith in the effectiveness of their theories on instruction and the belief that data showing the success of their students would eventually bring greater acceptance.

Table 4.6 Selected Engelmann Publications on Responses to Criticisms

---

Engelmann, S. (1988). Theories, theories, theories: A critique of logic of whole language arguments. *ADI News, 7*(3), 5–6.

Engelmann, S. (1999). A response: How sound is High/Scope research? *Educational Leadership, 56*(6), 83–84.

Engelmann, S. (2002). Response to Allington: Allington leveled serious allegations against Direct Instruction. *ADI News, 2*(2), 28–31.

Engelmann, S. (2003). *Science versus basic educational research.* Available from http://zigsite.com/PDFs/ScienceVersus.pdf. (Reprinted in 2008 in *Australasian Journal of Special Education, 32*(1), 139-157.)

Engelmann, S. (2004). The dalmatian and its spots: Why research-based recommendations fail logic 101. *Education Week, 23*(20), 34-35, 48. (Reprint available from http://zigsite.com/Dalmatian.htm)

Engelmann, S. (2008). Machinations of What Works Clearinghouse (33 pp.). Available from http://www.zigsite.com/PDFs/MachinationsWWC%28V4%29.pdf

Engelmann, S. (2010). The dreaded standards. Available from http://zigsite.com/PDFs/The-DreadedStandards.pdf

---

CURRENT DIRECTIONS

After decades of writing on instruction and the educational system, Engelmann's passion for helping students and perfecting the education system has not waned. He continues to be actively involved in the development of current and new Direct

Instruction programs and in writing about critical issues in education. Recently he has expanded his focus in education to work more with English as a second language (ESL) students. Along with his colleagues, Engelmann has worked on developing the Direct Instruction Spoken English (DISE) program to teach English, specifically to older children. In contrast to other ESL programs, the DISE program focuses on teaching the necessary skills to speak English, not just to read it. The program is designed to ensure the understanding of the construction of the language and that the students can use the language in day-to-day situations.

The challenge of teaching English to non-English speakers has garnered more focus from Engelmann recently. He and his colleagues have worked with employees at a call center in Panama to teach them English. This work may be expanded in the future to teaching English to people who speak different languages, revising the program to target the needs and specific problems these individuals would have in learning English. This project is just one example of Engelmann's desire to better understand how people learn in order to develop better programs.

The projects Engelmann could pursue are endless with the wealth of data and insight he has accumulated on the effectiveness of Direct Instruction. Where he goes next in his career is not clear, but whatever route he does take, he will continue his pursuit of helping students succeed and establishing the potential for success for all. Throughout his career, Engelmann has strived to help all students succeed in school so they can achieve in life. This goal has led to the development of theories of instruction and programs to allow for all students to compete on an equal playing field. To accomplish these goals he has had to reevaluate the entire education system, searching for a recipe for success and how to obtain all the ingredients in the face of rules and regulations designed to hinder change. Refusing to quit and allow children to continue to suffer, he has been an active voice in the call for a revolution in education to end what he calls the "academic child abuse" throughout the country.

Engelmann's career has consisted of a series of challenges, but it is these challenges that have kept him progressing over time. He has never been afraid of challenges, rather he embraces them, and strives to overcome them and achieve his goals. It was the challenge of creating the most effective and efficient programs that drove him to continue to revise his programs and create new programs to solve other problems he encountered along the way. He described the toughest challenge of his career as being a participant in the political battleground of education, over which he has little control. Discussing these challenges Engelmann stated,

We have probably been as unsuccessful politically as we have been successful educationally. Just zero points.

Engelmann has written extensively about the political side of education, the rules and regulations placed on school systems, and the problems they create. Yet, he devoted himself to the development and implementation of Direct Instruction programs, which hindered his ability to be more active in the political realm of education. In reflecting on his decision to focus on the development and implementation of Direct Instruction (what Engelmann refers to as "the hard road") he said,

I don't know if that [going the hard road and not pursuing the politics] was a mistake because in the end what good did we do? In terms of the kids we worked with, we served them and we served a lot of teachers, but in terms of changing anything so that when we're not here it is going to maintain itself? Not a chance. We are not close.

While he devoted himself to the programs and the students and teachers he served, Engelmann still always tried to account for the political element in education, which is evident in his publications on revolutionizing the educational system. Political themes became more apparent later in his career, possibly due to the greater establishment of Direct Instruction in education. He strived to find a definitive solution to an old problem, which had progressively gotten more difficult and complex over time.

The enigma of education and the quest for equality may never be fulfilled, but few people have devoted their lives to the pursuit of a solution in the way Engelmann has. With all the hardships he has encountered in his career, Engelmann still takes pride in his accomplishments, foremost his construction of both a format and an accompanying philosophy for designing effective instruction. This accomplishment has not been matched in the world of education and may be his legacy in the field, but he still continues to problem solve from all sides of the equation. The world and the lives of millions of students are no doubt much more greatly enriched for his efforts than they would otherwise have been.

PART II

TRANSLATING THE SCIENCE TO SCHOOLS

CHAPTER 5

A number of empirical studies conclude that Direct Instruction programs are most effective when teachers follow all of the instructional guidelines and when they have strong administrative support. The best results appear when the implementations involve the entire school and all curricular subjects. In Chapter 5, Kurt Engelmann describes the key principles underlying effective implementations of Direct Instruction. He discusses what teachers and administrators need to do to use the programs in the way that they are intended and how this will produce the best outcomes for their students. Just as the DI curriculum is developed through careful, scientific analysis, the implementation guidelines, the instructions for putting the programs into practice, have been tried and tested. Good implementation is technical and demanding of teachers and staff and can produce extraordinary outcomes for students.

CREATING EFFECTIVE SCHOOLS WITH DIRECT INSTRUCTION

Kurt E. Engelmann

Direct Instruction (DI) can be defined in several ways—as a theory of instruction developed by Siegfried Engelmann, as a set of curricula authored by S. Engelmann and colleagues that translate this theory into instructional materials, and as the actual practice of teaching in schools involving the use of the Direct Instruction curricula. Taken together, these definitions provide a comprehensive view of the Direct Instruction approach.

These definitions vary, however, in the degree to which they are generally accepted among practitioners. On the one hand, there is little disagreement on what constitutes the theory of Direct Instruction, as the eponymous monograph Engelmann co-authored with Douglas Carnine is accepted as the authoritative source on theoretical considerations of the DI approach (Engelmann & Carnine, 1982b). There is also relatively little disagreement on what constitutes the Direct Instruction curricula as the materials authored by Engelmann and colleagues. While there are some materials that are mistaken for Direct Instruction materials because they possess a peripheral feature of DI, such as a scripted presentation, the publication of the *Rubric for Identifying Authentic Direct Instruction Programs* by Engelmann and Colvin (2006) has provided a definitive guide for determining which materials are and are not DI.

The actual practice of teaching DI in schools, however, varies greatly across the hundreds of schools that implement Direct Instruction schoolwide, and even more so across the thousands of other schools that use Direct Instruction in a limited capacity. Schools and districts vary in all major aspects of implementing Direct Instruction—in the specific programs and levels used, the time devoted to instruction in the programs, the number of teaching staff involved, the student-teacher ratios in the instructional groups, the frequency and criteria used to adjust the placement and composition of the instructional groups, and so forth.

This chapter takes a *normative* approach to the issue of implementing Direct Instruction. Rather than looking at the variation in how DI programs are used in schools—all the ways that Direct Instruction *can* be implemented—this chapter describes the *best practices* of implementing Direct Instruction—the ways in which DI was *designed* to be implemented. It draws from a number of sources, including the published curricula themselves, to compile a description of best implementation practices. This chapter also references procedures used by the National Institute for Direct Instruction

(NIFDI) for implementing DI. NIFDI was founded by Siegfried Engelmann to provide schools and districts with a comprehensive set of exemplar practices and procedures that have been found to be highly effective in improving the performance of the full range of student learners in a schoolwide implementation of DI.

This chapter is divided into five sections with several subsections. The first section describes four principles governing the successful implementation of Direct Instruction. The second and third sections apply these four principles to two levels of implementation—the level of *instruction*, which addresses the direct interaction between teachers and students, and the level of *support*, which addresses factors that affect instruction indirectly. The fourth section addresses the key role of the school principal in effective implementations, and the last section discusses long-term challenges that can impede the success of a Direct Instruction implementation.

PRINCIPLES OF SUCCESSFUL IMPLEMENTATION

Four major principles underlie a successful implementation of Direct Instruction: (1) maximize all factors that affect performance, (2) teach students within their zone of proximal learning, (3) provide all students with effective instruction, and (4) provide all students with efficient instruction. These principles are related to each other in a roughly sequential hierarchy. In other words, the first two principles act as a necessary prerequisite for the remaining principles. The first two principles must be met in order for the remaining two principles to be met. And the third principle must be met in order for the final principle to be met. Additional principles of implementation can be derived from these primary principles.

Maximize All Factors That Affect Performance

The first operating principle for a DI implementation is *to maximize student performance, all factors that make a difference in student performance must be maximized.* Stated differently, if students are to achieve their maximum potential, all factors that can affect student performance must be used with maximum effect. If a factor that can positively affect student performance is not utilized to its maximum potential, then student performance isn't being maximized, by definition.

Factors that affect student performance encompass everything in a school or district's control, including the daily schedule, the assignment of personnel, the professional development of staff, the physical arrangement of classrooms, and the public announcement system. Even such seemingly peripheral factors as field trips should be arranged so they provide maximum academic benefit for students. This operating principle is an extension of the same principle applied to the development of the Direct Instruction curricula, which attempt to maximize the effect of each teacher's delivery through a written script detailing specific teacher wording, teacher actions, and expected student responses (Engelmann, 2014).

Note that the principle of controlling school-based factors does not imply arbitrary control. The implementation of Direct Instruction does not require control for control's sake. Rather, use of resources should be related to the functions that make a difference in student performance.

Teach Students within their Zone of Proximal Learning

The second operating principle for a DI implementation is *to maximize student performance, students should be taught skills and concepts that lie within their zone of proximal learning (ZPL).* The ZPL differs for each child and can be defined as the next most advanced skills and concepts each child is prepared to learn in each subject area. The ZPL is similar to Vygotsky's zone of proximal development (ZPD)–what a child can do with help (scaffolding) versus what a child can do independently–without reference to the individual student's historical experiences and the broader cultural context in which instruction occurs (Tudge & Scrimsher, 2003).

The ZPL can be visualized as the next most difficult or sophisticated step involved in learning a skill or concept. An example of the ZPL can be taken from the acquisition of prereading skills. If a child can say two words together quickly ("ham-burger = hamburger"), the next step is to teach the student to blend sounds together orally, such as "aaa-mmm = am" or "mmm-$\bar{e}\bar{e}\bar{e}$ = me." If a student who is at the step of blending sounds together orally is instead presented with a more difficult task, such as decoding a series of written letter symbols to form a single word, there is a very high probability that the student will fail the task because it is beyond the student's ZPL.

The incremental step design of the Direct Instruction programs facilitates providing students instruction in their respective ZPLs. Each DI lesson contains only about 10-15% new material as most of the lesson consists of review material or applications of concepts or skills previously introduced. If students are initially placed at their current instructional level in each subject area, they should be able to master all of the material they encounter in the next lesson since they already possess the prerequisite skills. If students are not placed in their zone of proximal learning, then the design of the DI programs is nullified. If students are placed in material that is too difficult, the percentage of new material that students must master will be much higher than 10 to 15%. If the percentage is too high, the situation will resemble traditional instruction in which most of the material presented to students is new to them and therefore unlikely to be mastered in a reasonable amount of time.

Presenting students with material that is well beyond their ZPL can also have a strong negative effect on student self-image and student behavior. If they are placed at an instructional level where they can be successful, students will tend to develop positive attitudes toward their school and themselves. The results of Project Follow Through, the largest educational experiment in the history of the United States, demonstrate the positive effect Direct Instruction has on student self-image in the primary grades. Students participating in the Direct Instruction model scored significantly higher in affective measures than students participating in other school reform models (Adams & Engelmann, 1996).

Provide All Students with Effective Instruction

The third principle in implementing Direct Instruction successfully is *to maximize student performance, all students should be provided with effective instruction every day.* Instruction is *effective* if all students learn the content and skills covered in each lesson. As discussed above, the DI programs contain a step-by-step design with an incremental increase in sophistication of skills and concepts for each lesson. Providing effective instruction daily is integral to keeping students within their zones of proximal learning as they acquire the skills and concepts presented in the programs.

Effective instruction implies that students learn what the program is designed to teach them. It does not take into account how much time is required for students to master the material or how many resources are used for students to achieve mastery. Effectiveness is just related to whether students learn the material they encounter—it is the "degree to which instructional materials or programs are successful in accomplishing their objectives" (*Instructional effectiveness*, n.d.). Note that this definition does not simply equate instruction with "best practices" or "high quality instruction," but instead involves the extent to which students actually learn the material to which they are exposed, paralleling the notion of program-referenced testing discussed in Chapter 1.

Providing effective instruction daily is particularly important in the DI context. With the progressive, step-by-step design of the DI programs, it is critical that students master each "step" or lesson before proceeding. If not, students will face an increasingly more difficult task of mastering each new lesson that is presented. Using a staircase metaphor, S. Engelmann (1999) explains how failure to teach to mastery eliminates the benefits of the progressive design of the DI programs:

The benefits of the design of the program are obliterated if a student falls below the level of a stair. This fact holds for students who are "smart" as well as those who have a history of failure. If a student is below the fifth stair and tries to reach the sixth stair with one step (which means thoroughly mastering the sixth lesson in one period), the student must learn substantially more than students who are firmly on the fifth stair. Furthermore, the student must learn this material during the same amount of time allotted for students who are firmly on the fifth stair. Therefore, the student who is below the fifth stair must learn the material at a faster rate. The student on the fourth stair must learn material at twice the rate of students who are correctly placed. The student who is on the third stair must learn at three times the rate. For the typical student, a step that requires three times the amount of new learning is too great. Even if the student is able to perform acceptably on lesson 6 after some repetition, the retention rate of the student on the subsequent lessons drops dramatically. (p. 3)

Provide All Students with Efficient Instruction

The fourth principle in implementing Direct Instruction successfully is *to maximize student performance, all students should be provided with instruction that is efficient as well as effective.* Efficiency of instruction refers to resource use in general and the use of time in particular. Instruction is more efficient if students learn a given amount of material in less time. An analogous concept is acceleration, which Engelmann defines as "teaching more in less time" (Engelmann, n.d., p. 1).

Effective instruction is a prerequisite for efficient instruction as students' acquisition of skills is inherent in increasing the rate of acquiring skills and concepts. Increasing the rate of lesson coverage without student mastery would not be efficient as students would have to repeat the material covered (an unfortunately common occurrence at many schools implementing Direct Instruction without sufficient support). The fact that efficient instruction requires effective instruction is incorporated into the widely quoted maxim that "mastery comes before lesson progress." An application of this maxim to reading is "accuracy before fluency," meaning that students should read with a high degree of accuracy before attempts are made to increase their reading rate.

Acceleration or efficiency of instruction is inherent in efforts to "close the performance gap" so lower-performing students learn at a greater rate and "catch up" to their peers. Engelmann (2004) describes the urgency of providing efficient instruction to lower-performing students:

Children at-risk are significantly behind middle-class children both in what they know and in their strategies about how to learn and retain information being taught to them. If these children are to catch up, the task facing teachers is a paradox: to achieve more learning for these children during each period than the middle-class child in a traditional program learns during the same amount of time. (p. xix)

While instructional efficiency is most urgent for at-risk children, acceleration can occur for higher performing students as well. Use of DI has led to many cases in which higher-performing students have outgained comparable students in a given time period or learned faster in comparison to their own performance history (Engelmann & Carnine, 1982a; Stockard, 2010). Thus, all students should be provided with efficient instruction as a means of maximizing their performance.

In the sections that follow, the principles outlined above are applied to two levels of implementation. The first level, the level of *instruction*, addresses the interactions that take place directly between teachers and students in the instructional setting. The second, the level of *support*, is concerned with the factors that affect student learning indirectly and allow for effective and efficient instruction to occur. The level of support addresses the environment in which teachers work, including the training and on-site coaching provided to teachers. Both levels are affected by actions taken by administrators, building coaches, district personnel, and external support providers. The actions needed to promote the most effective implementations are discussed in the next two sections.

THE INSTRUCTIONAL LEVEL OF IMPLEMENTATION

The level of instruction deals with the ways in which teachers interact directly with students to improve student achievement. Teachers must follow specific directions and guidelines to provide students with effective and efficient instruction that will accelerate their performance.

Following the Program Guidelines

To be effective, teachers must deliver the Direct Instruction programs as designed for the full amount of time scheduled. The programs were made to control as many instructional variables as possible to ensure an effective implementation by every practitioner. The teacher presentation books (TPBs) for each DI program specify the precise wording and actions that teachers are to follow. The TPBs also specify expected student responses and the correction procedures that teachers should follow if student responses do not correspond to those intended. In addition to providing scripted presentations, each program has specified guidelines for time allocation, grouping, presenting the program, and remediating student errors.

Two critical components of DI program delivery are the signal and unison response. Watkins and Slocum (2004) identify three advantages of group oral unison responses:

1. all students get high-quality practice on every item because they provide their own response and cannot echo other students,

2. all students are busy learning the material and are less likely to become distracted, and

3. teachers can assess the skills of all the students in an instant and be well informed about their skills. (p. 45)

Another critical presentation technique is to provide appropriate pacing. The pacing must be quick enough to capture students' attention, but not too quick that students cannot follow the presentation. The pace must be varied to allow pauses at the appropriate places. Teachers must give students enough "think time" on complicated or difficult items. This think time can be reduced as students master the material. Also, teachers must "pause and punch" to emphasize critical elements of a presentation. For instance, teachers should emphasize "an apple" in exercises requiring students to discriminate between the articles "a" and "an."

Motivating Students and Shaping Desired Behavior

While presenting the program, teachers must motivate students to attend to the presentation and respond appropriately. Teachers should establish and communicate to their students their behavioral expectations for group instruction, independent work, and transitions between activities. A critical technique (often attributed to Professor Wesley Becker, Direct Instruction co-founder) is to "catch students in the act of being good," i.e., to reinforce students for what they are doing that meets expectations.

The teacher's attention to students who conform to the expectations provides reinforcement to these students as well as a strong incentive for the other students to change their behavior and conform to the expectations. If, however, the teacher pays attention to students who are violating behavioral expectations, this can provide reinforcement to these students as well as a strong incentive for the other students to change their behavior and violate the behavioral expectations.

Teachers should use both verbal and graphic means of reinforcing students' appropriate behavior. Teachers can use a simple tally system divided into sections for student points and teacher points. Students get points for achievement—performing instructional tasks correctly—and teachers get points when students violate behavioral expectations. When a teacher gives herself a point, she should explain to the group the reason (saying that "not all students have their finger on Part B," for instance). The teacher should allocate enough points so that students always receive more points by the end of the instructional period and "win" the game.

Teachers should provide specific verbal feedback to students with far greater frequency of positive feedback than negative feedback. Praise should occur at least four times the rate of corrective feedback. The 4:1 positive-to-negative ratio includes corrections on student errors during instruction as well as feedback on student behavior. A correction can have a negative effect on student self-image regardless of how gently the teacher delivers the feedback. As discussed earlier, improper placement of students at a lesson that is too difficult will result in a higher rate of response errors. The inclusion of student performance in calculating the positive-to-negative ratio of teachers' feedback to students indicates the importance of proper placement in the DI programs.

A motivation system should also be in place for students engaged in independent work. Teachers should set a goal on the number of perfect independent worksheets students are to complete by a specific date. The date and number of perfect papers should be set so they are achievable. When the students reach the goal, they receive a short reinforcing activity for their accomplishments, and the teacher sets a new goal.

Ensuring Student Mastery

As discussed in the previous section, teachers must ensure that students master the material in each Direct Instruction exercise before proceeding to the next exercise. Teachers should correct student errors and repeat the material until the students are at mastery on every task. In addition, teachers should perform "delayed tests" on all instructional items where students committed errors to ensure that all students can perform correctly on all parts of each exercise by the end of a lesson.

Engelmann (1999) has identified two other criteria to determine whether students are placed properly in the DI programs. These mastery criteria are based on the percentage of responses that students answer correctly *the first time they encounter an exercise*:

Criterion 1. Students should be at least 70% correct on anything that is being introduced for the first time.

Criterion 2. Students should be at least 90% correct on the parts of the lesson that deal with skills and information introduced earlier in the program sequence. (Engelmann, 1999, p. 7)

Specific student mastery criteria are also applied to independent work and in-program assessments (discussed below). If students are placed properly in the program and taught to mastery every day, their progress through the lessons should correspond to pre-established expectations. These lesson progress expectations differ by the performance level of the students as well as the grade level of the instructional program.

Three types of in-program assessments allow for periodic checks on student mastery: mastery tests, cumulative tests, and reading checkouts. Mastery tests are periodic assessments designed to test students' knowledge of skills and concepts covered in a range of lessons. They vary in length and difficulty depending on the sophistication of the program level. In addition to mastery tests, several DI programs contain cumulative tests that summarize the material covered over a much larger number of lessons than the mastery tests. Checkouts are informal reading inventories designed to assess students' accuracy and fluency rate with familiar material.

Passing the tests should not be a goal in and of itself. Rather, the tests serve as indicators of the degree to which the students have mastered the instructional material and, thus, the effectiveness of the instruction the students have received. If the instruction is altered to "prepare" students for the tests, then the tests cannot serve as a clear indicator of the effectiveness of instruction.

Teachers should record student mastery test results, independent work scores, and daily lesson progress. The school's leadership team reviews the data to assess the performance of each instructional group, one of the schoolwide functions discussed below.

THE SUPPORT LEVEL OF IMPLEMENTATION

Teachers' implementation of the DI approach (the instructional level) is highly successful only when the school's leadership team provides an environment in which effective and efficient instruction can take place. School and district leaders are responsible for establishing the structural components needed for a successful DI implementation, training staff to implement the program properly, monitoring instruction to ensure that the program is implemented with fidelity, and increasing the capacity of the school and district to support the model fully.

Using DI for Core Instruction

Ensuring that the school implements DI as the sole instructional approach in the subject areas selected is a key structural component of a successful DI implementation. Direct Instruction programs were not designed to be used in conjunction with other programs or other instructional approaches. If students receive instruction in several approaches in the same subject matter, they can get confused. Other programs may be used for additional practice but not instruction. For instance, students may read stories and short selections from basal reading programs, novels or other outside reading material as long as these materials just provide practice on skills already mastered in the DI reading program.

Scheduling and Grouping

Another reason for not implementing other instructional approaches or programs is the time required for the DI programs. There are precise daily time requirements for each DI program. Providing sufficient time is critical for the successful implementation of DI as students' progress through the programs depends to a large degree on the amount of time they spend receiving instruction.

Common instructional times by subject for each grade level, and where possible across grade levels, allow for the creation of instructional groups that are homogeneous with respect to skill level. Students should be grouped homogeneously in order to increase the efficiency of instruction. If students in an instructional group all possess similar skills and knowledge, the teacher can target the instructional presentation to the same skill level. If, however, instructional groups are not homogeneous with respect to skill level, the instructor faces a serious dilemma: to whom should the instructor target the presentation? If the teacher teaches to the higher-performing members of the group, the lower-performing students will not be able to keep up, and their mastery of the lessons will decline precipitously over a short time. If the teacher teaches to the lower-performing members of the group, the higher-performing students will not be sufficiently challenged and will be learning at a lower rate than their maximum potential. If the teacher teaches to the performance middle, a combination of these effects will take place.

Note that the instructional groups are not permanent tracks but flexible groupings to accommodate the current skill level of students. A student can place into different levels in different programs—into a high-performing math group but a medium-performing language group, for instance—and can move into a different group as the student's performance dictates. So instructional schedules should provide the flexibility to group and regroup students within and across grade levels.

Initial placement of students into instructional groups is determined by student performance on the placement tests that accompany the teacher's guides for each program. Adjustments to group membership should be based on two types of data: direct observation by a reliable observer and written data on student performance.

Ensuring Proper Student-Teacher Ratios

Students in the lower levels of the DI programs require small student:instructor ratios to ensure that young students are mastering the content and skills covered in the programs. These ratios vary according to the skill levels of the students. The ratio of the lower-performing students can be two or three times as low as that for higher-performing students in the same grade. These ratios allow the instructors (teachers or paraprofessionals) to devote attention to the most fragile learners to ensure that they progress through the programs at mastery. The higher levels of the programs can be taught to whole-class groups as large as 25 or 30 students.

Providing Direct Instruction Support Personnel

A building coordinator—often referred to as a reading coordinator or reading coach in those schools implementing only the Direct Instruction reading and language programs—should be the primary staff member supporting the day-to-day operation of the Direct Instruction implementation. The building coordinator acts as the linchpin to the DI implementation and is responsible for material orders, overseeing placement testing, organizing teaching schedules, maintaining student lists for instructional groups, collecting student performance data, and arranging in-service training. The building coordinator should be a full-time position with 100% of the assigned duties in support of the DI implementation. An exception can occur in small schools with fewer than 150 students in which the building coordinator is a half-time position.

In addition to the duties listed above, the building coordinator acts as the lead coach and oversees peer coaches. (Peer coaches, discussed below, provide direct support to the teaching staff.) In order for the building coordinator to function as the lead coach, she must have experience teaching Direct Instruction. If she does not have prior experience with DI, she must develop it on the job for at least a semester by teaching a group of students during some part of the school day. Without experience teaching Direct Instruction, the building coordinator will only be able to provide superficial support to teachers.

The building coordinator will not be able to learn all levels of all DI programs even with the opportunity to teach the program. To provide additional program-specific coaching, the school can tap into the budding expertise of the teaching staff by developing peer coaches—usually one coach per grade level. Over time, the peer coaches can become resident resources for other teachers teaching the same levels of the program. To provide support effectively, the coaches need to receive training in specific aspects of coaching.

The National Institute for Direct Instruction (NIFDI), which provides such training, has defined four levels of coaches training that lead teachers must receive in order to function as effective peer coaches:

- The first level, which is usually scheduled during the first year of implementation, focuses on analyzing student performance data. During this stage, the peer coaches' primary role is to identify and describe problems of student performance in enough detail to permit the building coordinator and NIFDI personnel to implement an appropriate solution.

- The next two levels of training prepare peer coaches to perform 5-minute and extended observations of instruction with students present.

- The last level of coaches' training prepares coaches to lead grade-level meetings focusing on student performance and participate in data analysis and problem-solving sessions with the rest of the school's leadership team. (NIFDI, 2014, para. 4)

With trained peer coaches in place, the school greatly increases its capacity for delivering effective instruction to all students.

Peer coaches are prime candidates for becoming program trainers after they have taught the program with expert coaching for two years. Training is a different skill than coaching. A program trainer must create a sequential introduction to the critical skills and formats that teachers must master before they can start using DI successfully with students. A program trainer must learn when to provide hands-on practice in critical skills and formats, how to monitor participants to ensure they master fundamental DI delivery and correction techniques, how much time to spend explaining the rationale of the program's design versus practicing skills in a role-play format, and when to adjust the original sequence to accommodate participants who require additional practice in specific formats or additional explanation of the program's design.

Training and Professional Development

All teaching staff should receive a thorough preservice training before the start of the school year in the precise levels of the programs that correspond to their students' mastery level as determined through placement testing. Teachers should receive the equivalent of two full days training on any single level of the program. Some adjustments are possible if a small number of teachers is involved so the trainers can devote their attention to only a few participants.

During the school year, the teaching staff will require three different types of ongoing professional development on DI teaching techniques: in-class coaching, practice sessions and in-service training sessions. In-class coaching should be provided by an expert DI coach for the first three years of implementing the program. The coach observes student performance, relates the teacher's behavior and the classroom environment to the students' performance, and provides specific remedies that are designed to improve student performance. The feedback should include positive observations of the teacher's delivery of the program as well as a maximum of three remedies for the teacher or support staff to implement. The number of remedies is limited so that the teacher receiving the feedback isn't overwhelmed with too much to change at any one time.

Through in-class observations, the experienced coach identifies common problems of implementation across several classrooms that can be addressed more efficiently through a group in-service rather than through individual coaching. In-service sessions can involve just the teachers or aides teaching a specific level of a program, or they can involve the whole staff. The sessions may focus on a specific technique or format for a small group of teachers, such as a rhyming format, or on a more general topic for the whole staff, such as motivating students. In-services can last anywhere from 30 minutes to a whole day depending on the topic and the number of teachers involved.

In addition to in-services, teachers should practice upcoming lessons in formal practice sessions so they can present the scripts flawlessly and correct student errors fluently. Practice sessions should occur for at least 20 minutes at least once a week for all teaching staff during the first year of implementation and more often as needed. Practice sessions and in-service sessions need to be monitored if they are going to be effective. A member of the school's leadership team should ensure that the targeted teaching staff is present, that the sessions start on time, and that the main focus of the session is on practicing, not discussing the program.

Any type of training should be followed by in-class monitoring to ensure that teachers actually apply the techniques covered in the training to the instructional setting. Student performance won't improve if teachers don't incorporate the techniques into their teaching behavior. Coaches and administrators can ensure that *all* teachers master the skills covered during training sessions by conducting in-class observations after the training has been completed, tracking the use of the targeted techniques by individual teachers and providing feedback to individual teachers on their use of the techniques along with follow-up training on specific skills that still require improvement. Teachers should be informed of this follow-up process, which will convey to them the importance of mastering the techniques during the in-service training.

Weekly Problem-Solving Sessions with External Support

In addition to providing training based on direct observations, the school's leadership team—building coordinator and peer coaches—analyze student performance data in weekly problem-solving sessions to identify areas for improvement. Especially in the first years of implementation, this analysis is done with the assistance of an external support provider, an outside expert on the implementation of DI. The external support provider participates by phone, video conference or in-person if on-site.

Before a problem-solving session commences, the teaching staffs submit data on lessons completed by each instructional group, the results of in-program assessments by individual students, and a summary of the percentage correct on each student's independent work. The building coordinator and peer coaches screen these data for accuracy and completeness. The data are ordered by grade level and teacher, usually from the lowest to highest grade involved in the DI implementation, along with notes from observations taken since the last problem-solving session. The leadership team and external support provider then discuss the progress and mastery of each instructional group systematically. They identify students whose performance indicate that they either need additional firming in critical skills or are ready for more challenging work and can be moved to a higher-performing group. The data may also indicate that whole groups need to repeat material or can skip to a higher placement in a particular program. Such adjustments are made weekly to ensure that students are kept as close as possible to their performance level at all times.

A product of the problem-solving session is a summary of action items, with four separate sections on different aspects of the DI implementation. The first section is devoted to a review of the previous week's items—actions that were identified in previous problem-solving sessions. This follow-up ensures that remedies are actually implemented in the classroom and are effective in solving the instructional problems identified. If a problem has not been resolved since the previous session, it is not forgotten but is retained on the action list with possibly a modified remedy if the first remedy was applied but did not solve the problem. The second section is devoted to a review of the current week's data, with the goal of identifying specific remedies to instructional problems. The third section is devoted to accolades for student success— such student accomplishments as high performance on mastery tests or successfully completing a level of a program. This section provides a mechanism for the leadership team to give positive feedback to teachers for their students' success.

The final section addresses critical problems of implementation. These can be divided into two types: "red flag" and "redline" problems. Red flag problems are problems that have persisted for three weeks or more. Any problem can become a red flag problem because even a problem that seems innocuous can grow into a more serious problem over time. For instance, failing to remediate and retest a student who committed excessive errors on a mastery test will result in more serious problems for the student if he is presented with increasingly more difficult material as time goes on. In contrast to red flag problems, which involve the persistence of problems for three weeks or more, redline problems are problems that are so serious that they pose an immediate threat to the success of the DI implementation. These problems include violations of many of the implementation requirements discussed in this section. The red flag/redline section allows for the leadership team to quickly identify these and other serious problems and make them the highest priority in their daily efforts to support the implementation.

THE ROLE OF THE PRINCIPAL

A particularly important aspect of the support provided to teachers, and thus the probability that their students will succeed, is the role of the principal. An effective principal is one of the most critical prerequisites for a successful implementation of DI as the principal's statements and actions determine the upper limit of the impact of DI. A school implementing DI may be able to achieve substantial improvement in student performance without an effective principal, but improvements will be much greater with the principal's full participation. The principal should demonstrate leadership in four critical areas: (1) setting up the DI implementation initially, (2) monitoring the fidelity of implementation, (3) intervening decisively to ensure fidelity of implementation, and (4) acting as the spokesperson for DI to internal and external stakeholders. The principal may be able to delegate duties in some of these areas; in others the principal will need to execute the duties.

Setting up the DI implementation involves acquiring and allocating the resources needed to ensure success. The principal must ensure that sufficient staff members are hired and that the staff members fully understand their responsibilities in the DI implementation. The principal should communicate expectations to all staff explicitly and explain DI responsibilities as part of the hiring process for new staff. If the staff is involved in a vote on the implementation of DI, the principal should make clear to all that, regardless of their vote, they will be expected to deliver DI as designed if the school implements the program.

The principal should also ensure that there are sufficient funds for implementing DI successfully. Sufficient instructional materials that match the students' assessed needs as determined by placement test results should be purchased before the start of the year, with funds reserved for the purchase of additional materials as students finish program levels throughout the school year. In addition, sufficient funds should be allocated for an external support provider to supply training, on-site coaching and guidance in the implementation of DI as well as a weekly review of student performance data. The principal should also secure funds for visiting a model DI school and attending specialized training that would be too expensive for an external support provider to supply on-site.

Once the DI implementation has been set up properly, the principal should monitor the implementation to ensure that it is implemented with fidelity. The principal should conduct observations to see firsthand the implementation of DI in action and to reinforce the observations of the building coordinator and coaches. Most observations can be performed quickly—within two to five minutes—to accurately gauge the effectiveness of instruction. The principal should also meet with the building coordinator and designated coaches frequently as a means of monitoring the implementation indirectly.

When problems of implementation are identified through observations or data analysis, the principal should determine whether the problem is a "can't-do" or a "won't-do"—whether a teacher has the skills and ability to implement DI correctly, or, on the other hand, a teacher simply chooses not to implement DI correctly. If the problem is a "won't-do", the principal should remind the teacher of the expectations and then monitor the teacher's behavior to ensure that the teacher implements the program properly. If the problem is a "can't-do", the principal should determine whether the problem can be solved by increasing the skills of the teacher through training or, conversely, whether the problem is out of the control of the teacher, which requires structural changes in the implementation of DI.

The principal's communication with staff should include regular, positive feedback. Implementing DI is very stressful for many staff members because of the unique demands of presenting from a script with signals and the tremendous amount of attention and energy that is required to monitor all student responses, correct all student errors, and repeat exercises until students master all parts of every lesson. Positive feedback from the building coordinator and principal provides encouragement to teachers and paraprofessionals to overcome their doubts and persevere in implementing DI effectively for all students.

In addition to helping the school's staff dispel their doubts and fears about DI and their own abilities to deliver DI successfully, the principal should dispel the doubts and fears of other stakeholders–district administrators, parents, and community members. A great number of myths have proliferated about the DI programs, and these need to be addressed explicitly. Several publications list the myths along with the evidence rebutting the myths (Tarver, 1998; Adams & Engelmann, 1996). Principals should be familiar with these myths and how to rebut them.

LONG-TERM IMPLEMENTATION CHALLENGES

Schools and districts that adhere to the guidelines above for implementing DI will experience short-term success in improving student performance and student self-images. However, if the goal of the school or district is to experience sustained stellar improvement in student performance, several challenges must be overcome.

Importance of the Early Grades

The years during which DI can have its most profound and positive effect on student performance are the years of a child's first introduction to academic content–preschool, Kindergarten, and first grade. During these grades, carefully structured instruction can provide students with the fundamental skills and background knowledge they need to succeed in academic subjects in later years. The need for careful instruction in the early grades is particularly great for students in high-poverty areas. Research has identified the strong disparities that exist in language exposure and vocabulary acquisition among preschool children depending on their socio-economic status (Hart & Risley, 1995). Research has also demonstrated that children who enter school with language deficits experience difficulty learning to read, which can have negative repercussions on student performance and self-image for the rest of their time at school (Early Struggles in Vocabulary, 2001; Children of the Code, n.d.).

The Cohort Effect: Longevity Produces Better Results

If a school or district is able to accelerate student progress in the DI programs from the earliest grades as described above, the school or district will experience a wave of rising student performance as cohorts that started DI in preschool or Kindergarten work their way up the grades. The first cohort to start DI in preschool or Kindergarten will perform well but not as well as later cohorts. This is because teachers require several years of experience teaching DI with expert coaching before they are able to deliver the program with maximum effectiveness for all students. So the third or fourth cohort of students to start DI in preschool or Kindergarten is likely to be the cohort leading the wave of the highest performing students.

Note that this wave takes several years to reach the upper grades. Performance in the fourth and fifth grades may not increase appreciably in the first two years of implementing DI, especially if the students' performance in those grades was several years behind national norms. Performance will increase noticeably after three to four years, but it may take five or six years of implementing DI with fidelity before the performance reaches its height as the cohort of students who began DI in Kindergarten reaches the upper elementary grades. In schools that maintain the DI implementation for this long, student performance increases can be astounding (Stockard, 2011; Vitale and Joseph, 2008). Even in high poverty schools, approximately half of the fourth graders who start DI in Kindergarten exit the six-level *Reading Mastery* series and use *Understanding U.S. History*, a history text intended for middle school students, as their reading text.

Quite often, school and district staff do not understand the time requirements of the cohort effect. As Engelmann and Engelmann (2004) explain:

> If the model is evaluated on the basis of the performance of Grade 5 students after two years of implementation, the gains will not be impressive because the fifth-graders would have gone only through Grades 4 and 5 in the model, not Kindergarten through fifth grade. The principal, teachers, or central administrators who observe the trends may conclude that the program works in the lower grades but not in the upper grades. They may choose to maintain the model in the primary grades but use other material and approaches for the upper grades. (p. 118)

One of the primary tasks of the school and district leadership is to maintain the DI implementation at a high level for the number of years that it takes for the cohort of students who receive DI as Kindergartners to reach the higher grade levels. To show the maximum effect of the DI approach in a school system, the cohorts that begin DI in Kindergarten should be provided with effective instruction until they graduate from high school. Unfortunately, school systems are not set up to implement a single approach for so many years despite evidence of effectiveness with students in the system.

Preventative versus Remedial Strategies

Starting a DI implementation in the early grades is an effective strategy for accelerating student performance and preventing student failure. Beginning DI in preschool or Kindergarten ensures that students learn critical skills and concepts early, which prevents them from falling behind grade-level expectations. Their early success boosts their self-image and provides them with the confidence that they will succeed in later grades. This preventative strategy, which involves identifying students' needs and adjusting instruction to meet their needs, is the most humane and successful strategy for ensuring that students become successful learners as they meet the district's performance goals.

When a DI implementation is started, however, students in the upper grades have not had the benefit of receiving instruction with DI. Many of them perform well below grade level expectations, so a preventative strategy cannot work for them. A concerted effort with targeted and consistent instruction must be in place to close performance gaps and bring students' performance in line with grade level expectations. This involves prioritizing DI remedial instruction over grade-level instruction. Indeed, if students' skill levels do not permit them to access grade-level content courses, then time spent in these courses is wasted. The time could be much better spent double- or triple-dosing remedial instruction that will improve students' fundamental skills and prepare them for rejoining their grade-level peers in time. The time required to close these gaps will simply depend on the size of the gaps and the rate at which these gaps can be closed.

Middle school represents the last opportunity for many students to close sizable performance gaps. Ironically, stricter high school graduation requirements have resulted in fewer remedial students acquiring the skills they need to graduate. Most high schools do not offer remedial classes that meet the needs of students whose skill level is severely below grade-level expectations. Those schools that do offer remedial courses do not offer them for credit. Typically, high school students will not take courses unless they receive credit for them, with the result that students do not acquire the skills they need to succeed in content-area courses. Consequently, many students drop out of high school because they cannot meet graduation requirements. Offering remedial courses for credit and modifying the schedules of students who are severely at risk of not acquiring basic academic skills needed to graduate are two strategies that can help students who are struggling to succeed in high school.

Optimally, a district can employ both preventative and remedial implementations of DI simultaneously. A preventative implementation should be used as the primary long-term strategy for improving student performance because of the tremendous benefits it has for students' well being. But the needs of current students, many of whom perform below grade-level expectations, should also be met through remedial implementations of DI. A dilemma occurs when a district needs to choose between a preventative and a remedial strategy because of limited resources. District personnel and other stakeholders may feel compelled to try to meet the immediate needs of current students although this strategy will lead to a permanent remedial implementation. If students do not receive effective instruction in the early grades, there will always be a need for a remedial program because a steady stream of students will continue to perform below grade-level expectations when they reach the higher grades. If, however, students receive effective instruction in the early grades, there will not be a need for a large-scale remedial program because the vast majority of students will be performing at or above grade-level expectations. The moral challenge is to choose between the long-term benefit of future students versus the immediate benefit of current students.

Note that either a preventative or remedial strategy with DI is more proactive than a response to intervention (RTI) strategy for improving student performance. With RTI, all students are provided the same instruction initially. Then, instruction is modified for those students who demonstrate that the core instructional program is too difficult for them. In other words, students receive appropriate instruction only after they experience failure with the initial instructional program. Although this is an improvement over the practice of continuing to use a single instructional program for all students regardless of their differential skill levels, RTI is a "fail first" strategy that wastes precious time by requiring students to spend time in a program that does not match their needs, and it exacts a toll on the self-image and well-being of students who struggle with the core instructional program. In contrast, students who receive DI are assessed for placement in the DI programs as the first step of implementing the program, so all students receive appropriate instruction from the outset.

Developing Institutional Memory

One of the biggest challenges to implementing DI successfully over the long term is to develop an institutional memory of conditions that existed before DI was implemented and the effect of implementing DI on students' attitudes and performance. Specifically, districts and schools need to develop and retain a shared understanding of what student performance levels were like before DI was implemented, what types of instructional approaches were replaced by DI, and what progress has been completed to date toward the ultimate goal of maximizing the performance of all students with DI. Developing and sharing this understanding is comparatively easy if staff turnover is low. But if there is a high turnover of personnel, new staff members will not share the same perspective as staff members who have been present from the beginning of the DI implementation. A concerted effort by the school and district leadership to inform new staff members about the effect and ongoing need for DI–through discussions with experienced staff members, video clips of classroom instruction, and graphic displays of changes in student performance over time–can help new staff members develop a commitment to and understanding of the need to implement DI for all students.

The weakest link in the development of a shared commitment to implementing DI is turnover at the administrative level. When the administrator responsible for bringing DI into a district is replaced, DI is often quickly abandoned regardless of its record of improving student performance. Staff members who recognize the benefit of DI usually try to forestall replacing DI. But unless the administrator who is directly responsible for the DI implementation supports DI unequivocally, the DI implementation will tend to erode over time.

CONCLUSION

Implementing Direct Instruction successfully is a highly technical enterprise that involves increasing the efficiency and effectiveness of all factors in a school setting that can influence student performance. This includes factors at the instructional level, which affect teacher-student interaction directly, as well as factors at the support level, which affect teacher-student interaction indirectly. The success of the implementation is dependent on aligning all of these factors to achieve maximum effect. If any one of the factors is out of place, the effect of the other factors may be compromised. If, for instance, students are not properly placed in the Direct Instruction programs, the skills of a teacher to deliver the program are nullified.

In order for an elementary school to maximize student success in the long run, the school must implement the Direct Instruction model fully for at least the number of years equal to the number of grades at the school (six years for a K–5 school). Maximizing student success at middle and high schools involves implementing DI at the feeder elementary schools as well as the middle/high school itself for the number of years equal to the maximum grade of the school.

Implementing Direct Instruction for such a long period of time is complicated by staff turnover, especially of administrative staff. Schools and districts can develop institutional memory of the need for and effectiveness of the DI implementation, which can be used to orient new teaching staff to the school's goals and objectives for using Direct Instruction.

Orienting new administrative staff members is more difficult unless they have prior experience with DI, as administrators have a tendency to ignore the success of approaches used previously at schools and implement their own "innovative" alternative. Fortunately, many administrators who implement the comprehensive Direct Instruction model fully become strong advocates of the DI approach. Administrators who witness student success with DI in one school or district carry that knowledge with them to other districts. Many of them implement DI at new sites once they leave their original school or district because they have seen firsthand the unparalleled potential of the comprehensive Direct Instruction model to accelerate the performance of all students and raise their self-confidence as competent, successful learners.

REFERENCES

Adams, G. L., & Engelmann, S. (1996). *Research on Direct Instruction: 25 years beyond DISTAR.* Seattle, WA: Educational Achievement Systems.

Children of the Code. (n.d.). *Interview with Dr. Alex Granzin: Traumatized learning: The emotional consequences of protracted reading difficulties.* Retrieved from http://www.childrenofthecode.org/interviews/granzin.htm.

"Early struggles in vocabulary development can hamper economically disadvantaged children". (2001, April 11). *Penn State Newswire.* Retrieved from http://www.psu.edu/ur/2001/childrenvocabulary.html

Engelmann, S. (1999, July). *Student-program alignment and teaching to mastery.* Paper presented at 25th National Direct Instruction Conference, Eugene, OR.

Engelmann, S. (n.d.). *Achieving a full-school, full-immersion implementation of Direct Instruction: Developer's guidelines.* Retrieved from http://www.nifdi.org/pdfs/Dev_Guide.pdf

Engelmann, S. (2004). Foreword. In N. E. Marchand-Martella, T. A. Slocum, & R. C. Martella (Eds.), *Introduction to Direct Instruction* (pp. xix–xxvi). Boston: Allyn & Bacon.

Engelmann, S. (2014). Research from the inside: The development and testing of DI. In J. Stockard (Ed.), *The Science and Success of Engelmann's Direct Instruction* (pp. 3-24). Eugene, OR: NIFDI Press.

Engelmann, S., & Carnine, D. (1982a). Direct Instruction outcomes with middle-class second graders. *ADI News, 1*(2), 4– 5.

Engelmann, S. & Carnine, D. (1982b). *Theory of instruction: Principles and applications.* New York: Irvington Publishing, Inc.

Engelmann, S. & Colvin, G. (2006). *Rubric for identifying authentic Direct Instruction programs.* Eugene, OR: Engelmann Foundation.

Engelmann, S. E., & Engelmann, K. E. (2004). Impediments to scaling up effective comprehensive school reform models. In T. K. Glennan Jr., S. J. Bodilly, J. R. Galegher, & K. A. Kerr (Eds.), *Expanding the reach of education reforms: perspectives from leaders in the scale-up of educational interventions* (pp. 107–133). Santa Monica, CA: RAND Corporation.

Hart, B., & Risley, R. T. (1995). *Meaningful differences in the everyday experience of young American children.* Baltimore, MD: Paul H. Brookes.

Hempenstall, K. (2004). The importance of effective instruction. In N. E. Marchand-Martella, T. A. Slocum, & R. C. Martella (Eds.), *Introduction to Direct Instruction* (pp. 1–27). Boston: Allyn & Bacon.

Instructional effectiveness. (n.d.) *Glossary of education, Education.com.* http://www.education.com/definition/instructional-effectiveness/, retrieved April 21, 2013.

National Institute for Direct Instruction. (2014). *Developing Peer Coaches.* retrieved January 25, 2014 from http://www.nifdi.org/services/coaching/peer-coaches.

Stockard, J. (2010). Fourth graders' growth in reading comprehension and fluency: A pretest-posttest randomized control study comparing *Reading Mastery* and Scott Foresman basal reading program (Technical Report 2010-3). Eugene, OR: National Institure for Direct Instruction. Retrieved from http://www.nifdi.org/di-research-database

Stockard, J. (2011). Direct Instruction and first grade reading achievement: The role of technical support and time of implementation. *Journal of Direct Instruction* 11, 31–50.

Tarver, S. G. (1998). Myths and truths about direct instruction. *Effective School Practices,* 17(1), Winter: 18–22.

Tudge, J., & Scrimsher, S. (2003). Lev S. Vygotsky on education: A cultural-historical, interpersonal, and individual approach to development. In B. J. Zimmerman & D. H. Schunk (Eds.), *Educational psychology: A century of contributions* (pp. 207–228). Mahwah, NJ: L. Erlbaum Associates.

Vitale, M. R., & Joseph, B. L. (2008). Broadening the institutional value of Direct Instruction implemented in a low-SES elementary school: Implications for scale-up and school reform. *Journal of Direct Instruction,* *8* (1), 1–18.

Watkins, C. A., & Slocum, T. A. (2004). The components of Direct Instruction. In N. E. Marchand-Martella, T. A. Slocum, & R. C. Martella (Eds.), *Introduction to Direct Instruction* (pp. 28–65). Boston: Allyn & Bacon.

CHAPTER 6

Helping teachers manage students' behavior is a key element of Direct Instruction's goal of effective and efficient instruction. While embedded within each DI program, these elements of behavior management have also been an important influence on the fields of behavior management and applied behavior analysis. In Chapter 6 Caitlin Rasplica discusses these linkages. She describes intersections in their historical development and numerous similarities in effective instruction and effective behavioral management. She highlights the ways in which effective behavior management mirrors the basic principles of Direct Instruction, showing that all children can learn to behave appropriately when given proper instruction and that behavior problems do not result from bad children, but from ineffective environments.

DIRECT INSTRUCTION AND BEHAVIOR SUPPORT IN SCHOOLS

Caitlin Rasplica

A growing body of literature suggests that students' social behavior problems and academic skill deficits are closely related (McIntosh, Horner, Chard, Boland, & Good, 2006; Lee, Sugai, & Horner, 1999), and the vast history of the Direct Instruction methodology shows the success that can occur with the intersection of sound academic and behavioral principles. It shows that all children can learn and all can succeed. Students just need to be taught using an adequate curriculum at an appropriate level and in a supportive learning environment.

This chapter explores the intersection of academic and behavioral principles of learning. The first section discusses the importance of behavior support for the promotion of learning and contrasts traditional methods of behavior management in schools to the way in which Direct Instruction (DI) helps students develop the behaviors needed for academic success. Intersections in the historical development of Direct Instruction and the field of behavior support are then examined. The final, and most extensive, section discusses and illustrates parallels in specific design characteristics of the two fields. A brief discussion of implications of this analysis for schools and possible future trends concludes the chapter.

BEHAVIOR MANAGEMENT, DIRECT INSTRUCTION, AND LEARNING

This section describes traditional responses to behavior problems in schools and contrasts these responses to conceptualized understandings of why such problems occur. It then describes how Direct Instruction addresses these root causes of misbehavior in schools.

Typical Responses to Behavior Problems in Schools

Effective behavior management techniques are essential to student learning, but many educators are faced with the task of educating students whose behavior impedes their learning as well as that of others. Problematic behavior is one of the most frequent complaints of teachers and a major reason that they leave teaching. Yet, teachers are rarely trained in how to address these issues (Stockard & Lehman, 2004).

Educators have commonly addressed behavior problems differently than instructional problems (Colvin, Kame'enui, & Sugai, 1993). Students are often given reprimands for social behavior, but not typically given reprimands for poor academic performance (Colvin, et al., 1993). Historically, school discipline has been established on a punitive system of rules and consequences (Colvin, 2007; Gettinger, 1988). If a rule is broken, students receive consequences for their behavior intended to punish misbehavior. Although methods for dealing with problem behavior began to shift in the 1970s to include a more proactive approach, schools typically continue to respond to behavior problems with discipline procedures consisting of office referrals, suspensions, and expulsions.

Such punitive systems, including zero tolerance polices, have not been shown to be effective means to deal with behavior problems (APA Zero Tolerance Task Force, 2008; Mayer, 1995; Skiba & Peterson, 1999). A punitive response often presents a short-term fix to what is actually a chronic issue (Osher, Bear, Sprague, & Doyle, 2010) and is often associated with increased rates of aggression, vandalism, and school drop-out (Mayer & Butterworth, 1995). Additionally, schoolwide discipline plans are often built within systems that are unclear and inconsistent. The work of behavior analysts shows that students with the most challenging behaviors require use of discipline practices that have an instructional focus.

Researchers have identified two primary reasons that students may engage in disruptive behavior during classroom instruction (March & Horner, 2002). The first function of disruptive behavior is directly related to the instructional materials presented to the learner. Students may find the materials aversive if they are either too difficult or too easy. They may then engage in disruptive behavior in order to escape the difficult or boring task. In short, if the material does not have a payoff for the students, there is little incentive for them to stay on task (Engelmann, 1997). The second primary function of problem behavior involves the student seeking attention from adults or from their peers. The student will engage in disruptive behavior in order to obtain this attention, as it is, at the time, the most efficient means to access attention.

Direct Instruction Addresses the Source of Behavior Problems

The traditional approach to behavior management, involving a punitive system of rules and consequences, has been called a "reactive" method, focusing on actions after the behavior occurs (Gettinger, 1988) and ignoring the root causes of problem behavior. Direct Instruction approaches behavior management and discipline in a strikingly different manner, one based on behavioral principles of prevention, positive reinforcement and carefully designed instruction. The main difference between DI and other approaches to instruction is the large emphasis placed on antecedent stimuli, on the pathways that produce behavior problems (Gersten, Carnine, & White, 1984). This involves the careful design and presentation of instructional materials, including the manner in which the teacher presents the materials to the students, as well as the emphasis placed on the structure of the environment and the setting in which instruction is delivered.

DI is based on the theory that clear instruction, limited of misinterpretation, can promote learning in all students, accelerate the acquisition of skills, and enable students to generalize these skills to other examples. Moreover, the Direct Instruction tradition shows that behavior problems are dramatically reduced if all students are sufficiently engaged in the instructional process (Walker, Colvin, & Ramsey, 1995). Classroom management involves keeping the children engaged in the lesson by maintaining interest and decreasing behaviors that disrupt work on the assigned tasks (Engelmann, 1997).

Instruction that addresses potential problem behaviors begins by attending to careful and effective placement of students in levels of instruction that balance challenge and attainability. Once a student is effectively placed in an appropriate level, pacing and explicit instructional delivery minimize learner failure and maximize student engagement. These criteria ensure that the students are given work that is neither too difficult nor too boring, which decreases the need to avoid or escape the work and ultimately decreases disruptive behaviors (Filter & Horner, 2009).

Misbehavior within the classroom may also be a result of the need for attention from peers or staff. The DI programs incorporate continual and frequent reinforcement for students. This reinforcement comes in the form of teacher praise for their success as well as the students' knowledge that they are progressing through the curriculum and continually learning.

In short, the Direct Instruction programs embody, within their structure, mechanisms that address the two sources of behavior problems. Careful placement of students within the program ensures that students are not given material that is too difficult or too easy. The fast pacing of instruction ensures that they are not bored. Continual and systematic reinforcement, both from learning the material and from teachers' consistent and frequent praise, mitigates needs for additional attention. All of these elements of behavior management have been part of the Direct Instruction programs from their inception.

BEHAVIOR MANAGEMENT FROM THE BEGINNING

Many scholars who are now prominent in the field of behavior management trained or worked with Wesley Becker, a psychologist who was an early colleague and long-term collaborator of Engelmann's. Becker first joined Engelmann in his work in the third year of the Bereiter-Engelmann preschool (Engelmann, 2007). Becker became the new director of the preschool and demonstrated how one could change student behavior by changing teacher behavior (Engelmann, 2007). Becker's motto was to "catch kids in the act of being good." In other words, he advocated setting the environment so students can succeed and offering praise when they do, thus reinforcing their positive behaviors (Engelmann, 2007).

After this initial experience, Engelmann concluded that teaching requires good acting. Teachers must learn to say the right things at the right times and to act in a manner that will help the children develop positive attitudes about school and appropriate behaviors (Engelmann, 2007). Perhaps reflecting Becker's early involvement in the 1960s, the conceptual beginnings of Direct Instruction included the theoretical application of applied behavior analysis (Becker, Engelmann, & Thomas, 1975; Engelmann, Granzin, & Severson, 1979). Becker's research in applied behavior analysis concerning explicit statement of classroom expectations, contingencies of behavior, and the influence of teacher attention (Becker, Madsen, Arnold, & Thomas, 1967; Madsen, Becker, & Thomas, 1968) are all key elements in the DI model. In subsequent years the work expanded to involve behavior modification with individual students (Engelmann, 2007), as Engelmann, Becker, and colleagues extended their instructional work to engage students with severe behavior problems. When training new teachers, the importance of a teacher's response to a student, the alteration of instruction and the environment, was always stressed.

The link between behavior and instruction was clear from the beginning, and researchers soon began to realize the potential impact that many of the principles and concepts derived from Direct Instruction could have in other fields and environments including special education (Gersten, 1985), teacher behavior, and classroom organization. Becker, Madsen, and colleagues published several studies identifying the importance of establishing classroom expectations to allow for effective classroom environments (e.g., Becker et al., 1967; Madsen et al., 1968). In 1968, the first issue of the *Journal of Applied Behavior Analysis (JABA)* was published, which represented a time at which behavioral principles were extended to educational settings (Sugai & Horner, 200). Baer, Wolf, and Risley's (1968) landmark publication, along with the work of Becker, Engelmann and colleagues, set the stage for future work involving the application of applied behavior analysis (ABA) to the study of human behavior. To date, DI and behavior analytic principles have been studied with numerous populations and settings including general case programming with students with severe developmental disabilities (Colvin & Horner, 1983) and classroom management in general education settings (Colvin, Kame'enui, & Sugai, 1993; Gettinger, 1988; Lewis & Sugai, 1999; Simonsen, Fairbanks, Briesch, Myers, & Sugai, 2008).

Engelmann's instructional programs focus on the use of behavioral principles on the classroom level, but the principles can also be viewed at an organizational or systemic level. Horner, Sugai, and colleagues have expanded the use of behavior analytic principles to apply within a systems-wide, or school-level, approach. An extensive literature base indicates that School-Wide Positive Behavior Support (SWPBS; Sugai & Horner, 2002) is an effective means of addressing problem behavior in schools by explicitly teaching school expectations and acknowledging appropriate behavior (Horner, Sugai, & Anderson, 2010; Horner, Sugai, Smolkowski, et al., 2009; Sugai & Horner, 2006). For the success of SWPBS, it is expected that environments are designed so that the students can be successful, paralleling the key role of student success in behavior management within classrooms. Thus, the theory of SWPBS is strongly tied to that of Direct Instruction as both approaches focus on adapting the environment rather than changing the child as the key to solving problems. The next section looks at the parallels of behavior management, including SWPBS, and Direct Instruction in greater detail.

PARALLELS AMONG DISCIPLINES

Several components of the Direct Instruction model are well-represented in behavioral models including systematic use of reinforcement, frequent assessment of learner behavior, breaking large tasks into small components by use of task analysis, teaching pre-skills, and use of a mastery learning approach (Gersten et al, 1984). Although not commonly acknowledged in contemporary literature, there are significant parallels between the DI instructional principles and the fields of applied behavior analysis and behavior support in schools. Both approaches, DI instructional programs and behavior support techniques, are often used side by side within educational settings, but, in actuality, are rarely used to influence one another. The two fields have tended to become separate within the academic and applied world. However, the intersection of academic and behavioral skills is an important component, which should be examined in great detail. It is in response to such practices that Colvin and colleagues (1993) have argued for using an instructional approach to manage chronic problem behavior in the school system.

The sections below describe five areas where an instructional approach to teaching academic skills parallels methods of teaching social behavior skills and can be applied within a school system: teaching academic and behavioral expectations, rules, and strategies; correction procedures; managing misrules; pre-correction; and assessment. Four assumptions underlie this discussion (Sugai & Horner, 2002). The first is that behavior is learned, just as an academic skill is learned. Teachers outline and describe rules and expectations, and students interpret these and demonstrate their understanding of them. The second assumption is that behavior can be taught. In order for behavior to be learned, one can expect that behavior can be taught. Just as a child must be taught how to read, appropriate behaviors are also taught. The third assumption is that if problem behavior is learned, the appropriate behavior has not been taught correctly. Therefore, behavior has not been learned in cooperation with the expectations of the present environment. The final assumption is that if problem behavior has been learned, then appropriate behavior can be taught to replace these problem behaviors. *Note that each of these assumptions parallels those that are inherent within the Direct Instruction curricular programs and mirror basic principles of Direct Instruction: All children can learn to behave appropriately when given proper instruction, and behavior problems do not result from bad children, but from ineffective environments.*

Teaching Academic and Behavioral Expectations, Rules, and Strategies

The principle that separates Direct Instruction from most other instructional design programs and philosophies is that in the initial stages of instruction, every step in applying principles or rules is explicitly taught (Gersten et al., 1984). Engelmann and colleagues focused on the concept of "faultless instruction" where instruction was specifically sequenced to lead to accurate communication of the concepts to be taught, which therefore limits the possibility of confusion.

Explicit Instruction of Behavioral Expectations

Explicit instruction can be considered a preventive approach. It limits the likelihood that new learners will acquire errors and thus limits the likelihood that skills will need to be re-learned. For example, when teaching the rule for a "long a," students are explicitly told the rule. Instruction might include the following, "When there's an e at the end of a word, you read the letter name." Students are then given a carefully designed sequence of examples in order to demonstrate this new rule through guided practice. In addition to the explicit approach to instruction, DI ensures that learning involves mastery of the concepts that are taught. Once a skill is mastered, it can be built upon with more advanced skills.

Intervention plans for managing behavior in the classroom and other school settings must also be explicit to be effective. Effective behavior plans typically begin with establishing and teaching expectations to the students. Establishing staff expectations greatly impacts both student academic performance, as well as social behavior (Walker, Colvin, & Ramsey, 1995). Behavior expectations should clearly outline and define desirable behaviors of students. Effective strategies for establishing behavioral expectations within the classroom encourage direct teaching of the desired social behavior (Colvin, 2004).

A common issue in developing a productive behavioral program is acknowledging that behavioral expectations should be taught to students. This is not considered a phenomenon in teaching academic skills, as Engelmann's instructional principles have been developed and described in the literature. Therefore, teachers can apply these instructional principles to behavioral difficulties as well. Desirable behaviors can be taught to students by establishing expectations for the students or teaching desirable behaviors to students rather than using punitive techniques to retroactively attempt to resolve problematic behaviors. This argument encourages a proactive approach when establishing a behavior support system, involving explicit instruction and attention to generalization of the learned behaviors.

Modeling, Monitoring and Practice

Instructional principles provide guidelines for teaching desirable behaviors. They show that behaviors can be modeled through example. Desirable behaviors can be considered a skill set that needs to be taught to students through modeling. Expected behaviors must then be monitored to ensure the task and expectations are communicated and were received by the learner. If the communication was not received, feedback should be given to the learner to then ensure that the student is successful in performing that behavior in the future.

Within instruction, rules are typically taught using examples or non-examples to model the rule. A specified series of positive examples of a concept, negative examples of the concept, as well as minimally different examples help the learner to distinguish what is included in the concept of interest. For example, when teaching the color "red," one would not present four red fish. Instead, one would present one red fish, one red bird, and one red car. Then one would teach that something is "not red" by presenting the same three objects, but in a color that is not red. This provides examples and non-examples to the learner. Similarly, when teaching about a behavioral expectation such as "sitting with your hands and your feet to yourself," one would model an example by sitting upright with hands folded in their lap. Next, one would provide a minimally different non-example where hands are on the peer's desk rather than in their lap.

Once the rule has been taught, guided practice is used to ensure the learner is successful. This is typically followed by supervised independent practice where the learner can demonstrate the skill. Skills are maintained through repeated practice at a later time. Repeated practice is critical, and is needed far more than is often considered. The integration of previously learned concepts and skills in continuous review helps students maintain mastery. Thus, teachers may continually need to remind students of behavioral expectations, such as talking at only appropriate times or not running in the halls, so that the appropriate behavior is maintained. When teaching and reteaching these behavioral expectations, it is important that a consistent operational definition of the appropriate behavior is used.

Generalization of Learned Behaviors

Generalization refers to the use of a trained skill in an untrained setting. If two examples that are treated in the same manner share the same quality, and the learner has the ability to identify the sameness, the learner can generalize. Based on Engelmann's theory of instruction, generalizations are treated as an outcome of communication (Engelmann & Carnine, 1991).

General case programming is a key principle of the Direct Instruction academic model and has long been used within Direct Instruction strategies (Horner & McDonald, 1982; Horner, Jones, & Williams, 1985; Horner, Albin, & Ralph, 1986). A general case strategy uses the fewest number of rules to enable a child to solve a variety of tasks. For example, a child who learns to decode regular words is learning a general case. Children learn the strategy of decoding with one set of words by understanding letter-sound correspondence. They can then apply this strategy to a different set of words that were not previously encountered. When possible, general case strategies should be taught across all content areas (Gersten et al., 1984).

In behavior management, general case instruction refers to the behaviors performed by a teacher that increase the probability that the behaviors performed in one setting will also occur in a different setting. The goal is to provide a strategy for the students that they can use when they come across an example they have not yet encountered.

If a learner fails to generalize, one can assume that inadequate instruction was provided, which limited the ability to generalize (Engelmann & Carnine, 1991). In the previous instructional example, the strategy for reading words with "long a" can be applied to most words ending with a vowel, consonant, and final e. Therefore, the learner can generalize the rule to other examples. This also applies to behavior management in schools and how likely it is that a behavior generalizes from one setting to another. For instance, transitioning into the classroom at the start of the day could involve the same behavioral expectations as transitioning out of the classroom at the end of the day.

Correction Procedures

Mistakes will inevitably occur during the learning process, whether it involves academic content or behaviors. Typically errors are a result of a lack of information or from misapplication of a general case strategy. The way in which these errors are corrected is crucial. Mistakes must be corrected in a way that assures that the student can continue with the instructional program in a quick and efficient manner (Engelmann & Carnine, 1991) or, with respect to behavior, that the corrections do not detract from instructional time.

According to Engelmann and Carnine (1991), students may make a discrimination mistake, a response mistake, or a combination of the two. A discrimination mistake is made when the student provides an incorrect response, although capable of making the correct response. In order to correct a discrimination mistake, additional information is provided to the student to display what controls the response, or in other words, what differentiates the correct response from incorrect responses (Engelmann & Carnine, 1991). A response mistake occurs when the student is unable to produce the response. In order to correct a response mistake, the teacher or interventionist must shape the response.

Correcting with Model-Lead-Test

Despite the two types of correction procedures, there are commonalities in corrections. All corrections should include a remedy to the main problem, use of juxtapositions allowing for quick repetition of the skill in need of discrimination, inclusion of sufficient opportunities to practice, and an opportunity for the learner to respond to the task in the same context in which the task was originally presented (Engelmann & Carnine, 1991). A common procedure for correcting mistakes is to first model the correct response, test the missed response, and then repeat the test at a later time. This approach is often referred to as the three-step firming procedure. The following exchange provides an example of the procedure:

TEACHER SAYS:	STUDENT RESPONSE:
	(Student incorrectly reads the word trick) Tick.
1. My turn, *trick.*	
Say it with me: *Trick.*	*Trick.*
2. Your turn. Get ready.	
	Trick.
3. Go back to the beginning of that sentence.	

Step 1 provides the student with information regarding the correct response, step 2 tests whether this information was received by the learner through a direct test, and step 3 tests whether the student is able to correctly perform the task when it is given in the original context at a later time (Engelmann & Carnine, 1991). Through this approach the student receives feedback on the mistake and is then supplied with the essential steps to ensure that the student has developed the needed skills to perform the task at a later time.

Correcting with Prompting

Errors that occur through misapplication of a general case strategy are corrected by prompting the student to use the steps in the strategy. For example, the following teaching sequence could be used to correct an error made on the word "fad" if the student says "fade."

Teacher: Is there an e at the end of the word?

Student: No.

Teacher: Do you say the letter name then?

Student: No.

Teacher: (points to underlined a) What's the underlined sound?

Student: aaa (short a sound)

Teacher: What word?

Student: Fad.

Correcting Behavior

Strategies for correcting errors in behavior management models in schools are conceptualized in ways that are similar to the instructional procedures for correcting errors provided by Engelmann and Carnine (1991). Engelmann and Carnine's instructional approach involves five steps: focus on the rule that was taught, teach the rule again through guided practice, allow for supervised independent practice, check for understanding of the rule at a later time, and, finally, allow for additional practice in order to establish maintenance and generalization of the rule. Colvin (2007) applies these strategies to behavior management. He recommends that students be provided feedback that specifies that unacceptable behavior has occurred, followed by identifying specific strategies to ensure that the students learn the expected behaviors for the future. Colvin has identified a system, based upon instructional principles, to correct problem behaviors, emphasizing that it should include a continuum of responses for the problem behavior and systematic procedures for managing consequences for behavior problems.

Errors made during instruction or in behavior should be corrected immediately. This correction is intended to ensure that the student will perform correctly in subsequent tasks, similar to tasks where the mistake originally occurred (Engelmann & Carnine, 1991). The first step in correcting a behavior should be to acknowledge the other students who are displaying the expected behaviors (Walker, Colvin, & Ramsey, 1995). This acknowledgement can be delivered in the form of praise or other strategies using positive reinforcement. Students should also be provided with times at which they can receive feedback on their behaviors, as well as suggestions and encouragement for improving such behaviors in the future (Walker et al., 1995). On a schoolwide level, students displaying the appropriate behavior may intermittently receive some form of reinforcement in order to increase the likelihood that the appropriate behavior will occur again in the future.

The behavioral correction procedure can be determined as successful if the student displays appropriate behavior during the next opportunity to respond (Walker et al., 1995). The ultimate goal is "errorless learning," or a school and classroom with minimal levels of behavioral problems, parallel in many respects to the notion of mastery learning of academic materials.

Managing Misrules

A misrule occurs when the child learns the wrong rule, possibly through miscommunication. Misrules are critical to immediately identify and remedy. If they are not immediately corrected the likelihood for repeated academic errors to be made on later tasks is increased. When a misrule occurs, tasks can be teased apart into smaller tasks in order to understand where the breakdown occurred and to reteach the rule. After the tasks have been broken down, the teacher will assess where the error occurred. The instructor can then have the child practice the rule correctly, while firming the individual parts where the error was previously made.

Misrules can also occur with social behavior. When misrules occur in behavior management, it is commonly identified as problem behavior, which is occurring through continuous rehearsal of that problem behavior. Similarly to academics, analyses of where the behavior routine is breaking down must be made in order to formulate a remedy for the problem. The school staff member can then identify an alternative routine, while modeling the appropriate behavior or reminding the student of the rule.

When identifying problem behavior, it is commonly an issue of stimulus control, so the teacher or interventionist must weaken this stimulus control relationship, by first trying to identify the environmental stimuli that set the occasion for problem behavior. For example, problem behavior may be more likely to occur when a student is presented with an independent worksheet or during whole group math instruction, or when a particular staff member is present. This problem behavior may also be more likely to occur due to a more distant variable such as skipping breakfast.

This procedure for managing misrules of social behavior is in direct contrast to the traditional approach of applying punishment in schools such as suspension. While the traditional approach applies sanctions after the behavior has occurred, the error correction approach sets the environment and expectations in a manner that reduces the probability that problem behavior will occur.

Pre-Correction

Students will likely make errors even when effective instructional practices are in place. Some errors can be anticipated by the teacher ahead of time. Pre-correction procedures are used when academic and problem behaviors are anticipated, and therefore, often predictable if they are following a pattern. Through mastery learning, carefully designed instruction, frequent opportunities for practice, and judicious review of previously learned concepts, the type of student mistakes can often be predicted (Gersten et al., 1984). As noted above, it must be assumed that both appropriate and inappropriate behaviors are learned. Importantly, appropriate behaviors can then be taught by using principles of instruction (Colvin, Patching, & Sugai, 1991). Pre-correction procedures within an instructional procedure are achieved by systematically manipulating the antecedent and consequence, or the initial teacher behavior and the feedback provided, respectively.

Direct Instruction principles instruct teachers to use a systematic error correction procedure. One example is "model, lead, test" (Engelmann & Carnine, 1991). Model-lead-test involves showing the appropriate behavior or requested task, leading the student in practicing the appropriate behavior or task, and then evaluating whether the student performs the task or behavior independently. If it is likely that students will predictably repeat an error, a teacher may use pre-correction procedures by setting up the student to successfully complete the next academic task. Through pre-correction procedures, a teacher responds before the student has engaged in the task or the behavior and, therefore, has manipulated the antecedent. It is critical to understand the difference between correction and pre-correction procedures. Correction procedures are reactive in that they deal with the error after it has occurred. In other words, correction procedures place focus upon the consequence, whereas pre-correction procedures focus on the antecedent.

Pre-correction is an effective instructional approach that is also used to establish appropriate behavior. For example, Walker and colleagues (1995) describe a situation in which a teacher anticipates that a student will transition into the classroom in a disruptive manner. Since this has been anticipated, the teacher can remind the student before making the transition of the expectations and have a task ready for them to transition to immediately upon entering the classroom. This strategy reduces the potential need to act reactively to problem behaviors (Walker et al., 1995).

Assessment

Assessment of student skills, whether they are behavioral or academic in nature, is essential at all phases of learning, and Direct Instruction and Applied Behavior Analysis share a common commitment to the collection and use of data for several purposes. Assessment allows for modifications to the teaching techniques to be made if needed, intervention development, or use as a universal screening or individual progress monitoring tool.

Engelmann and Carnine (1991) discuss the diagnosis of the problem when a child is not supplying the expected responses. The diagnosis assumes that the instruction is flawed, and therefore, a misrule developed (Engelmann & Carnine, 1991). When identifying a problem, it can be assumed that the errors performed are not based on the knowledge of the learner, but rather on the communication the learner received. Through assessment of the learner, modifications to instruction can be acknowledged. DI programs are comprised of periodic assessments to determine if students mastered previously learned concepts or if more practice is needed before advancing in the program. Similarly, behavior problems in schools should be seen as resulting from faulty teaching and, with appropriate modification of the environment, students can learn the behaviors that will promote their learning and future success. For example, when pre-correction is used, teachers should collect student performance data to determine whether the pre-correction procedure identified and implemented was effective (Walker et al., 1995).

Several universal screening tools for behavior have been developed for use with individual students, classrooms, and entire schools (Walker & Severson, 1992; Walker, Cheney, Stage, & Blum, 2005). These developments parallel Engelmann's emphasis on continually assessing learning progress and mastery of concepts. When the focus is on social behavior, assessment lends the ability to see how students have mastered social behavior skills and where additional practice, support, or intervention is needed. These assessments build on the assumption that undesired behaviors result from communication errors, just as errors in academic learning result from faulty teaching. Thus, behavioral monitoring procedures evaluate whether behavioral expectations are being met and ways in which the communication, or instruction, could be improved.

CONCLUSIONS

As budgets shrink, teachers are increasingly faced with the burden of larger class sizes, enabling behavior problems to heighten. Disruptive behaviors including aggression, defiance, and insubordination are the most common reasons students are asked to leave school and amplify the burden on teachers. However, suspension and expulsion do not provide the most effective means for dealing with problem behavior, and if the disruptive behavior of these students is not dealt with effectively, these behaviors contribute to poor student and community outcomes (Osher et al., 2010).

School staffs are also simultaneously confronted with new pressures to incorporate state initiatives aimed at improving the outcomes for students. Such initiatives are sometimes viewed as troublesome to many staff members. Therefore, appropriate systems for both instructional and behavior support continue to be in demand within the educational system today.

The instructional principles embodied in the Direct Instruction programs developed by Siegfried Engelmann, Wes Becker, and colleagues are embodied in the behavior management techniques of the field of applied behavior analysis (ABA) found in schools today. Many contemporary leaders in the field of behavior management were influenced by their own work with DI and their interactions with those working with the programs. More specifically, key elements of behavior management, including behavioral expectations, correcting errors, correcting misrules, and using pre-correction techniques, parallel key aspects of DI instructional systems. It is also clear that both a strong behavioral management system and effective instruction are necessary in order to have effective schools and improve outcomes for students. Such systems can help individual students, much as Engelmann's instructional and behavioral support have helped many thousands of students have successful academic outcomes. They can also help entire school systems be more successful.

The striking parallels between the fields probably reflect their common origins. One could also argue that each field is more effective when used with the other. In other words, a DI teacher is more effective if there is an understanding of the elements of ABA, and someone using ABA is more effective in the classroom if they are simultaneously using Direct Instruction. As any teacher or school staff member who has been working with children knows, you must have an engaging instructional lesson to minimize behavioral difficulties; you must also have a supportive environment to engage the learner in the instruction.

As SWPBS and other behavior management frameworks continue to be implemented across schools today, the sustainability of such approaches may lead the research in the field of education for the future. Engelmann, Becker and colleagues provided a strong foundation for instructional and behavior support over 40 years ago, but the sustainability of the principles will require additional attention of researchers and practitioners in the field due to the constant evolution of beliefs about school systems and the seemingly continual eruption of new educational fads.

State mandates will also continue to be a driving force for implementation of such practices, but the sustainability of interventions is critical as significant resources are used to implement and maintain interventions and techniques intended to provide positive student outcomes. As these systems evolve we, as educators, must remember the basis of behavioral change in schools, possibly through the application of Becker's motto to "Catch kids in the act of being good," and use the time-tested and highly validated methods of behavior management embedded within Direct Instruction and the allied behavioral fields.

REFERENCES

American Psychological Association Zero Tolerance Task Force. (2008). Are zero tolerance policies effective in the schools? *American Psychologist, 63*(9), 852–862.

Baer, D., Wolf, M., & Risley, T. (1968). Some current dimensions of applied behavior analysis. *Journal of Applied Behavior Analysis, 1,* 91–97.

Becker, W. C., Engelmann, S., & Thomas, D. R. (1975). *Teaching 1: Classroom management.* Chicago: Science Research Associates.

Becker, W., Madsen, C., Arnold, C., & Thomas, D. (1967). The contingent use of teacher attention and praise in reducing classroom behavior problems. *Journal of Special Education, 1,* 287–307.

Colvin, G. (2004). *Managing the cycle of acting-out behavior in the classroom.* Eugene, OR: Behavior Associates.

Colvin, G. (2007). *7 steps for developing a proactive schoolwide discipline plan: A guide for principals and leadership teams.* Thousand Oaks, CA: Corwin Press.

Colvin, G., & Horner, R. (1983). Experimental analysis of generalization: An evaluation of a general case programme for teaching motor skills to severely handicapped learners. *Advances in Mental Handicap Research, 2,* 309–343.

Colvin, G., Kame'enui, E., & Sugai, G. (1993). Reconceptualizing behavior management and school-wide discipline in general education. *Education and Treatment of Children, 16*(4), 361–381.

Colvin, G., Patching, B., & Sugai, G. (1991). Pre-correction: A strategy for managing predictable problem behaviors. *Direct Instruction News, 10*(2), 34–40.

Engelmann, S. (1997). *Preventing failure in the primary grades.* Association for Direct Instruction: Eugene, OR.

Engelmann, S. (2007). *Teaching needy kids in our backwards system: 42 years of trying.* Eugene, OR: ADI Press.

Engelmann, S., & Carnine, D. (1991). *Theory of instruction: Principles and applications.* Eugene, OR: ADI Press. (Originally published in 1982).

Engelmann, S., Granzin, A., & Severson, H. (1979). Diagnosing instruction. *The Journal of Special Education, 13*(4), 355–363.

Filter, K. J. & Horner, R. H. (2009). Function-based academic interventions for problem behavior. *Education and Treatment of Children, 32,* 1-19.

Gersten, R. (1985). Direct Instruction with special education students: A review of evaluation research. *The Journal of Special Education, 19*(1), 41-58.

Gersten, R., Carnine, D., & White, W. A. (1984). The pursuit of clarity: Direct Instruction and applied behavior analysis. In W. Heward, T. E. Heron, D. S. Hill, & J. Trap-Porter (Eds.), *Focus on behavior analysis in education.* Columbus, OH: Charles Merrill.

Gettinger, M. (1988). Methods of proactive classroom management. *School Psychology Review, 17*(2), 227–242.

Horner, R., Albin, R., & Ralph, G. (1986). Generalization with precision: The role of negative teaching examples in the instruction of generalized grocery item selection. *Journal of the Association of Person with Severe Handicaps, 11*(4), 300–308.

Horner, R., Jones, D., & Williams, J. (1985). Teaching generalized street crossing to individuals with moderate and severe mental retardation. *Journal of the Association for Persons with Severe Handicaps, 10,* 71–78.

Horner, R., Sugai, G., & Anderson, C. (2010). Examining the evidence base for School-Wide Positive Behavior Support. *Focus on Exceptional Children, 42*(8), 1-14.

Horner, R., Sugai, G., Smolkowski, K., Eber, L., Nakasato, J., Todd, A., & Esperanza, J., (2009). A randomized, wait-list controlled effectiveness trial assessing school-wide positive behavior support in elementary schools. *Journal of Positive Behavior Interventions, 11,* 133-145.

Horner, R., & McDonald, R. (1982). A comparison of single instance and general case instruction in teaching a generalized vocational skill. *Journal of the Association for Persons with Severe Handicaps, 7*(3), 7–20.

Lee, Y., Sugai, G., & Horner, R. (1999). Using an instructional intervention to reduce problem and off-task behaviors. *Journal of Positive Behavior Interventions, 1,* 195–204.

Lewis, T. J., & Sugai, G. (1999). Effective behavior support: A systems approach to proactive schoolwide management. *Focus on Exceptional Children, 31*(6), 1–24.

Madsen, C., Becker, W., & Thomas, D. (1968). Rules, praise, and ignoring: Elements of elementary classroom context. *Journal of Applied Behavior Analysis, 1,* 139–150.

March, R., & Horner, R. (2002). Feasibility and contributions of functional behavioral assessment in schools. *Journal of Emotional and Behavioral Disorders, 10*(3), 158–170.

Mayer, G. (1995). Preventing antisocial behavior in the schools. *Journal of Applied Behavior Analysis, 28,* 467–478.

Mayer, G., & Butterworth, T. (1995). A preventive approach to school violence and vandalism: An experimental study. *Personnel and Guidance Journal, 57*(9), 436–441.

McIntosh, K., Horner, R., Chard, D., Boland, J., & Good, R. (2006). The use of reading and behavior screening measures to predict non-response to school-wide positive behavior support: A longitudinal analysis. *School Psychology Review, 35,* 275–291.

Osher, D., Bear, G., Sprague, S., & Doyle, W. (2010). How can we improve school discipline? *Educational Researcher, 39*(1), 48–58.

Simonsen, B., Fairbanks, S., Briesch, A., Myers, D., & Sugai, G. (2008). Evidence-based practices in classroom management: Considerations for research to practice. *Education and Treatment of Children, 31*(3), 351–380.

Skiba, R., & Peterson, R. (1999). The dark side of zero tolerance: Can punishment lead to safe schools? *The Phi Delta Kappan, 80*(5), 372–376, 381–382.

Stockard, J., & Lehman, M. B. (2004). Influences on the satisfaction and retention of first-year teachers: The importance of effective school management. *Educational Administration Quarterly, 40,* 742–771.

Sugai, G., & Horner, R. (2002). The evolution of discipline practices: School-wide positive behavior supports. *Child and Family Behavior Therapy, 24,* 23–50.

Sugai, G., & Horner, R. (2006). A promising approach for expanding and sustaining school-wide positive behavior support. *School Psychology Review, 35*(2), 245–259.

Walker, H., Cheney, D., Stage, S., & Blum, C. (2005). Schoolwide screening and positive behavior supports: Identifying and supporting students at risk for school failure. *Journal of Positive Behavior Interventions, 7*(4), 194–204.

Walker, H., Colvin, G., & Ramsey, E. (1995). *Antisocial behavior in school: Strategies and best practices.* Pacific Grove, CA: Brooks/Cole Publishing.

Walker, H., & Severson, H. (1992). *Systematic screening for behavior disorders.* Longmont, CO: Sopris West.

CHAPTER 7

The preceding chapters describe the strong scientific base of Engelmann's Direct Instruction, the vast research showing its efficacy, the guidelines DI provides for effective schools, and the politically fraught, often illogical nature of educational policymaking. Education is too often driven by fads that ignore and indeed seem impervious to the findings of science. Will it always be so? In the final chapter, Shepard Barbash argues both sides of the question, and offers two starkly contrasting visions of DI's future.

DEBATING DI'S FUTURE*

Shepard Barbash

If Direct Instruction works so well, why do so many people hate it? If illiteracy and innumeracy are problems DI can solve, why don't more people use it? If Siegfried Engelmann is a genius, why don't more people know it? Why have so many educators been blind for so long, and how can more be made to see?

A tiny fraternity has asked and answered these questions for 50 years. For 50 years Engelmann has created new programs and new members have joined the fraternity. And yet for all their efforts, DI's share of the K–12 market remains tiny, and the nation's literacy rate has barely changed. One in fifty teachers uses DI. One in three students is a poor reader.

Even DI's successes end in failure: hundreds of places over the years have adopted DI, taught better, then disowned it and taught worse again when new leaders came in with other ideas.

Is this DI's destiny—to drift in the backwaters like a rare bird, seen and enjoyed by the lucky few, perhaps to go extinct? Is this Engelmann's destiny—to be a glittering footnote in the dull history of public education? The optimist cries no!—the ugly duckling may yet turn into a swan! The pessimist sighs yes—Engelmann will soon be forgotten, and DI will disappear or at best remain an endangered species. Which will it be? Of course no one knows. "History arranges things—badly," Talleyrand says. Life for DI has always been a great and terrible struggle.

---

* This chapter is based on three bodies of work. The first is my book, *Clear Teaching*, published in 2012. The second is my research since 2012 on IDEA Public Schools, a charter school network in Texas. I followed IDEA because DI remains my primary interest and IDEA is the largest and fastest-growing district in the United States that uses DI as its K-2 academic program. In December 2013, I began to research Tennessee's education policies and their potential impact on the market for Direct Instruction. My interest was piqued by the state's unprecedented gains on the National Assessment of Educational Progress.[1]

I make the case for optimism and pessimism, but I am not committed to either. As I joked in a speech not long ago, I remain of three minds: "On Mondays, Wednesdays and Fridays I'm an optimist. On Tuesdays, Thursdays and Saturdays I'm a pessimist. On Sundays I'm confused." Readers looking for the keys to a brighter future will be disappointed. The only assurance I can give is that Direct Instruction is a great invention that can lift our nation like no other invention of our time. Its growth is worth fighting for, and it will not grow without a fight.

THE OPTIMIST: RESULTS WILL CONQUER

The success of most things depends upon knowing how long it will take to succeed.
–Montesquieu

The Gathering Storm

Americans want educators to do a better job preparing their children to go to college, find good work and become good citizens. Anything they can be persuaded will do so, they will demand. They are not clamoring for DI, but they have enacted policies that are encouraging its use. The greatest of these are measures that require states to collect better data on how schools are performing, evaluate educators based on this data, and promote more competition among schools for students. These policies if sustained in enough places will turn teaching into a behavioral science that embraces Zig Engelmann as its pioneer. So says the optimist.

Better Tests, Higher Stakes

A good test of student performance is DI's best friend–so long as the results are easy for the public to understand and hard for educators to ignore. For years DI was all but friendless because few educators kept meaningful data on how their students were doing, much less used it to improve instruction. Scoreboards comparing schools were rare because few schools kept score, much less disclosed the score to anyone who might care enough to affect the outcome. Successes went unrewarded, failures unamended. DI programs came and went, achievement rose and fell, the hopes of children were lifted and dashed–and the public stood by, none the wiser.

This rudderlessness is fitfully giving way to a culture that relies on data to guide its actions. The growing unhappiness with K–12 education, the fear that nations with better schools and harder-working students are eroding our prosperity, the growing conviction that educators should be held more accountable for their work–these and other sentiments have prompted Americans to demand better information from their schools, and better outcomes. [2]

More testing is the first bittersweet fruit of the public's awakening. Educators today have more testing data on their students than ever before. They do not always know how to use this data to improve their teaching, and indeed their data is not always very useful, but they are less inclined to ignore or do without it because the people are less inclined to let them.

Better assessments help DI because students taught with DI tend to do better on them than students taught with something else. What is needed is a system that measures student achievement on a range of meaningful tasks. As schools move halt-ingly toward this ideal, more of them will feel pressed to try DI because more of them will be exposed for their inadequacies. "DI is not plain vanilla, it's the medicine," says a sales representative from McGraw-Hill Education, which owns and sells the major DI programs. "Schools adopt DI because they have a problem and DI solves it." Better tests are a double boon: they force more schools to face their problems, and they generate more proof that DI is an effective solution.

Progress in Tennessee

Tantalizing evidence that a better scoreboard will lead to more DI comes from Tennessee. The state was the first to adopt an assessment system that measures not only the absolute performance of schools and students but their progress over time. The Tennessee Value-Added Assessment System (TVAAS) estimates the "value added" by individual districts, schools and teachers by comparing the results of their students from year to year on a set of achievement tests required by the state. Teachers are expected and encouraged to use the TVAAS data to improve their teaching; administrators are required by law to use the data to evaluate their teachers; and the public is given a report card that includes TVAAS and a range of other data for every school and district and for the state.[3] Tennessee also improved its scoreboard by strengthening the standards and tests on which the TVAAS data is based.

The most promising sign that the policies are working is Tennessee's impressive performance on the 2013 National Assessment of Educational Progress. The Volunteer State (long one of the lowest performing) showed the biggest improvement of any state in a single two-year testing cycle since NAEP started nationwide assessments in 1992.[4]

The state's progress probably was not much helped by Direct Instruction, but Direct Instruction definitely has been helped by the state's progress. Sales of DI programs by McGraw-Hill Education in 2013 soared nearly 250 percent in Tennessee over the prior year. The growth was stimulated by the state's requirement that schools monitor student progress more closely in Grades K–3 and use scientifically validated instruction to meet the needs of any child not performing at grade-level norms.[5]

DI has friends in Tennessee. The commissioner of education, Kevin Huffman, was trained by Engelmann's staff on *Reading Mastery* when he was an elementary school teacher in Houston. He liked the program enough that he wrote his own version to teach reading to his students who didn't speak English. As commissioner, Huffman cannot order schools to teach with DI (or any other specific curriculum), but he has been a strong advocate for the policies that encourage its use, such as using TVAAS data to evaluate teacher effectiveness and requiring schools to use scientifically validated programs to teach children who are behind their peers.

The Power of Publicity

The most outspoken advocate for DI in the state is John Stone, president of the Education Consumers Foundation (ECF), a nonprofit group that Stone likens to the Consumers Union (publisher of *Consumer Reports*). ECF holds award ceremonies to recognize top-performing schools, creates easy-to-read charts of data to facilitate school comparisons, and publishes research on policies and practices to highlight what works and what doesn't. [6]

Stone is a full-throated optimist:

For decades, ineffective schools have blamed poor reading outcomes on poverty, and the public has had little choice but to accept their explanation. Today, ECF's third-grade reading charts let people see for themselves the vast differences in outcomes at demographically similar schools. The days of playing the education policy game without keeping score are over.

If DI keeps growing in Tennessee, and if enough schools using it get better scores on the state report card, other states will pay attention. [7]

Trust the Market

DI's other best friend is competition. The argument goes like this: K–12 education functions like a monopoly. Nothing really threatens its survival. It pays no great price when its students fail and reaps no great reward when they succeed. It does not learn from experience or replace old ways with new ways that work better because it does not have to. It is big enough to behave as it wants, and it does not want DI.

DI is anathema to the monopoly because it gives teachers less freedom to do what they want in the classroom and because it defies the monopoly's vast stake in the conventional wisdom about how children learn.[8] It has survived in a trickle of sites, most of them serving the poor and the disabled. These sites have shown to anyone who cared to look that children can learn much more than teachers typically teach them or indeed believe they can learn. They have also shown that teachers not only can learn DI, they grow to love it once they do because it makes them so much more successful. But because these sites are aberrations abhorrent to the monopoly, they have never grown large enough or lasted long enough to command much attention or inspire emulation. The best way to promote their growth and survival is to create a marketplace that attracts better talent into education and drives everyone to do better.

Until new players can open new schools that seriously compete with public schools for students, DI will remain an alien in unfriendly terrain. Encourage smart people from outside the monopoly to start schools that compete for its customers and DI will thrive as never before.

This prosaic hypothesis—that more competition will lead to more DI—has only recently gone from wish to possibility. The evidence comes from an unlikely source: a charter school network, IDEA Public Schools, founded by two Teach for America (TFA) alumni near the Texas-Mexico border. The case is unlikely because the talented and ambitious don't normally flock to poor, hot, out-of-the-way places to make their careers, and also because TFA resolutely disdains DI.[9] IDEA is thus a robust confirmation of the theory: if competition in the form of charter schools can attract talent strong enough to overcome TFA's bias and plant DI in the remote fields of south Texas, it can attract the talent to grow DI anywhere with almost anyone. Give a smart competitor access to customers and the sale can be made: parents of children ill-served by their schools will send them to DI schools when given the chance.

Charters: A New Kind of Public School

Competition makes the unlikely more likely and the future harder to predict. IDEA for all its unlikelihood is in fact the natural-born child of competition. It was born of Texas' charter school law—which is a child of the school choice movement—which is the child of popular discontent with the public school. The Texas law, passed in 1995, authorized the state to approve and fund 215 charters; a law passed in 2013 raises the cap to 305 by 2019.

Charter schools must be tuition-free and open to all students. They are more *public* than public schools in that students need not live in a defined geographic area to apply and attend. If a campus attracts more applicants than it has slots, admission is determined by blind lottery. They are *less* public than public schools in that they are nonprofit corporations governed by nonprofit boards that are appointed and not elected by the public. They are *schools of choice* in that they must persuade people to apply to them over the neighborhood public school, where children are expected to attend and are guaranteed a place.

A charter may operate more than one school. (In 2013, there were 209 charters operating 506 campuses in Texas.) Entities like IDEA that run multiple schools are called charter management organizations (CMOs). CMOs are treated by the state as districts even if they operate campuses in disparate regions. The IDEA *district* is based in Weslaco and comprises elementary and secondary schools in Austin, San Antonio, and nine communities across the Rio Grande Valley.

Funding is based on average daily attendance (ADA), as it is for other public schools. Charters receive about 20 percent less than public schools from the state. Unlike public schools, they get no public money for facilities and no money from local taxes. Start-up costs are often covered by philanthropy. Even so, average state funding exceeds $7,000 per student per year, enough to enable a well-managed charter to generate enough of a surplus to borrow money through the sale of tax-exempt bonds to pay for facilities. IDEA ran a $16 million surplus and budgeted $7,494 in state revenue per student for the 2012–2013 school year, based on an ADA of 98 percent.

College Prep for the Poor

IDEA is among the most ambitious CMOs in the country dedicated to serving the poor. It has grown from 1 school, 11 employees, 140 students and a budget of $1.2 million in 2000 to 30 schools, 1,600 employees, 15,500 students, and a budget of $163 million in 2013. It opened 8 new campuses in the 2012 alone. IDEA's board has approved a plan to grow to 60 schools by 2017, ultimately enrolling 50,000 students. Its co-founder and chief executive officer, Tom Torkelson, says he expects IDEA to be enrolling 100,000 students before he reaches retirement age.

IDEA deliberately recruits poor families and takes pains to avoid advertising to the affluent and middle class. Four out of five students qualify for free or reduced-price lunch. That percentage has held steady as the organization has grown. Nine of ten students are Hispanic. Torkelson says he wants IDEA to become the largest source of Hispanic college graduates in the nation.

"College for All" is the mission. For seven straight years, every graduating senior has been accepted to college. Although not every student who enrolls at IDEA stays there and graduates, the achievement is significant on several counts:

- Students enrolled at IDEA go to college and graduate within four years at about six times the rate of comparable students elsewhere.

- Three of four IDEA graduates are the first in their family to go to college.

- Fewer than 20 percent of adults in the communities IDEA serves hold a college degree.

- Fewer than 4 percent of IDEA's students leave for other schools each year–and even fewer drop out.

• The district has grown 30 percent annually for the last five years and enrolls more than 15 times the number of seniors it enrolled when it began (419 as of May 2013, up from 27 in 2007).

IDEA does well on other measures also. It received a rating of *exemplary* from the Texas Education Agency, TEA's highest rating, for six straight years, every year since its founding. (No other K–12 public school district with a high percentage of low income students ever earned an exemplary rating.) It was one of only three charter organizations to win a grant from the U.S. Department of Education's Race to the Top program in 2012. (The grant was for $31 million, one of the largest awarded.) Three of its high schools were ranked in the top 1 percent of all public high schools and the top 40 charter schools by *U.S. News & World Report* in 2013.[10]

Parents evidently prefer IDEA to their traditional public school. The district has taken market share from the independent school districts (ISDs) where it competes. According to state records, from 2012 to 2013 enrollment at IDEA in the Rio Grande Valley grew by 3,062 students, or 32 percent, and *dropped* in several neighboring ISDs, including Brownsville, San Benito and Harlingen. Even with its rapid growth, the district had a waitlist of 18,000 students in June 2013, the second longest of any CMO in the country.[11]

Stronger Leaders, Higher Expectations, Better Results

Most schools adopt DI when they are failing and under pressure to improve. IDEA was already exemplary and beating the competition when Torkelson decided to install it as his core curriculum for Grades K–5. When a board member asked why he bothered, he replied: "Because *better than* is not the same thing as *good enough*."

This drive to *keep getting better* is not uncommon among the better CMOs, who tend to be mission-driven and who must compete for students to survive. It is rare in traditional public schools because the leadership to sustain it is fleeting and rare– hence the schools' tendency to do DI *until* they get better, then drift from it and fall back again because the leader gets distracted or complacent or loses district support or leaves for another job. Torkelson has no plans to leave because the mission he has set for himself will take a lifetime to achieve. He has district support because he is the CEO of a district he himself is creating. He recruits the talent he needs for his board because they are appointed, not elected. He has more control over staffing and compensation because his hands are not tied by unions. He is less prone to the complacency and cronyism that afflict traditional public schools because as a school of choice he is in more danger of losing students if he fails to serve them well.

Optimists say he is the sort of leader education needs and the better CMOs provide. He is younger and more energetic than most superintendents. (When he started IDEA he was 24, and the youngest founder ever of a charter school in Texas.) He is also more competitive. ("Tom wants to crush the competition," a board member says.) He is an accomplished triathlete. (When frustrated he'll go off on a seven-mile run.) He did not go to college to become a teacher and so was not taught (as so many teachers are) to believe myths about learning. He graduated Georgetown University with a degree in economics.

He has high hopes for everyone. He expects all children at IDEA to be taught to read by the end of Kindergarten, even the thousands who arrive speaking no English. (He taught his own two sons to read when they were three using Engelmann's book, *Teach Your Child to Read in 100 Easy Lessons*.) He says that when he was first assigned by Teach for America to teach fourth grade, at Donna ISD, he was stunned and appalled that his students were already so far behind—they could barely read—and that no one at TFA or in his district could tell him how to catch them up. He found a DI remedial program that worked well, *SRA Corrective Reading*, opened an afterschool academy with a TFA colleague, got good results for two years, then quit and launched IDEA (taking many of his students with him) after the district refused to let them expand what they were doing into the school day.

He says he uses DI programs because they work for all students and because ordinary teachers can be trained to use them. They make it possible for him to maintain consistency and quality across schools as he expands. He says he uses Engelmann's training organization, the National Institute for Direct Instruction, because NIFDI's full-immersion model has produced the best results. The model uses DI programs to teach language, reading, writing, spelling and math in elementary school. Secondary schools use DI remedial programs for students performing below grade level. Sixth-grade teachers use *Understanding U.S. History*, another DI program.

Doing What Elected Officials Can't

Torkelson's choice of NIFDI was ambitious even by DI standards. The full-immersion model is so different from what schools do now and so much work that it gets few takers. Just a few dozen schools use it in the U.S. outside IDEA. It needs a strong executive because it takes time to learn and is often unpopular at first. When Torkelson announced its adoption to his board, he warned them that IDEA would lose a lot of students and teachers the first year. "Buy-in will not be a prerequisite *for* the program," he told them, "it will be an outcome *of* the program."

He was right. Teacher and student retention dropped when he made the change and recovered the following year. By the fall of 2013, IDEA's waiting list was longer than ever, and more people than ever were applying to be IDEA teachers. In surveys of faculty and parents that year, DI was popular with both groups. Optimists were vindicated. The surveys proved not that DI works, but that it can gain traction in a competitive market *because* it works. The groups who start out fighting DI wind up liking it best and wanting it most.[12] All they need, all DI needs, is a stouthearted leader to open more schools for them, and charter school laws that make room for more stouthearted leaders.

A hundred years ago Mark Twain wrote: "In the first place God made idiots. This was for practice. Then he made school boards." Without strong, stable governance, DI never grows and never lasts. The optimist's faith in competition boils down to a belief that it will ultimately lead to better governance, and that better governance will emerge first from the better charters. Torkelson's board, handpicked to support IDEA's mission, approved his radical shift even after being warned of the upheaval it would cause. Traditional school boards are not so visionary, nor can they afford to be so brave. Short-term pain for long-term gain is not a tradeoff much less rallying cry that people who face re-election find attractive. Nor is DI a strategy many superintendents are likely to propose, educated as they are among people who detest and defame DI (if they have heard of it at all). Freed from the democratic process of elections, good charters serve democracy better by harnessing its citizens to act not like idiots out for themselves, but statesmen competing to serve children.

Charter Management Organizations: Allies of the Future?

Of course, most charter schools don't understand DI either. They remain in thrall to the same myths that dominate the rest of K–12 education. Like the old Dairy Queen ice cream shops, they boast an assortment of flavors, all variations on vanilla. The better ones tend to get their results not by teaching better, but by creating a better *school culture* and working longer and harder: more school days per year, more hours per day, tighter discipline, stronger social support, higher expectations. But precisely because they have the work ethic and the systems in place to motivate kids and watch their performance closely, they are more likely than the typical public school to outgrow the myths and finally start *teaching* better, too—especially if they are growing and want to get better as they grow. Torkelson may be a maverick among mavericks, but he is not the only ambitious charter operator facing the dilemma of how to get big and stay good—a dilemma DI solves. Fast-growing CMOs *could* become DI's best friends. What DI needs are more laws like Texas' that allow CMOs to grow fast.

The trends are encouraging. The number of charter-friendly states is growing. Charter schools are growing faster than traditional public schools, and the good ones are learning faster, too. They will do to public schools what the Japanese automakers did to the U.S. auto industry and win a big chunk of the market unless public schools improve. Either way, time favors DI. Competition in K–12 education is increasing. The stiffer it gets, the stronger the impetus to use things like DI that serve students well.[13]

The Power of Science and Free People

The case for Direct Instruction is growing stronger, the opportunity greater. All it needs is a spark. It has been hidden away, vilified, starved and slandered—yet people keep discovering its power. It explodes our myths about childhood, myths dearer to us than religion—yet lovers of children come willingly to its truths. It abandons popular practice for behaviors that are awkward and strange—yet converts keep mastering its ways. Even in barebones, bastard form it helps children learn. It solves a terrible problem. So it endures.

You can't fool all of the people all of the time. Tiny, scattered minorities cling to DI like apostates clinging to the good. Ennobled by the love of their students, nourished by their success, solemnized by their trust, they are an army of thousands waiting to be gathered and led. The right leadership could swell their ranks to millions, so great is their weapon. Such an army could remake the profession, so fierce would be its ardor.

It would take time. Remaking education so that it respects evidence is the work of generations. But time is good to science and invention, which are the heart of DI. Every year new research confirms the effectiveness of DI programs—more than 70 studies in the last decade—and every year Engelmann works on new programs.[14] Every year science discovers things about the mind that explain *why* DI works and why other programs don't.[15] Mother Nature will not be fooled, and cannot be ignored forever. In time educators will accept DI.

Time is also good to democracies. Hence the Irishman's quip quoted in our Congress: "Americans will always do the right thing—after exhausting all the alternatives." The growing engagement of governments, businesses, philanthropists, and so many others in the minutiae of education, the growing conviction that serious problems in the classroom are weakening the republic, and that solutions must be found—in short, the growing attentions of a vast and enterprising democracy, focused on a thing vital to its health, can only help DI.[16]

THE PESSIMIST: IGNORANCE WILL REIGN

Optimistic. adj. Mistaken at the top of one's voice.
–Ambrose Bierce, *The Devil's Dictionary*

DI's most passionate devotees tend also to be the most pessimistic about its prospects. Those who have worked in education longest and know DI best are convinced it will never be used by more than a tiny percentage of teachers in a tiny number of classrooms. I have talked with many such disciples over the years. Few have ever sounded more dispirited about the future of DI than DI's creator himself.

Engelmann's pessimism is chronic and comes in waves. Foremost among his concerns in the summer of 2013 was the adoption by the states of a set of common instructional standards that he says are so poorly conceived they will make the programs, teachers and assessments infected by them even less effective than they are now–a dark future indeed.

Why the Common Core Will Fail

Sponsored by the National Governors Association and the Council of Chief State School Officers, the Common Core State Standards purport to specify a list of things all students should master in the core academic subjects before they go to college. The standards were meant to replace the states' own standards with a single system that states would voluntarily adopt. As of January 2014, 45 states (including Tennessee) had done so. The problem is that the new standards were written by the same people that have reviled or ignored DI for decades, and so give DI's antagonists that much more power to impose their failed ways and misconceptions across the country.

Engelmann says the Core's dictates are opaque and wrong, particularly in Grades K–4:

> *Both for math and language arts they are wrong for two main reasons. Some standards require teaching things that are too difficult for students who are below the 50th percentile (which is most of our students in large cities). Also some standards are not grade appropriate. For instance, one requires second graders to compare adjectives and adverbs, something that only a few adults are able to do with precision.*[17]

Engelmann would ignore the standards if he could but he cannot. States and districts will only buy programs they think *align* to the Core, so DI if it wants any takers will have to be changed to conform to appearances: a bit like reformulating the polio vaccine to win a popularity contest.[18] Engelmann assures me he will be able to do so without ruining his programs. Even so, his forecast for the harm the Core will do is apocalyptic. He writes:

> *The Common Core standards will have the greatest negative effect on urban schools that has occurred in the last century. Its failures in reading will result in the adoption of far less ambitious standards and a return to poor practices.*[19]

What he doesn't write is that a return to poor practices means a departure from DI practices.

Acts of Blindness

As an expression of the industry's best thinking, the Core is a sure sign that teachers, principals, superintendents, school board members, education commissioners, legislators, governors, curriculum writers, college professors, accreditation bodies—all the people who matter in K–12 education—are little closer now than they were 50 years ago to understanding what Engelmann learned back then about how kids learn and how to design programs to teach them. If no one appreciates Direct Instruction for the advance that it is, then no one can be counted on to preserve it. Like a delicate flower, it will always be vulnerable to being trampled by the blind. The Core is only *today's* blindness. As sure as night follows day, there will be others, and it is only a matter of time (says the pessimist) before DI gets trampled down for good.

Hope in charter schools is misplaced because most charters will be ruled by the Common Core. Few understand instruction well enough to see where the Core goes wrong. Nor do they understand how DI can help them do better. CMO founders are entrepreneurs who have succeeded not by following scripts but by building their own models and learning from each other. What works for them (so they think) will work for their teachers, but only if their teachers are smart and hard-working and enterprising. So they hire smart people, work them hard, and turn them loose to be entrepreneurs in the classroom. Asking CMOs to embrace DI is like asking a libertarian to embrace big government. The good ones are already beating the competition. Why should they overturn the established order and install an alien regime? Only the most farsighted will see that teachers need well-designed programs to teach well, and that program design is not something teachers or curriculum directors know how to do. Despite its success, IDEA has yet to inspire a single CMO to adopt DI.[20] Torkelson remains a maverick.

Things that are popular are often easy to comprehend. The mysteries of how DI works are impenetrable to all but a few. *Theory of Instruction*, the book that most thoroughly explains them, is a dense work read by almost no one. Beethoven's late quartets were thought to be unplayable when they were written, and are not often performed. DI programs, though quite teachable, are like late Beethoven—understood and enjoyed by a tiny Druid elite.

And whereas few would presume to rewrite Beethoven, many think they can improve on Engelmann. Tinkering with DI programs is common and harmful, and hard to resist. Engelmann years ago coined a phrase to explain the impulse. He calls it *premature elucidation*. People often *think* they understand DI methods before they do, and so feel competent to violate them.

IDEA has already weakened the programs with ill-advised changes. Beginning in August 2013, students in Grades 3–5 were placed in the DI curricula for reading and math at their *grade* level instead of at their *ability* level. They were given tasks that the state expects they should be able to perform at their age, instead of tasks they actually *can* perform. Kids below grade level were thus given tasks much too difficult for them—like manipulating fractions before they know their times tables, or reading long, complex sentences before they can read simple ones.

No one who understands how children learn would drop them in over their heads in a DI program. IDEA's actions were brought on by Torkelson's fear of not doing well on the state test. He wanted students who were not performing at grade level neverthe-less to learn grade-level content in time for the test. But students who are presented with tasks that require them to master too much too quickly learn less, not more. Three months into the school year, the children who were not placed appropriately were progressing through DI lessons at less than half the rate they had been when they were placed according to Engelmann's guidelines. At that point, Torkelson decided to drop DI entirely in Grades 3–5 and use a mix of unproven materials that he hoped would improve test scores in those grades. [21]

State Tests: Not Good Enough

State testing regimes are another debilitating form of blindness. They tell teachers much less about their students than do the mastery tests that are built into DI programs, but they drive instruction because states care about them so much more. That wouldn't be bad if the states knew what concepts to teach and when, but they don't, and so more often than not they drive instruction in the wrong direction.

Flawed testing is in fact why Engelmann rejects school choice as grounds for optimism. "There is no truth in education," he says. Tennessee is as much a maverick as Torkelson. Most state tests reveal little about how students are doing—indeed they often *hide* how students are doing—so there is no reliable way for consumers to make informed choices. As parents shop around for schools, they will be prone to the same misconceptions about DI that afflict so many educators, and they will be prey to these same educators' propaganda and puffed-up results as they shop around.

An Orphan in the Marketplace

Engelmann's pessimism is steeped not only in his reading of the tea leaves but bitter experience: revenues from the sale of DI products at McGraw-Hill Education (MHE) fell by more than 50 percent between 2005 and 2012. The drop was due less to changes in the marketplace than to turmoil at MHE, which went through several reorganizations and cut its DI sales force by 40 percent.[22]

DI is a good horse on a sloppy track at MHE. The programs are profitable but MHE is not. The company was sold in 2012 to Apollo Global Management. Pessimists predict the new owners won't be much smarter about selling DI than were their predecessors, and can't afford to be any braver. They face the same dilemma: DI is more profitable and effective than anything else the company sells, but given the market's biases and blind spots, everything else is easier to sell! Crowded into MHE's big bag of products, DI has been orphaned. It requires more time and expertise to create (which slows product development), more training to learn (which adds to costs), and more work to sell and support. In an ideal world, MHE salespeople would be free to declare that DI works best, but how can they—why *should* they?—when they must also sell other things they've invested heavily in that don't work as well?

No, DI will only thrive as an only child, if it thrives at all. That means finding an investor rich enough to buy it from Apollo and smart enough to see its potential. But investors who actually know what works in education are as rare as educators who know what works because they are blinded by the same myths, and indeed are rewarded by educators for believing them.

DI's owners whoever they are must also confront the fact that educators crave not what works but *novelty*. Pediatricians don't stop prescribing erythromycin, patients don't tire of taking aspirin, surgeons don't switch protocols on a whim, but K–12 education is designed as if teachers get *series fatigue* and demand new stories to teach reading, even when the old stories work better. Who will write the new stories? Who will design the new programs that align to the ever-changing, evermore intrusive standards of an unknowing public? No one writes programs as well as Engelmann, and few could learn how, or even want to. But Engelmann is over 80 and has no stomach for fads and caprice. Abandon science after 50 years as a scientist? It would be like eating your own children. No wonder he's gloomy. His time is running out, and he is spending too much of it responding to insensate demands. The insatiable hunger for *something new* will be the death of DI because there will be no way to feed the beast.

Other programs do not depend on authors. They are made by large teams untethered by science. Like sprawling romance novels, they can be made quickly and to suit varying tastes, and lots of people can make them. They are ever new yet always the same. They thrive in a rudderless market because they are rudderless themselves. They demand little of anyone, whereas DI's devotion to evidence—stern mistress!—will be its undoing. There are more DI knockoffs than ever—less well designed, less effective, but easier to use—and they are winning the struggling schools that DI most needs to win.

No Leaders or Public Will

"It is easy to imagine a great painting," Yeats said. "The hard part is realizing it in materials." Who will realize the optimist's vision for growth? Who will insure that competition leads to more DI and not less? Who will woo the CMOs and the public schools they threaten? Who will insure that states learn the right lessons from Tennessee?[23] Such a campaign would require more resources than MHE is likely to risk and more than the DI training organizations possess. The latter are notoriously poor salesmen.[24] And wealthy philanthropists are as bad at picking winners as the educators themselves. (Bill Gates, Mark Zuckerberg, Eli Broad, Mark Cuban: Prove me wrong!)

Who will train the troops? It takes two years of intensive training to make a good DI school. If a few large districts suddenly decided to adopt DI, there would be no way to train them and no system in place to produce more trainers. The colleges of education don't know how to teach DI, much less train others to teach it, and they don't want to learn. They don't like DI. MHE won't help because MHE sees training as a specialized skill outside its core business. Training outfits like NIFDI *can't* help because they are tiny: few employ as many as 10 people, and none more than 30. IDEA alone may soon employ more people than NIFDI can train.

Most schools that use DI fail to give their teachers adequate training, and they give DI a bad name because when things go poorly the programs get blamed. If this happens now, when demand for DI is weak and trainers are available, it will happen even more if demand picks up—which means it will never pick up for very long, because schools will keep doing DI on the cheap and dumping it when they fail. Like a bad web connection that keeps freezing the video, lack of bandwidth will be a constant brake on DI's progress.

More accountability might generate the resolve and attract the talent needed
to overcome these growing pains, but Americans don't *want* more accountability.
Whenever our leaders try to impose tougher standards on our schools, they get hooted
down as soon as the first bad report card arrives. Parents want their children to come
home with good grades more than they want them to be taught better. Grades they can
understand. *Teaching better* would require massive changes in our education system that
they cannot comprehend and that the system will never accept. Long before an honest
test makes schools worried enough to try DI, that test will be abandoned, and DI will
remain on the shelf.

There is no way out, the pessimist says. Educators will never understand DI, much
less lead the charge to embrace it. State dictates will always trump DI and never be as
good. Parents whose kids need DI will never know enough to demand it. Competition
for students will never be stiff enough, and scoreboards will rarely be good enough, to
drive many schools to adopt it. And publishers who sell DI will forever be constrained
by the above. Ignorance will reign, and the poor will continue to suffer.

TWO VISIONS, ONE HOPE

Whence genius? Whither its path?

Siegfried Engelmann was born November 26, 1931. His grandmother called him
the Wunderkind, but not even she foresaw what he would become, or how what he did
would affect others. No one could have foreseen that he would invent a better way to
teach. No one could have known that he would disprove so many myths. No one knew
he would prove that the disabled can be taught, good schools can defeat poverty, and
black schoolchildren can learn as well as whites. No one knew that his methods would
be despised and his achievements discounted, or that he would persist for so long in
the face of such vilification and neglect. And no one knows what will happen now.

Great works endure–but not always, and sometimes only barely, by accident or
surprise. Bach's St. Matthews Passion, a Christian masterpiece, disappeared for a
century and was resurrected by Mendelssohn, a Jew. Direct Instruction has survived its
unpopularity because it is there and it works: in the face of enormous resistance, amid
lies and calumny, it keeps making people smarter, and so people keep discovering it,
and using it, and being amazed by it, like so many astonished Mendelssohns. There
will always be such people, but if the programs get dropped or diluted terribly to suit
the market's taste, there won't be much left for them to discover or defend. An enfeebled DI is no help to the enfeebled, and may as well go extinct. Oblivion is possible.

But a renaissance is also possible. DI may yet find an evangelist worthy of its creator and spread. New geniuses may spring up and build on Engelmann's work. New ranks of disciples may at last break through. Better policies may pass. IDEA and Tennessee may lead the way. Such things if they were to happen would be no more marvelous than what has happened already: Engelmann's singular odyssey, and his vast corpus of luminous, uplifting works. Optimists and pessimists can argue which fate is more likely, but can anyone argue which fate would be better, and which should be sought, with every fiber of humanity? Carpe diem. Repeat to mastery. The cause can be won, and there is no greater cause.

NOTES

1. I describe my research for *Clear Teaching* in an appendix:

"This book is based on ten years of intermittent research during which the author read the major writings on Direct Instruction; monitored its implementation in twelve schools in the Atlanta Public School system over a three-year period; worked as an education research assistant for APS for three years and then at the Georgia Governor's Office for 18 months; wrote articles about DI and education for the national press; tutored a seven-year-old girl who had been left back in first grade with the DI reading program, Funnix; and interviewed hundreds of people with direct experience in DI, including teachers, teacher aides, students, principals, parents, school superintendents and other district staff, trainers, implementation managers, sales representatives, government officials, program authors, professors and researchers" (p. 70).

So far I have visited IDEA headquarters and campuses eight times for a total of 35 days as an imbedded reporter. I have observed staff meetings at all levels of the organization, classrooms in twenty schools, trainings, performance reviews, job interviews, planning retreats and other events and meetings. I have read strategic plans, internal reports and unpublished minutes to meetings I did not attend. In addition to visiting IDEA, I have done phone interviews with a range of sources, including IDEA personnel, funders of the school choice movement, and leaders at other charters. The visits and phone interviews began in May 2012 and continue to the present.

The main sources for my research in Tennessee have been the Education Consumers Foundation, in particular its president, John Stone, staff at McGraw-Hill Education, independent DI training consultants, and materials published by the Tennessee Department of Education.

2. Americans are also concerned about rising costs. The country has invested more and more in K-12 education, but the return on investment has been poor. Student performance has not improved much.

3. The "report card" (so the state calls it) includes data on test scores, TVAAS growth rates (compared to the state average), demographics, attendance, graduation rates and other items. The TVAAS data, for the first time, allow the public to see which schools teach their students the most. Thus a school with wealthy students who get high scores but who don't grow much may be rated no better, and in fact might be rated worse, than a school with poor students who get lower scores but who grow more.

4. The state improved and bettered its national ranking in all four NAEP tests—fourth and eighth grade reading, and fourth and eighth grade math. In statistical terms, the gains were significantly greater than the gains (or losses) in 42 states for fourth grade math, and in 34 states for eighth grade reading. The state's fourth-graders jumped from 46th to 37th in the nation in math and from 41st to 31st in reading.

5. This approach to monitoring and instruction is known as Response to Intervention, a concept that comes from public health. The state's definition of *scientifically validated* is more rigorous than it is in most states.

6. ECF published my book, *Clear Teaching* in 2012. I was not paid to write it, and I get no royalties from its sale.

7. Personal interview, January, 2014.

8. For a description of how DI refutes the popular myths about teaching, learning and child development, see *Clear Teaching*, p. 38

9. Teach for America in Texas told IDEA's founders in 2012 that it would stop sending teachers to IDEA's elementary academies because the schools had started using DI. TFA in Maryland advises its teachers not to teach at City Springs Elementary because the school uses DI. IDEA and City Springs employ TFA teachers but have to retrain them because much of what they are taught by TFA ignores or contradicts DI principles and practices.

10. Data obtained from http://www.usnews.com/education/best-high-schools/national-rankings/page+3; http://www.usnews.com/education/best-high-schools/national-rankings/page+3; http://www.usnews.com/education/best-high-schools/national-rankings/charter; and http://www.usnews.com/education/best-high-schools/national-rankings/charter-school-rankings

11. Harmony Public Schools, based in Houston, had the longest waitlist.

12. This has in fact been the pattern at DI schools for years; well-run DI sites are almost always killed off by new administrators who don't like DI, not by teachers or parents. High turnover in district leadership has hurt DI since its inception.

13. Another trend favorable to DI is the growing power of computers. Computer power can help everyone, but it can help DI more than other programs because the burdens it would lift from the DI teacher are so much heavier. DI programs require that teachers present more tasks per minute than any other mode of instruction. The programs generate a uniquely large torrent of student performance data that teachers must collect and analyze to guide their teaching. Computer power will make DI an easier sell because it will make these tasks easier. It will also make objectionable practices less objectionable by making them easier to manage and understand (grouping students by ability, for instance).

14. The major new programs are *Essentials for Writing* and *Essentials for Algebra* for secondary school students and *Direct Instruction Spoken English* for students in second grade or above who speak no English.

15. For instance, recent research shows that learning to read, write, and do math requires far more memorization—hence practice over time—than most educators realize or accept. (Hence their mischaracterization of DI as "drill and kill"—drill and *prosper* would be closer to the truth.)

16. Two examples, one from philanthropy, one from business: The Elgin Foundation in Knoxville, Tennessee, has persuaded six school districts in the coal region of Appalachian Kentucky, Virginia and Tennessee to train their teachers to use DI programs to teach reading to children who are performing below grade level norms. Districts and the foundation share the costs. The project was launched in 2010 and is the largest commitment ever by a private philanthropist to promote DI. (As of fall 2013, 45 schools were participating.) In Michigan, the Engineering Society of Detroit published a report in 2013 that explicitly endorses Direct Instruction. As the book went to press, the Society was negotiating with a school district in Michigan to create a DI demonstration site. The Society's members include the major U.S. automakers and other large corporations.

17. Personal e-mail from Engelmann, September, 2013.

18. The task may be impossible. Engelmann and his co-authors spent more than three years revising the main DI math series, *Connecting Math Concepts*, in part to align it to the Common Core Standards—to no avail. The California State Board of Education ruled in November 2013 that schools could not purchase the series with state funds earmarked for textbooks because it did not adequately cover the standards.

19. Personal e-mail from Engelmann, September, 2013.

20. In October 2012, I published an article about IDEA and five other well-regarded CMOs. None of the five had plans to adopt DI. http://www.chron.com/default/article/Bid-to-expand-charter-schools-could-boost-3923749.php

21. The irony is that IDEA's spring 2013 state test results showed that almost every student who was performing at grade level in the DI programs also did well on the test. The most sensible strategy thus would have been to place students at their ability level and accelerate their lesson progress as much as possible, so that more of them caught up to their grade level and passed the test. IDEA's placement strategy did the reverse.

22. The company rebuilt its DI sales force and sales increased 2 percent in 2013.

23. Those lessons are both technical and political. Building a better scoreboard requires technical sophistication. Putting in place the policies that force educators to live by its results requires leadership and public will.

24. "These guys couldn't sell sex on a troop train!" venture capitalist Bob Cook exclaimed after meeting a group of authors and trainers in Eugene, Oregon, several years ago.

APPENDIX A: ENGELMANN'S DIRECT INSTRUCTION PROGRAMS
AN ANNOTATED BIBLIOGRAPHY

Timothy W. Wood

Siegfried Engelmann and colleagues began developing Direct Instruction curriculum in the 1960s, starting with *DISTAR Language, Reading*, and *Mathematics* programs. The early *DISTAR* reading and language programs were designed to be taught in tandem because students required particular language skills in order to develop reading skills. The *DISTAR* programs went through series of revisions in response to teacher feedback, student performance, and in-class observations to increase their efficiency and effectiveness. Later programs followed the same principles of the Direct Instruction model used in these programs to expand the focus to different areas of study and to include larger groups of students in terms of skill, age, and language of origin. Additionally Engelmann authored trade books for parents to teach their children at home, and assessment manuals for critical skills for students in different academic subjects.

The following sections describe the Direct Instruction programs designed by Engelmann and his colleagues. The goals of these programs are detailed as well as the rationale behind their design. Descriptions of the revision processes of the programs are included when deemed necessary. Following these summaries is a chronological listing of all of Engelmann's Direct Instruction programs and related publications with additional notes for clarification.

SUMMARIES OF MAJOR DI PROGRAMS

Brief descriptions are given below of the major DI programs in reading, language, mathematics, spelling, and writing. Engelmann and colleagues have also developed programs related to science and social studies, have written trade books for parents, manuals for teachers, and learning assessments. All of these materials are included in the chronological listing in the second part of this appendix.

Reading

Engelmann and his colleagues developed four major reading programs: *DISTAR, Reading Mastery, Corrective Reading*, and *Horizons.*

DISTAR-Reading and Reading Mastery

Reading Mastery is the continuation of the *DISTAR Reading* program under a new name. *Reading Mastery* is designed to help students in Grades K-6 learn efficiently by using intensive, explicit, and systematic teaching. The program is broken into daily lessons. Each lesson is composed of exercises that teach different skills. In each lesson some exercises provide review on previously taught skills and some introduce new skills. The program covers the five essential components of reading: phonemic awareness, phonics and word analysis, fluency, vocabulary, and comprehension. The first two levels of *Reading Mastery* focus on the acquisition of accurate and fluent decoding skills. An artificial orthography is used to make the beginning reading experience easier for the naïve reader. The third through sixth levels of *Reading Mastery* emphasize the development of comprehension and vocabulary. The third and fourth levels focus on using reading as a vehicle to learn new information. Stories at these levels integrate a great deal of science and social studies content and are used to help students learn to use reading to acquire new information. The last two levels of *Reading Mastery* focus on literature. While the upper levels of *Reading Mastery* focus on comprehension and vocabulary, the programs continue work on developing decoding, word recognition, and fluency. Revisions to *Reading Mastery* have been designed to make the instruction easier and more efficient for teachers and students.

Corrective Reading

Corrective Reading was designed for struggling readers in Grades 3 through 12 and for use with adults who have not mastered basic reading skills. *Corrective Reading* utilizes carefully planned sequenced lessons, which provide the structure and practice necessary for struggling readers to acquire the skills to become fluent and accurate readers and be able to comprehend text. The pacing of the lessons is faster than in the *Reading Mastery* program due to its narrower focus of instructional goals. *Corrective Reading* consists of two major sequences: *Decoding* and *Comprehension*. Decoding levels A, B, and C focus on basic decoding skills, reading fluency, and reading narrative and informational text. The program is unique in that it integrates the teaching of word attack skills with extensive reading of text that contains only word elements that have been previously taught in the program. Lessons are specifically designed to deal with the common errors made by the corrective reader. Comprehension levels A, B, and C teach a wide range of language and comprehension skills. The words introduced in the comprehension program are carefully selected to ensure students are able to decode them. A placement test provides guidance for the teacher to determine where in the sequence of programs to begin instruction.

Horizons

Horizons is another Direct Instruction program designed to teach beginning reading to children using systematic and explicit Direct Instruction techniques. The program features sequenced instruction on word attack, story reading, comprehension, vocabulary, fluency, and spelling. Unlike *Reading Mastery*, *Horizons* uses a regular orthography throughout all levels. *Horizons* was designed to be more palatable to mainstream educators. While *Horizons* can be used with at risk students, it can more readily accelerate the reading development of students who enter school with moderate to high levels of literacy. *Horizons* has 3 levels: Levels A and B teach students how to break the code. There is a fast-cycle program (*Horizons A-B*) that presents the content of levels A and B in one year. The third level of *Horizons* is an accelerated comprehension program that combines content from *Reading Mastery 3* and *Reading Mastery 4* into a year-long program.

Funnix Reading

Funnix Reading is a Direct Instruction-based CD program consisting of a series of 220 lessons. The lessons in *Funnix* use the same approach and much of the same content presented in the *Horizons* reading program. *Funnix* is a computer program that pairs the child and parent together at the computer. As the child makes oral responses to questions presented by the program, the parent provides feedback to the student and moves on or repeats tasks. *Funnix* is designed for the non-reader and continues through second grade content. While *Funnix* was initially designed for the beginning non-reader, it can be adapted for use with first or second graders who are behind in their acquisition of reading skills, and can be used in small groups in a school setting. *Funnix* is composed of two sequenced components: *Funnix Beginning Reading* and *Funnix 2*.

Language

Engelmann and his colleagues' first language programs were the *DISTAR Language* series, which they continued to revise over the following years and eventually renamed as *Language for Learning, Language for Thinking*, and *Language for Writing*. They later designed programs specifically for English as a Second Language (ESL) students. The language programs' many exercises in vocabulary, background knowledge, statement analysis, questions, and concept application prepare students for the literal and inferential comprehension of the books and other materials they will read both in and out of school.

Language for Learning (DISTAR I)

Language for Learning is a continuation of the *DISTAR Language I* program. The program is designed to teach young children (pre-Kindergarten to Grade 2) the basic vocabulary, concepts, and sentence forms used in typical classroom instruction. Like other Direct Instruction programs, *Language for Learning* is a highly systematic and explicit program. New content is introduced carefully and integrated with previously taught content. The program can be used with four year-old children in preschool programs, primary-age children in bilingual and ESL programs, primary-age children in Title I and Special Education programs, and children in speech correction and language classes.

Language for Thinking (DISTAR II)

Language for Thinking is the latest revised version of *DISTAR Language II*. It builds on the concepts, vocabulary, and statement patterns used in *Language for Learning*. However, the general format of *Language for Thinking* exercises are more complex and require more independent work from students. *Language for Thinking* can be used with students who have completed, or almost completed, *Language for Learning*, or students who know the basic concepts taught in *Language for Learning*, but are in first or second grade and need more explicit language instruction.

Language for Writing (DISTAR III)

Language for Writing is a revision of *DISTAR Language III*. The program focuses not only on writing, but also on the vocabulary, syntax, and organization skills that underpin writing. Students learn how to convey details, how to indicate a sequence of events, how to make clear statements, and how to present events that lead to a conclusion. The program teaches students the conventions of clear writing; the vocabulary needed to describe actions, events and objects; and the sentence structure required to put complex ideas into writing. The program can be used with second or third graders who have completed *Language for Thinking* or who can pass the placement test for *Language for Writing*.

Español to English

Español to English is a Direct Instruction program designed for young children who speak little or no English, or who are marginally bilingual. The lessons in *Español to English* are designed to phase the children into the lessons in *Language for Learning*. Initial lessons include explanations in Spanish. The proportion of the lessons taught in Spanish systematically decreases as the students gain proficiency in English.

Direct Instruction Spoken English (DISE)

The *Direct Instruction Spoken English (DISE)* program is designed for non-English speakers in Grade 3 and above and will help students achieve a functional mastery of the English language in one year or less. The program features an explicit, systematic instructional model that supports English language learners in developing a functional mastery of spoken English. Students are taught both social and academic vocabulary. The program consists of 100 90-minute lessons.

Comprehensive Core Reading Programs

Beginning in 2000, Direct Instruction reading and Direct Instruction language programs were integrated into literacy programs designed to meet state requirements for a comprehensive literacy program. The first comprehensive Direct Instruction literacy program produced was *Journeys*, a K-3 program that combined components of the Direct Instruction language programs and the *Horizons* reading program. *Journeys* was specifically designed to meet the Texas State Standards.

In 2002, a comprehensive program called *Reading Mastery Plus* was published specifically to meet Florida standards. *Reading Mastery Plus* was a K-5 program that utilized all the levels of *Reading Mastery* and components of *Language for Learning, Learning for Thinking*, and *Reasoning and Writing*.

In 2008, the *Reading Mastery Signature Edition* appeared. The Signature edition includes all the *Reading Mastery* levels, and additional components from the *Language for Learning, Language for Thinking*, and *Reasoning and Writing* programs.

Mathematics

Engelmann and colleagues developed four major mathematics programs: *DISTAR, Corrective Mathematics, Connecting Math Concepts* and *Essentials for Algebra*. The more recently published versions have incorporated technology.

DISTAR Arithmetic

DISTAR Arithmetic was the prototype for the Direct Instruction mathematics programs. *DISTAR Arithmetic I* was originally developed for preschool or Kindergarten students. The program, which teaches the most basic math concepts, is still used as a vehicle to teach the highly naïve beginning learners.

Corrective Mathematics

Corrective Mathematics is a series of seven modules intended as an intervention program for students in Grade 3 through adults who have trouble with grade level work. Four of the modules deal with basic operations: Addition, Subtraction, Multiplication, and Division. Each of these modules has three basic strands. One strand focuses on teaching facts, a second strand focuses on computation operations, and the third on word problems. The other three modules teach fractions, decimals, and percentages and ratios. *Corrective Math* is designed to provide systematic and explicit instruction on critical skills, but does not include all the content students need to learn. It should be considered an intervention program that supplements a core math program.

Connecting Math Concepts

Connecting Math Concepts is a six level program (Levels A-F) designed to accelerate the math learning performance of students in Grades K through 5. The program provides highly explicit and systematic instruction in the wide range of content specified in the Common Core State Standards for Mathematics. Specific strategies are taught for all content. For example, rather than just presenting an array of story problems and giving students general directions, the program teaches specific strategies for attacking and solving different types of word problems. Instruction is designed to provide ongoing success for students. *Connecting Math Concepts* carefully and realistically controls the introduction and integration of math content so that students learn connections between related skills and are not overwhelmed by too much content being presented at one time. For example, math facts are introduced systematically over the first four levels of the program with daily practice on new facts and review of previously taught facts. While students are learning facts, all problems the students work on contain only facts that have been previously introduced.

Funnix Beginning Math

Funnix Beginning Math is a Direct Instruction–based CD program. The computer-based program consists of 100 lessons and was designed for preschool and Kindergarten children with no math or counting skills. It is also applicable for older students who have not learned beginning math operations. The program was intended to be used primarily with home-schooled children.

Essentials for Algebra

Essentials for Algebra is designed for students in middle school or high school who are at risk of failing to meet graduation requirements in math. The program teaches essential pre-algebra content and provides students with an introduction to traditional Algebra I content that is cohesive and clear.

Spelling

Engelmann and colleagues developed two programs to specifically teach spelling: *Spelling Through Morphographs* and *Spelling Mastery.*

Spelling Through Morphographs

Spelling Through Morphographs is a one-year program designed to teach spelling to older students (4th grade and older). Students learn that words are composed of morphographs, which roughly are prefixes, suffixes, and bases or roots. The program presents rules for combining the morphographs and provides extensive practice in applying these rules. The program uses specific strategies that encourage students to think their way through spelling rather than to memorize weekly word lists. These strategies combined with repeated practice and application enable students to spell unfamiliar words and to remember familiar words more successfully than they would by using other methods. Upon completion of the program, students will have learned 750 morphographs and be able to spell between 12,000 and 15,000 words, including most words on the complete Dolch word list and words most commonly misspelled in high school and college. The program can be used with regular education students as well as students with disabilities or students with English as a second language. The more at-risk students will likely need additional practice.

Spelling Mastery

Spelling Mastery is a six-level Direct Instruction series that teaches students dependable spelling skills by blending three approaches: the phonemic approach, the whole word approach, and the morphemic approach. Each approach has advantages and possible disadvantages. *Spelling Mastery* is designed to maximize the advantages of each approach and minimize the disadvantages. The whole word approach focuses on memorization. *Spelling Mastery* does not use memorization for words that contain predictable phonemic elements, but reserves memorization for words that have irregular letter-sound relationships (i.e. feud, break, gone). Prompts are used to make the initial learning easier and systematic practice is provided to facilitate retention. The phonemic approach is used for letter-sound correspondences that are predictable. For example, the sound /ar/ is highly consistent. In about 95 percent of the words in which the sound /ar/ is said, the sound is spelled with the letters a-r. A careful analysis of phoneme-grapheme relationships was made by the authors and the generalizable relationships are systematically introduced and practiced. The morphemic approach is used for combining the roots, bases, prefixes, and suffixes into words. The morphemic approach used is highly similar to the approach used in *Spelling Through Morphographs*. Students combine morphographs to write words and do exercises in which they indicate the morphographs in words. The use of morphographs to figure out the meaning of words gradually increases as students progress through the levels.

Writing

Engelmann and colleagues developed three major writing programs: *Expressive Writing, Reasoning and Writing* and *Essentials for Writing*.

Expressive Writing

The *Expressive Writing* program is composed of two levels, *Expressive Writing 1* and *Expressive Writing 2*. *Expressive Writing 1* consists of 50 lessons. *Expressive Writing 2* consists of a ten-lesson pre-program followed by 50 regular lessons. The program can be used with students of any age who can read at the third grade level or above.

Expressive Writing 1 is designed for students who haven't mastered foundational writing skills. Students learn to construct simple sentences by reporting on what a picture shows. They learn that a sentence has two parts, the part that names and the part that tells more. Students write sentences by naming a person or thing and telling what that person or thing did. As the program develops, students learn to tell the main thing a person did and to construct paragraphs for a sequence of pictures. A process through which students first discuss a writing assignment, then write, and then systematically edit for specific points becomes an integral part of the program. At the end of *Expressive Writing I*, students can write a paragraph that describes a sequence of related actions using simple declarative sentences, punctuate sentences correctly, write consistently in the simple past tense, and write paragraphs that include sufficient detail and stay on topic.

Expressive Writing 2 is designed for students who can construct a basic paragraph, but who have problems with clarity, are unable to punctuate quotes and other sentence types correctly, and use a narrow variety of sentence forms. Writing exercises begin with simple one paragraph assignments, and then increase gradually to two, three, and more paragraphs. Students learn to infer important detail that must have happened between pictures in a sequence. By the end of *Expressive Writing 2*, students can write a multi-paragraph narrative that is written clearly (using clear pronoun referents and including details necessary for clarity), uses a variety of sentence types, and includes correctly punctuated direct quotes.

Essentials for Writing

Essentials for Writing was designed for students in middle school and high school who are at risk of failing to meet high-school graduation requirements in English Language Arts. The program can be used to prevent failure on high-school exit exams by scheduling it for ninth grade or earlier, or it can be used to prepare high-school students at risk of failing the high-school exit exam. The program is not a "test-prep" program. Instead, it teaches the essentials: complex behaviors needed to compose narrative passages, stories with a specific theme, descriptive essays, autobiographical sketches and biographies, responses to literature and persuasive arguments, and position papers.

Reasoning and Writing

Reasoning and Writing is a Direct Instruction program designed to teach the critical thinking skills needed to analyze situations clearly, reach conclusions logically, and to equip students to express themselves with precision and clarity as they write. The *Reasoning and Writing* series consists of six levels (A-F). Levels A and B are designed for students in late Kindergarten through second grade. Students need to have learned the language skills and content from *Language for Learning* to be able to benefit fully from the instruction in these programs. These programs teach pre-writing foundational skills by means of workbook activities, verbal responses, and stories that the teacher reads aloud. Stories the teachers read to the students are uniquely designed with a strong emphasis on story grammar and narrative patterns. Students learn to identify the story grammar elements and make predictions of what various characters will do. Level C teaches the students to write narrative passages. The content of level C is similar to that found in *Expressive Writing* levels 1 and 2. *Reasoning and Writing* levels D through F move into expository writing. Students learn to analyze commentaries and advertisements, to identify misleading claims and faulty or inadequate arguments, and to indicate contradictions in conflicting reports. Students also learn to write persuasive and descriptive passages, and passages that compare and contrast.

BIBLIOGRAPHIC REFERENCES

This section contains bibliographic references to all of the instructional programs that have been developed by Engelmann and his colleagues. It includes references to all of the materials described in the first part of this appendix as well as guides for teachers, textbooks for teachers in training, assessment materials, and other lesser-known programs, such as those involving drawing and music. Entries within each section are chronological and, within each year, alphabetical by author and title.

Reading

Engelmann and his colleagues developed four major reading programs: *DISTAR*, *Reading Mastery*, *Corrective Reading*, and *Horizons*.

DISTAR Reading

Engelmann, S., & Bruner, E. C. (1969a). *DISTAR Reading I*. Chicago: Science Research Associates.

Engelmann, S., & Bruner, E. C. (1969b). *DISTAR Reading II*. Chicago: Science Research Associates.

Engelmann, S., & Bruner, E. C. (1969c). *DISTAR Reading Fast Cycle*. Chicago: Science Research Associates.

Engelmann, S., & Hanner, S. (1969). *DISTAR Reading III*. Chicago: Science Research Associates.

Engelmann, S. (1975). *DISTAR Training Program for DISTAR Reading I*. Chicago: Science Research Associates.

Engelmann, S., & Bruner, E. C. (1977). *DISTAR Library Series.* Chicago: Science Research Associates.

Engelmann, S., Becker, W. C., & Carnine, L. (1978). *Continuous Tests for DISTAR Reading.* Eugene, OR: E-B Press.

Engelmann, S., & Bruner, E. C. (1978). *DISTAR Reading: An Instructional System.* Chicago: Science Research Associates.

Engelmann, S. (1979). *DISTAR Reading Activity Kit.* Chicago: Science Research Associates.

Reading Mastery

Engelmann, S. E., & Bruner, E. (1983). *Reading Mastery I.* Chicago: Science Research Associates.

Engelmann, S., & Bruner, E. C. (1988). *Reading Mastery: Fast Cycle (DISTAR).* Chicago: Science Research Associates.

Reading Mastery Fast Cycle presents the content in *Reading Mastery I* and *II* in one school year. Stories and exercises in *Fast Cycle* are basically the same as *Reading Mastery I* and *II*, except half the lessons are not included. *Fast Cycle* can be used with younger children who can progress at an accelerated pace or students in second and third grade who are behind.

Engelmann, S., & Bruner, E. (1988a). *Reading Mastery I: DISTAR Reading.* Chicago: Science Research Associates.

Engelmann, S., & Bruner, E. (1988b). *Reading Mastery I: Teacher's Guide.* Chicago: Science Research Associates.

Engelmann, S., & Bruner, E. (1988c). *Reading Mastery II: DISTAR Reading.* Chicago: Science Research Associates.

Reading Mastery Rainbow Edition

The Rainbow edition was a revision of the original *Reading Mastery* program.

Engelmann, S., & Bruner, E. (1995a). *Reading Mastery I* (Rainbow Ed.) (Teacher's Presentation Book, Student Material, Literature Guide, and Teacher's Guide). Columbus, OH: SRA/McGraw-Hill.

Engelmann, S., & Bruner, E. (1995b). *Reading Mastery II* (Rainbow Ed.) (Teacher's Presentation Book, Student Material, Literature Guide, and Teacher's Guide). Columbus, OH: SRA/McGraw-Hill.

Reading Mastery Plus

Engelmann, S., Osborn, J., Bruner, E. C., & Seitz-Davis, K. L. (2002). *Reading Mastery Plus: Level K* (Teacher's Presentation Books, Student Material, and Teacher's Guide). Chicago, IL: SRA/McGraw-Hill.

Engelmann, S., Bruner, E. C., Osborn, J., & Seitz-Davis, K. L. (2002). *Reading Mastery Plus: Level 1* (Teacher's Presentation Books, Student Material, and Teacher's Guide). Chicago, IL: SRA/McGraw-Hill.

Engelmann, S., Bruner, E. C., Engelmann, O., Seitz-Davis, K. L., & Arbogast, A. (2002). *Reading Mastery Plus: Level 2* (Teacher's Presentation Books, Student Material, and Teacher's Guide). Chicago, IL: SRA/McGraw-Hill.

Engelmann, S., & Hanner, S. (2002a). *Reading Mastery Plus: Level 3* (Teacher's Presentation Book, Student Material, Literature Guide, and Teacher's Guide). Columbus, OH: SRA/McGraw-Hill. (Originally published 1969 as *DISTAR Reading III*, Chicago: Science Research Associates)

Engelmann, S., & Hanner, S. (2002b). *Reading Mastery Plus: Level 4* (Teacher's Presentation Book, Student Material, Literature Guide, and Teacher's Guide). Columbus, OH: SRA/McGraw-Hill. (Originally published 1983.)

Engelmann, S., Osborn, J., Osborn, S., & Zoref, L. (2002a). *Reading Mastery Plus: Level 5* (Teacher's Presentation Book, Student Material, Literature Guide, and Teacher's Guide). Columbus, OH: SRA/McGraw-Hill. (Originally published 1984.)

Engelmann, S., Osborn, J., Osborn, S., & Zoref, L. (2002b). *Reading Mastery Plus: Level 6* (Teacher's Presentation Book, Student Material, Literature Guide, and Teacher's Guide). Columbus, OH: SRA/McGraw-Hill. (Originally published 1984.)

Reading Mastery Classic Edition
Engelmann, S., & Bruner, E. C. (2003a). *Reading Mastery Level I* (Classic Ed.) (Teacher's Presentation Book, Student Material, Literature Guide, and Teacher's Guide). Columbus, OH: SRA/McGraw-Hill. (Originally published 1969 as *DISTAR Reading I*, Chicago: Science Research Associates.)

Engelmann, S., & Bruner, E. C. (2003b). *Reading Mastery Level II* (Classic Ed.) (Teacher's Presentation Book, Student Material, Literature Guide, and Teacher's Guide). Columbus, OH: SRA/McGraw-Hill. (Originally published 1969 as *DISTAR Reading II*, Chicago: Science Research Associates.)

Engelmann, S., & Bruner, E. C. (2003c). *Reading Mastery Levels I/II Fast Cycle* (Classic Ed.) (Teacher's Presentation Book, Student Material, and Teacher's Guide). Columbus, OH: SRA/McGraw-Hill. (Originally published 1969 as *DISTAR Reading Fast Cycle*, Chicago: Science Research Associates.)

Reading Mastery Signature Edition
Engelmann, S., & Bruner, E. C. (2008a). *Reading Mastery Reading, Level K* (Signature Ed.) (Teacher's Presentation Book, Student Material, Literature Guide, and Teacher's Guide). Columbus, OH: SRA/McGraw-Hill.

Engelmann, S., & Bruner, E. C. (2008b). *Reading Mastery Reading, Level 1* (Signature Ed.) (Teacher's Presentation Book, Student Material, Literature Guide, and Teacher's Guide). Columbus, OH: SRA/McGraw-Hill.

Engelmann, S., & Hanner, S. (2008a). *Reading Mastery Reading, Level 2* (Signature Ed.) (Teacher's Presentation Book, Student Material, Literature Guide, and Teacher's Guide). Columbus, OH: SRA/McGraw-Hill.

Engelmann, S., & Hanner, S. (2008b). *Reading Mastery Reading, Level 3* (Signature Ed.) (Teacher's Presentation Book, Student Material, Literature Guide, and Teacher's Guide). Columbus, OH: SRA/McGraw-Hill.

Engelmann, S., Osborn, J., Osborn, S., & Zoref, L. (2008a). *Reading Mastery Reading, Level 4* (Signature Ed.) (Teacher's Presentation Book, Student Material, Literature Guide, and Teacher's Guide). Columbus, OH: SRA/McGraw-Hill.

Engelmann, S., Osborn, J., Osborn, S., & Zoref, L. (2008b). *Reading Mastery Reading, Level 5* (Signature Ed.) (Teacher's Presentation Book, Student Material, Literature Guide, and Teacher's Guide). Columbus, OH: SRA/McGraw-Hill.

Engelmann, S., & Osborn, J. (2008a). *Reading Mastery Language Arts Strand, Level K* (Signature Ed., Grade K) (Teacher's Presentation Book, Student Material, Literature Guide, and Teacher's Guide). Columbus, OH: SRA/McGraw-Hill.

Engelmann, S., Osborn, J., & Davis, K. L. S. (2008). *Reading Mastery Language Arts Strand, Level 1* (Signature Ed.) (Teacher's Presentation Book, Student Material, Literature Guide, and Teacher's Guide). Columbus, OH: SRA/McGraw-Hill.

Engelmann, S., Davis, K. L. S., & Silbert, J. (2008). *Reading Mastery Language Arts Strand, Level 2* (Signature Ed.) (Teacher's Presentation Book, Student Material, Literature Guide, and Teacher's Guide). Columbus, OH: SRA/McGraw-Hill.

Engelmann, S., Silbert, J., & Hanner, S. (2008). *Reading Mastery Language Arts Strand, Level 3* (Signature Ed.) (Teacher's Presentation Book, Student Material, Literature Guide, and Teacher's Guide). Columbus, OH: SRA/McGraw-Hill.

Engelmann, S., Silbert, J., & Osborn, S. (2008). *Reading Mastery Language Arts Strand, Level 4* (Signature Ed.) (Teacher's Presentation Book, Student Material, Literature Guide, and Teacher's Guide). Columbus, OH: SRA/McGraw-Hill.

Engelmann, S., Grossen, B., & Osborn, S. (2008). *Reading Mastery Language Arts Strand, Level 5* (Signature Ed.) (Teacher's Presentation Book, Student Material, Literature Guide, and Teacher's Guide). Columbus, OH: SRA/McGraw-Hill.

Corrective Reading

Engelmann, S., Becker, W. C., Carnine, L., Meyer, L., Becker, J., & Johnson, G. (1975). *Corrective Reading Program*. Chicago: Science Research Associates.

Engelmann, S., & Haddox, P. (1978). *Corrective Reading Placement Test*. Chicago: Science Research Associates.

Engelmann, S., Hanner, S., & Johnson, G. (1978). *Corrective Reading: Series Guide*. Chicago: Science Research Associates.

Engelmann, S., Becker, W. C., Hanner, S., & Johnson, G. (1978). *Implementing the Corrective Reading Series*. Eugene, OR: E-B Press.

Engelmann, S., Meyer, L., Carnine, L., Becker, W., Eisele, J., & Johnson, G. (1988). *Corrective Reading: Decoding Strategies*. Chicago: Science Research Associates.

Engelmann, S. (1989). *Corrective Reading: Series Guide*. Chicago: Science Research Associates.

Engelmann, S., Osborn, S., & Hanner, S. (1989). *Corrective Reading: Comprehension Skills*. Chicago: Science Research Associates.

Engelmann, S., Haddox, P., Osborn, J., & Hanner, S. (2008). *Corrective Reading: Comprehension A* (Teacher's Presentation Book, Student Material, and Teacher's Guide). Columbus, OH: SRA/McGraw-Hill. (Originally published 1978, and revised 1998.)

Engelmann, S., Osborn, S., & Hanner, S. (2008). *Corrective Reading: Comprehension B1 and B2* (Teacher's Presentation Book, Student Material, and Teacher's Guide). Columbus, OH: SRA/McGraw-Hill. (Originally published 1978 as *Comprehension B*, and revised 1998 as *Comprehension B1 and B2*.)

Engelmann, S., Hanner, S., & Haddox, P. (2008). *Corrective Reading: Comprehension C* (Teacher's Presentation Book, Student Material, and Teacher's Guide). Columbus, OH: SRA/McGraw-Hill. (Originally published 1980, and revised 1998.)

Engelmann, S., Johnson, G., & Carnine, L. (2008). *Corrective Reading: Decoding A* (Teacher's Presentation Book, Student Material, and Teacher's Guide). Columbus, OH: SRA/McGraw-Hill. (Originally published 1978, and revised 1998.)

Engelmann, S., Meyer, L., Carnine, L., Becker, W., Eisele, J., & Johnson, G. (2008a). *Corrective Reading: Decoding B1* (Teacher's Presentation Book, Student Material, and Teacher's Guide). Columbus, OH: SRA/McGraw-Hill. (Originally published 1978, and revised 1998.)

Engelmann, S., Meyer, L., Carnine, L., Becker, W., Eisele, J., & Johnson, G. (2008b). *Corrective Reading: Decoding B2* (Teacher's Presentation Book, Student Material, and Teacher's Guide). Columbus, OH: SRA/McGraw-Hill. (Originally published 1978, and revised 1998.)

Engelmann, S., Meyer, L., Johnson, G., & Carnine, L. (2008). *Corrective Reading: Decoding C* (Teacher's Presentation Book, Student Material, and Teacher's Guide). Columbus, OH: SRA/McGraw-Hill. (Originally published 1978, and revised 1998.)

Horizons

Engelmann, S., Engelmann, O., & Seitz-Davis, K. L. (1997). *Horizons: Fast Track A-B* (Teacher's Presentation Book, Student Material, Literature Guide, and Teacher's Guide). Columbus, OH: SRA/McGraw-Hill.

Engelmann, S., & Hanner, S. (1998). *Horizons: Fast Track C-D* (Teacher's Presentation Book, Student Material, Literature Guide, and Teacher's Guide). Columbus, OH: SRA/McGraw-Hill.

Engelmann, S., Engelmann, O., & Seitz-Davis, K. L. (1998). *Horizons: Level A* (Teacher's Presentation Book, Student Material, Literature Guide, and Teacher's Guide). Columbus, OH: SRA/McGraw-Hill.

Engelmann, S., Engelmann, O., & Seitz-Davis, K. L. (2000). *Horizons: Level B* (Teacher's Presentation Book, Student Material, Literature Guide, and Teacher's Guide). Columbus, OH: SRA/McGraw-Hill.

Funnix

Engelmann, S., Engelmann, O., & Seitz-Davis, K. L. (2001). *Funnix, Beginning Reading.* Eugene, OR: Royal Limited Partnership.

Engelmann, S., & Engelmann, O., (2002). *Funnix Reading 2.* Eugene, OR: Royal Limited Partnership.

Journeys

Engelmann, S., Engelmann, O., & Seitz-Davis, K. L. (2000a). *Journeys: Level K* (Teacher's Presentation Books, Student Material, and Teacher Guide). Columbus, OH: SRA/McGraw-Hill.

Engelmann, S., Engelmann, O., & Seitz-Davis, K. L. (2000b). *Journeys: Level 1* (Teacher's Presentation Books, Student Material, and Teacher's Guide). Columbus, OH: SRA/McGraw-Hill.

Engelmann, S., Engelmann, O., Seitz-Davis, K. L., & Arbogast, A., (2000). *Journeys: Level 2* (Teacher's Presentation Books, Student Material, and Teacher's Guide). Columbus, OH: SRA/McGraw-Hill.

Engelmann, S., & Hanner, S. (2000). *Journeys: Level 3* (Teacher's Presentation Books, Student Material, and Teacher's Guide). Columbus, OH: SRA/McGraw-Hill.

Supplementary Reading Guide

Engelmann, S., & Jensen, J. (1982). *I Love Library Books.* Eugene, OR: E–B Press.

Language

Engelmann and colleagues' first language programs were the *DISTAR Language* series, which they continued to revise over the following years and eventually renamed as *Language for Learning, Language for Thinking,* and *Language for Writing.* They later designed programs specifically for English as a Second Language (ESL) students.

DISTAR Language

Engelmann, S., Osborn, J., & Lundeen, B. (1968). *Learning Language: Concept and Action Stories.* Urbana, IL: University of Illinois Press.

Engelmann, S., & Osborn, J. (1970). *DISTAR Language II* (Teacher's Presentation Book, Student Material, and Teacher's Guide). Chicago: Science Research Associates.

Engelmann, S., Olen, L., & Concillo, P. (1978). *Continuous Tests for DISTAR Language.* Eugene, OR: E-B Press.

Engelmann, S. (1979). *DISTAR Language Activity Kit.* Chicago: Science Research Associates.

Engelmann, S., & Osborn, J. (1986a). *DISTAR Language I* (Teacher's Presentation Book, Student Material, and Teacher's Guide). Chicago: Science Research Associates. (Originally published 1969.)

Engelmann, S., & Osborn, J. (1986b). *DISTAR Language I Mastery Test.* Chicago: Science Research Associates.

Engelmann, S., & Osborn, J. (1986c). *DISTAR Language III* (Teacher's Presentation Book, Student Material, and Teacher's Guide). Chicago: Science Research Associates. (Originally published 1970.)

Engelmann, S., & Osborn, J. (1987). *DISTAR Language.* Chicago: Science Research Associates.

Language for Learning (DISTAR I)

Engelmann, S., & Osborn, J. (1998). *Language for Learning* (Teacher's Presentation Book, Student Material, and Teacher's Guide). Columbus, OH: SRA/McGraw-Hill.

Language for Thinking (DISTAR II)

Engelmann, S., & Osborn, J. (2002). *Language for Thinking* (Teacher's Presentation Book, Student Material, and Teacher's Guide). Columbus, OH: SRA/McGraw-Hill.

Language for Writing (DISTAR III)

Engelmann, S., & Osborn, J. (2006). *Language for Writing* (Teacher's Presentation Book, Student Material, and Teacher's Guide). Columbus, OH: SRA/McGraw-Hill.

Miscellaneous

Engelmann, S., & Gill, R. (1971). *Language Concepts Through Drawing.* St. Paul, MN: EMC.

Engelmann, S. (1971). *Language Concepts in Song.* St. Paul, MN: EMC.

Engelmann, S., Ross, D., & Bingham, V. (1982). *Basic Language Concepts Inventory.* Tigard, OR: C & C Publications, Inc.

English as a Second Language

Engelmann, S., Osborn, J., Garza, M., & Snyder, T. (2001). *Español to English* (Language for Learning) (Teacher's Presentation Book, Student Material, and Teacher's Guide). Columbus, OH: SRA/McGraw-Hill.

Engelmann, S., Johnston, D., Engelmann, O., & Silbert, J. (2010). *Direct Instruction Spoken English (DISE).* Dallas, TX: Sopris West.

Assessments

Engelmann, S. (1967a). *Basic Concept Inventory.* Chicago: Follett Publishing Company.

Engelmann, S. (1967b). *Manual for the Basic Concept Inventory.* Chicago: Follett Publishing Company.

Engelmann, S., Ross, D., & Bingham, V. (1982a). *Basic Language Concepts Test, Manual.* Chicago: Science Research Associates.

Engelmann, S., Ross, D., & Bingham, V. (1982b). *Basic Language Concepts Test.* Chicago: Science Research Associates.

Mathematics

Engelmann and colleagues developed four major mathematics programs: *DISTAR, Corrective Mathematics, Connecting Math Concepts,* and *Essentials for Algebra.* They also developed other mathematics related programs.

DISTAR

Engelmann, S., & Carnine, D. (1975). *DISTAR Arithmetic I* (2nd Ed.) (Teacher's Presentation Book, Student Material, and Teacher's Guide). Chicago: Science Research Associates. (Originally published 1970.)

Engelmann, S., & Carnine, D. (1976a). *DISTAR Arithmetic II* (2nd Ed.) (Teacher's Presentation Book, Student Material, and Teacher's Guide). Chicago: Science Research Associates. (Originally published 1970.)

Engelmann, S., & Carnine, D. (1976b). *DISTAR Arithmetic III* (2nd Ed.) (Teacher's Presentation Book, Student Material, and Teacher's Guide). Chicago: Science Research Associates. (Originally published 1972.)

Engelmann, S., Carnine, D., Becker, W. C., & Davis, G. (1978). *Mastery Tests for DISTAR Arithmetic I & II.* Eugene, OR: E-B Press.

Engelmann, S., & Carnine, D. (1990). *DISTAR Arithmetic.* Chicago: Science Research Associates.

Mathematics Modules

Engelmann, S., & Steely, D. (1978a). *Mathematics Modules: Fractions, Decimals, Percents* (Teacher's Presentation Book, and Student Material). Chicago: Science Research Associates.

Engelmann, S., & Steely, D. (1978b). *Mathematics Modules: Basic Fractions* (Teacher's Presentation Book, and Student Material). Chicago: Science Research Associates.

Engelmann, S., & Steely, D. (1981). *Mathematics Modules: Ratios and Equations* (Teacher's Presentation Book, and Student Material). Chicago: Science Research Associates.

Corrective Mathematics

Engelmann, S., & Carnine, D. (1981a). *Corrective Mathematics Series Guide.* Chicago: Science Research Associates.

Engelmann, S., & Carnine, D. (1981b). *Corrective Mathematics: Division* (Teacher's Presentation Book, and Student Material). Chicago: Science Research Associates.

Engelmann, S., & Carnine, D. (1981c). *Corrective Mathematics: Multiplication* (Teacher's Presentation Book, and Student Material). Chicago: Science Research Associates.

Engelmann, S., & Carnine, D. (1981d). *Corrective Mathematics: Subtraction* (Teacher's Presentation Book, and Student Material). Chicago: Science Research Associates.

Engelmann, S., & Carnine, D. (1981e). *Corrective Mathematics: Addition* (Teacher's Presentation Book, and Student Material). Chicago: Science Research Associates.

Engelmann, S., & Steely, D. (1981). *Corrective Mathematics Comprehensive Placement Test*. Chicago: Science Research Associates.

Connecting Math Concepts

Engelmann, S., & Carnine, D. (2003a). *Connecting Math Concepts: Level A* (Teacher's Presentation Book, Student Material, and Teacher's Guide). Chicago: Science Research Associates. (Originally published 1992, and revised 1997.)

Engelmann, S., & Carnine, D. (2003b). *Connecting Math Concepts: Level B* (Teacher's Presentation Book, Student Material, and Teacher's Guide). Chicago: Science Research Associates. (Originally published 1992, and revised 1997.)

Engelmann, S., & Carnine, D. (2003c). *Connecting Math Concepts: Level C* (Teacher's Presentation Book, Student Material, and Teacher's Guide). Chicago: Science Research Associates. (Originally published 1992, and revised 1997.)

Engelmann, S., Engelmann, O., & Carnine, D. (2003). *Connecting Math Concepts: Level D* (Teacher's Presentation Book, Student Material, and Teacher's Guide). Chicago: Science Research Associates. (Originally published 1992, and revised 1997.)

Engelmann, S., Kelly, B., & Carnine, D. (2003). *Connecting Math Concepts: Level E* (Teacher's Presentation Book, Student Material, and Teacher's Guide). Chicago: Science Research Associates. (Originally published 1992, and revised 1997.)

Engelmann, S., Engelmann, O., Kelly, B., & Carnine, D. (2003). *Bridge to Connecting Math Concepts* (Teacher's Presentation Book, Student Material, and Teacher's Guide). Chicago: Science Research Associates. (Originally published 1995, and revised 1997.)

Engelmann, S., Kelly, B., & Carnine, D. (2003). *Connecting Math Concepts: Level F* (Teacher's Presentation Book, Student Material, and Teacher's Guide). Chicago: Science Research Associates. (Originally published 1996, and revised 1997.)

Engelmann, S., & Engelmann, O. (2012). *Connecting Math Concepts: Level A* (Comprehensive Ed.) (Teacher's Presentation Book, Student Material, and Teacher's Guide). Columbus, OH: SRA/McGraw Hill.

Engelmann, S., Engelmann, O., & Carnine, D. (2012). *Connecting Math Concepts: Level B* (Comprehensive Ed.) (Teacher's Presentation Book, Student Material, and Teacher's Guide). Columbus, OH: SRA/McGraw Hill.

Engelmann, S., Kelly, B., & Carnine, D. (2012). *Connecting Math Concepts: Level C* (Comprehensive Ed.) (Teacher's Presentation Book, Student Material, and Teacher's Guide). Columbus, OH: SRA/McGraw Hill.

Engelmann, S., Silbert, J., Engelmann, O., & Carnine, D. (2012). *Connecting Math Concepts: Level D* (Comprehensive Ed.) (Teacher's Presentation Book, Student Material, and Teacher's Guide). Columbus, OH: SRA/McGraw Hill.

Engelmann, S., Engelmann, O., Kelly, B., & Carnine, D. (2012). *Connecting Math Concepts: Level E* (Comprehensive Ed.) (Teacher's Presentation Book, Student Material, and Teacher's Guide). Columbus, OH: SRA/McGraw Hill.

Engelmann, S., Kelly, B., Engelmann, O., & Carnine, D. (2012). *Connecting Math Concepts: Level F* (Comprehensive Ed.) (Teacher's Presentation Book, Student Material, and Teacher's Guide). Columbus, OH: SRA/McGraw Hill.

Funnix

Engelmann, S., & Engelmann, O. (2011). *Funnix Beginning Math*. Eugene, OR: Royal Limited Partnership.

Videodisc Programs

Engelmann, S., & Carnine, D. (1985). *Mastering Fractions.* Washington, DC: Systems Impact, Inc.

Engelmann, S., & Carnine, D. (1986a). *Mastering Decimals & Percents.* Washington, DC: Systems Impact, Inc.

Engelmann, S., & Carnine, D. (1986b). *Mastering Ratios.* Washington, DC: Systems Impact, Inc.

Engelmann, S., & Carnine, D. (1989). *Beginning Algebra.* Washington, DC: Systems Impact, Inc.

Engelmann, S., & Carnine, D. (1991). *Mastering Informal Geometry.* Washington, DC: Systems Impact, Inc.

Pre-Algebra

Engelmann, S., Kelly, B., & Engelmann, O. (2008). *Essentials for Algebra.* (Teacher's Guide, Textbook, and Workbook). Columbus, OH: SRA/McGraw Hill.

Spelling

Engelmann and colleagues developed two programs to specifically teach spelling: *Spelling Through Morphographs* and *Spelling Mastery.*

Dixon, R., & Engelmann, S. (1979). *Spelling Through Morphographs.* Columbus, OH: SRA/McGraw-Hill. (Originally published 1976.)

Dixon, R., & Engelmann, S. (1990). *Spelling Mastery Series Guide.* Chicago: Science Research Associates.

Dixon, R., Engelmann, S., & Meier, M. (1998a). *Spelling Mastery A* (Teacher's Presentation Book, Student Material, and Teacher's Guide). Columbus, OH: SRA/McGraw-Hill. (Originally published 1980.)

Dixon, R., Engelmann, S., & Meier, M. (1998b). *Spelling Mastery B* (Teacher's Presentation Book, Student Material, and Teacher's Guide). Columbus, OH: SRA/McGraw-Hill. (Originally published 1980.)

Dixon, R., & Engelmann, S. (1998a). *Spelling Mastery C* (Teacher's Presentation Book, Student Material, and Teacher's Guide). Columbus, OH: SRA/McGraw-Hill. (Originally published 1981.)

Dixon, R., & Engelmann, S. (1998b). *Spelling Mastery D* (Teacher's Presentation Book, Student Material, and Teacher's Guide). Columbus, OH: SRA/McGraw-Hill. (Originally published 1981.)

Dixon, R., & Engelmann, S. (1998c). *Spelling Mastery E* (Teacher's Presentation Book, Student Material, and Teacher's Guide). Columbus, OH: SRA/McGraw-Hill. (Originally published 1988.)

Dixon, R., Engelmann, S., Steely, D., & Wells, T. (1998). *Spelling Mastery F* (Teacher's Presentation Book, Student Material, and Teacher's Guide). Columbus, OH: SRA/McGraw-Hill. (Published in 1981 as *E* and in 1988 as *F*.)

Writing

Engelmann and colleagues developed two major writing programs: *Expressive Writing* and *Reasoning and Writing.*

Cursive Writing

Miller, S., & Engelmann, S. (1980). *Cursive Writing* (Teacher's Presentation Book, Student Material, and Teacher's Guide). Chicago: Science Research Associates.

Expressive Writing

Engelmann, S., & Silbert, J. (1985a). *Expressive Writing I* (Teacher's Presentation Book, Student Material, and Teacher's Guide). Chicago: Science Research Associates.

Engelmann, S., & Silbert, J. (1985b). *Expressive Writing II* (Teacher's Presentation Book, Student Material, and Teacher's Guide). Chicago: Science Research Associates.

Engelmann, S., & Grossen, B. (2010). *Essentials for Writing.* Columbus, OH: SRA/McGraw-Hill.

Reasoning and Writing

Engelmann, S., & Seitz-Davis, K. L. (1991). *Reasoning & Writing: Level A* (Teacher's Presentation Book, Student Material, and Teacher's Guide). Chicago: Science Research Associates.

Engelmann, S., Brown-Arbogast, A., & Seitz-Davis, K. L. (1991). *Reasoning & Writing: Level B* (Teacher's Presentation Book, Student Material, and Teacher's Guide). Chicago: Science Research Associates.

Engelmann, S., & Silbert, J. (1991). *Reasoning & Writing: Level C* (Teacher's Presentation Book, Student Material, and Teacher's Guide). Chicago: Science Research Associates.

Engelmann, S., & Silbert, J. (1993). *Reasoning & Writing: Level D* (Teacher's Presentation Book, Student Material, and Teacher's Guide). Chicago: Science Research Associates.

Engelmann, S., & Grossen, B. (1994). *Reasoning & Writing: Level E* (Teacher's Presentation Book, Student Material, and Teacher's Guide). Chicago: Science Research Associates.

Engelmann, S., & Grossen, B. (1995). *Reasoning & Writing: Level F* (Teacher's Presentation Book, Student Material, and Teacher's Guide). Chicago: Science Research Associates.

Science and Social Studies

Engelmann, S., Davis, K., & Davis, G. (1982a). *Your World of Facts I* (Teacher's Presentation Book and Student Material). Chicago: Science Research Associates.

Engelmann, S., Davis, K., & Davis, G. (1982b). *Your World of Facts II* (Teacher's Presentation Book and Student Material). Chicago: Science Research Associates.

Engelmann, S., & Carnine, D. (1987). *Understanding Chemistry and Energy.* Washington, DC: Systems Impact, Inc.

Engelmann, S., & Carnine, D. (1988). *Earth Science.* Washington, DC: Systems Impact, Inc.

Miscellaneous

Engelmann, S. E., & Carnine, D. W. (1972). *DISTAR and Strategy Games.* Chicago: Science Research Associates.

Engelmann, S., Becker, W. C., Carnine, L., Meyer, L., Becker, J., & Johnson, G. (1975). *Management and Skills Manual.* Chicago: Science Research Associates.

Engelmann, S., & Colvin, G. (1983). *Generalized Compliance Training: A Direct-Instruction Program for Managing Severe Behavior Problems.* Austin, TX: Pro-Ed Publishing.

College Level Textbooks

Becker, W. C., Engelmann, S., & Thomas, D. R. (1971). *Teaching: A Basic Course in Applied Psychology.* Chicago: Science Research Associates.

Becker, W. C., Engelmann, S., & Thomas, D. R. (1975). *Teaching 1: Classroom Management.* Chicago: Science Research Associates.

Becker, W. C., & Engelmann, S. (1976a). *Teaching 2: Evaluation of Instruction.* Chicago: Science Research Associates.

Becker, W. C., & Engelmann, S. (1976b). *Teaching 3: Evaluation of Instruction.* Chicago: Science Research Associates.

Trade Books - Parents

Engelmann, S., Haddox, P., & Bruner, E. (1983). *Teach Your Child to Read in 100 Easy Lessons.* New York: Simon & Schuster.

This book consists of 100 short step-by-step lessons for beginning readers. The program was originally designed for parents to help their children become good readers. The program is an abbreviated version of *Reading Mastery* levels I and II, using the same orthography and sequence of introduction for letter-sound correspondences.

Engelmann, S., & Engelmann, T. (1981). *Give Your Child a Superior Mind.* New York: Simon and Schuster. (Originally published 1966. Published in 17 languages.)

Give Your Child A Superior Mind teaches parents to play games and teach concepts to children from birth to five years of age, with the intent of increasing their I.Q.

APPENDIX B

ENGELMANN'S OTHER WRITINGS: AN ANNOTATED BIBLIOGRAPHY OF ENGELMANN'S ARTICLES, CHAPTERS, AND BOOKS

Timothy W. Wood

This listing of Engelmann's writings was developed by reviewing the National Institute for Direct Instruction's bibliography, the vitas of prominent Direct Instruction developers and researchers, and Engelmann's website, zigsite.com. Citations were verified by examining the original documents, comparing citations of the publications in various bibliographies, and consulting the authors of these publications. Documents were obtained from the National Institute for Direct Instruction, electronic journals, the libraries and archives of various universities and colleges, and the personal libraries of education researchers. Three publications were not located, as none of these libraries, publishers, or researchers had physical or electronic copies of the documents. These publications are included in the listing below, but no abstract is given. Bibliographic entries are grouped by the decade of publication. Within each decade grouping, the entries are ordered by year and, within each year, ordered alphabetically.

1960s

Effectiveness of Direct Instruction on IQ Performance and Achievement in Reading and Arithmetic

Bereiter, C., & Engelmann, S. (1966a). Effectiveness of Direct Instruction on IQ performance and achievement in reading and arithmetic. ERIC Documentation Reproduction Service No. ED030496.

Based on the assumption that the academic failure of disadvantaged and middle-class children was due to inappropriate instruction, Bereiter and Engelmann conducted a study that tested the theory that instruction designed to efficiently maximize attainment of basic academic concepts can substantially increase the rate at which disadvantaged and middle-class children learn new behaviors and skills. The second purpose of this study was to determine if the increased achievement could be maintained in the second year of preschool instruction. Bereiter and Engelmann's experiment consisted of 43 African American and Caucasian 4 year old students of high, middle, and low intelligence who would be eligible for the Head Start program. Adjustments were made so that each classroom had approximately equal number of African American and Caucasian students as well as males and females. 15 of the children were placed in an experimental group (I) and the remaining 28 in a control group (II). A 2-year program consisting of a group (III) of 18 middle-class 4 year olds was conducted with a control group (IV) of middle-class 4 year olds at a Montessori preschool. Groups I and III received a 2 year experimental program that was designed for rapid attainment of basic academic concepts. Group II received traditional preschool education instruction. Results indicated students in Group I achieved greater gains on the Stanford-Binet IQ test than Group II, and maintained those gains over the 2 year program. The mean IQ of the experimental subjects after two years was 121.08, well above the mean of normal, middle-class children. Children in Group III demonstrated greater achievement in multiple areas in comparison to Group IV. Additionally, examples of the teaching procedures used for the experimental groups are detailed.

Language Learning Activities for the Disadvantaged Child

Bereiter, C., & Engelmann, S. (1966b). *Language learning activities for the disadvantaged child.* New York: Anti-Defamation League of B'nai B'rith.

This book discusses the importance of developing language skills in early education, especially for disadvantaged children, while also providing useful techniques to develop critical language skills. Engelmann and Bereiter devised language learning activities, which they determined to be the most efficient methods. The activities are designed to be fun and give the children a sense of accomplishment. The book is divided into five sections; language fundamentals, reading readiness activities, counting, singing, and hints for conducting language learning activities.

Observations on the Use of Direct Instruction with Young Disadvantaged Children

Bereiter, C., & Engelmann, S. (1966c). Observations on the use of Direct Instruction with young disadvantaged children. *Journal of School Psychology, 4*(3), 55–62.

In this article Bereiter and Engelmann discuss their thoughts and experiences about the use of Direct Instruction with young disadvantaged children in their preschool. One of the greatest difficulties encountered in implementing Direct Instruction was overcoming the widespread belief that rigorous and or demanding programs used in preschools would be harmful to children, causing extreme anxiety, fear of school, and robot-like conformity. The authors discuss the teaching methods administered, observations, and results on the feasibility, educational effectiveness, and apparent effects of the program on the children's attitudes, motivations, and personal adjustment. Additionally this paper was intended to motivate fellow educators to seek better methods for instructing disadvantaged children and to question long held beliefs, which had suppressed experimentation in the past.

Teaching Disadvantaged Children in the Preschool

Bereiter, C., & Engelmann, S. (1966d). *Teaching disadvantaged children in the preschool.* Englewood Cliffs, NJ: Prentice-Hall.

In this book Bereiter and Engelmann confront the issue of the academic failure of disadvantaged children by addressing the importance of preschool education. The authors devised effective teaching procedures and curriculum to fit the needs of disadvantaged students in order to make them competitive with their more affluent peers. Other teaching techniques and procedures for preschoolers had been proven ineffective for disadvantaged preschoolers and thus the authors believed a new program designed specifically for their needs was necessary. Topics covered include why a new system of instruction is necessary, cultural deprivation, academic objectives, preschool management, teaching techniques, language instruction, music, arithmetic, and reading.

An Academically Oriented Pre-School for Culturally Deprived Children

Bereiter, C., Engelmann, S., Osborn, J., & Reidford, P. A. (1966). An academically oriented pre-school for culturally deprived children. In F. M. Hechinger (Ed.), *Pre-school education today: New approaches to teaching three-, four-, and five-year-olds* (pp. 105–135). Garden City, NY: Doubleday & Co.

In this article the authors discuss the process of creating an academically oriented preschool for culturally deprived children and their experiences in teaching disadvantaged children in the Bereiter-Engelmann preschool. They discuss their objectives for the preschool and how they were to be obtained, specifically the development of language skills. Key goals outlined for the preschool included analysis of the formal characteristics of language, reading and arithmetic that were pertinent for their students, creating instructional goals based on these characteristics, determining feasible means of implementing Direct Instruction with the students, determining how much these particular students could learn, and assessing the rate of learning that could be achieved. Additionally the paper discusses three individual instructional programs and the children's achievements following a three month period. Examples of the lessons taught are included.

The Structuring of Language Processes as Tool for Thought

Engelmann, S. (1966). The structuring of language processes as tool for thought. In D. Kestel (Ed.), *National Catholic Educational Association bulletin: Curriculum for renewal, 63*(1), 459–468.

In this article Engelmann addresses the importance of language skills in child learning, specifically how teachers must adapt teaching strategies to fit students' particular language skills. Engelmann explains his careful process of structuring language as a tool of thought. Key components of the process include viewing language as a behavior, drawing inferences about the cognitive structure the child must have, demonstrating the relationship between language and non-language behavior, and clarifying the role of diagnosis and remediation in order to give the teacher clearer guidelines for instruction. He provides examples of language tasks and analyzes the role of language in the child's thought process. Engelmann stresses that the language program must be more than a vocal-auditory program. It needs to be a conceptual program because basic language must be taught simultaneously with its content.

Give Your Child a Superior Mind: A Program for the Preschool Child

Engelmann, S., & Engelmann, T. (1966). *Give your child a superior mind: A program for the preschool child.* New York: Simon and Schuster. (Published in 17 languages. Reprinted in 1981.)

This book, designed for parents, provides a clear and concise step-by-step guide to increasing a child's intelligence from age 18 months to five years old. It consists of lessons, examples, experiments, and guidelines for each age group. Parents are introduced to the theories behind the instructional programs used in the book as well as instructions on the proper methods for instruction. The teaching methods and programs are based on Siegfried Engelmann's firsthand experiences with preschool children. The lessons in this book will better prepare children for entering school and succeeding.

A Study of How a Child Learns Concepts about Characteristics of Liquid Materials

Engelmann, S., & Gallagher, J. J. (1966). A study of how a child learns concepts about characteristics of liquid materials: Final report. ERIC Documentation Reproduction Service No. ED014428.

This study was conducted to test the validity of Jean Piaget's theory on children's ability to comprehend the concept of the conservation of liquid. The study consisted of 45 Kindergarten and first grade students from the Prairie elementary school in Urbana, Illinois. The children were tested on their understanding of conservation through tasks using solid objects, verbal prediction of liquid behavior, compensation problems, and the manipulation and prediction of liquid transfer. The children were also given the Peabody Picture Vocabulary Test (PPVT) in order to establish their mental competence and level. Results of the pretests identified 30 children as non-conservers. These 30 students were divided into 15 pairs, matched according to mental age scores and their scores on the PPVT. The pairs were separated into the experimental and control groups. Children in the experimental group received 15-20 minutes of training per day for five days. Training was intended to help the children establish the ideas of conceptual independence and compensation. The sessions were done in small group sessions with an emphasis on observation, but not active participation. Following the training both groups were retested on conservation inventory and the PPVT. Results indicated a significant improvement by the children in the experimental group on the conservation inventory test and no changes on the PPVT. The study provided evidence that the properties of liquids that had been assumed to stand for conservation can be taught through instruction and the skills are not dependent upon cognitive development as Piaget claimed.

Cognitive Structures Related to the Principle of Conservation

Engelmann, S. (1967a). Cognitive structures related to the principle of conservation. In D. W. Brison & E. V. Sullivan (Eds.), *Recent research on the acquisition of conservation of substance* (pp. 25–51). Toronto, Ontario, Canada: Ontario Institute for Studies in Education.

In this article Engelmann examines the debate between Piaget's view of the conservation of substance as a developmental phenomenon and his conceptualization of the matter as strictly an educational problem. He describes an experiment he conducted on the conservation of liquid quantity. The participants consisted of 87 Kindergarten and first grade students attending a middle class school in Urbana, Illinois. All students were given a series of tests to determine the necessary skills present for the conservation of substance. The students were divided according to the results, placing them into three groups: an Experimental group, a Control group, and a Conservator group. Engelmann lists the questions and models used to determine the students' skills as well as the training programs used with the experimental group. He discusses the results and their implications in relation to the differences between conserving and non-conserving students. He concluded that since significant results were achieved through the training process, the conditions for learning implied by the Piagetian description were not necessary for developing the skills for conservation of substance.

Communications Skills as an Objective: Teaching Communications Skills to Disadvantaged Children

Engelmann, S. (1967b). Communications skills as an objective: Teaching communications skills to disadvantaged children. In *Education for the culturally disadvantaged: Proceedings of the National Conference on Educational Objectives for the Culturally Disadvantaged* (pp. 67–86). Little Rock, AR: South Central Region Educational Laboratory.

In this article Engelmann addresses the difficulties in teaching communication skills to disadvantaged children and provides guidelines on how to do so effectively and efficiently. He asserts one of the primary causes of this problem is the unclear definition of what teaching is and how the teaching environment places limitations on what the educator, curriculum designer, and teacher can do. Engelmann argues the solution to these educational problems is describing every step of teaching procedures in specific terms to avoid misinterpretations that would result in more problems. Additionally Engelmann provides a guideline to designing teaching programs and describes the problems that can arise by not following his model. The model described was shown to be effective when used with a small group of students in the Bereiter-Engelmann Kindergarten in 1967.

Relationship Between Psychological Theories and the Act of Teaching

Engelmann, S. (1967c). Relationship between psychological theories and the act of teaching. *Journal of School Psychology, 5*(2), 93–100.

In this article Engelmann examines the use of psychological theories in instructional practices and their effectiveness. He argues psychological theories may be useful in determining the rate at which a student should progress academically as well as behavioral norms that are expected at certain ages. He does not believe these theories are useful for helping teachers induce particular behaviors of students and believes that often the explanations are too broad and inclusive or irrelevant. Engelmann states that psychological theories are designed to relate to teaching or they are not. He argues an educational diagnosis is more effective than a psychological theory because it is more specific to the situation. Additionally Engelmann describes the program he and Carl Bereiter designed in 1966 to educate young children, explaining how the specificity of their model is more effective than psychological theories.

Teaching Formal Operations to Preschool Advantaged and Disadvantaged Children

Engelmann, S. (1967d). Teaching formal operations to preschool advantaged and disadvantaged children. *Ontario Journal of Educational Research, 9*(3), 193–207.

In this article Engelmann discusses an experiment he conducted, which was designed to test children's ability to pass Piaget's test of the conservation of water. He intended to disprove Piaget's theory by demonstrating how a child's ability to pass the conservation of water test is not dependent upon his/her cognitive development and the child could be taught the rules of water behavior before the age Piaget determined to be necessary. Engelmann's study consisted of 10 preschool children ages 3 ½–5 ¾ years. Half of the students were categorized as "culturally disadvantaged" and the other half as "culturally advantaged." The inclusion of both groups was designed to show the effect of Direct Instruction over a broader range of development among students and allow for more precise conclusions about the training. Engelmann extensively detailed the training used in the experiment and included illustrations to clarify the lessons taught. Results indicated four of the five "culturally advantaged" students and three of the five "culturally disadvantaged students" solved the criterion problem presented. Additionally Engelmann discusses the flaws in Piaget's theories and the relationship of cognitive development to understanding the rules of the conservation of water.

Teaching Reading to Children with Low Mental Ages

Engelmann, S. (1967e). Teaching reading to children with low mental ages. In F. E. McDowell (Ed.), *Education and training of the mentally retarded* (pp. 193-201). Washington, DC: Council for Exceptional Children.

In this article Engelmann draws from his experience in working with at-risk children in preschools to discuss the challenges in teaching reading to children with low mental ages. He examines traditional reading instruction, its flaws with teaching children with low mental ages, and how to create effective reading instruction for all children. Engelmann uses task analysis to specifically break down all the different elements to reading and determine problem areas and procedures for solving them. He discusses the program used at the Bereiter-Engelmann preschool and its design and goals and then contrasts it to the traditional programs. The article concludes by describing the development of a program designed to give children the necessary skills to succeed and progress in school.

An Academically Oriented Preschool for Disadvantaged Children: Results from the Initial Experimental Group

Bereiter, C., & Engelmann, S. (1968). An academically oriented preschool for disadvantaged children: Results from the initial experimental group. In D. W. Brison & J. Hill (Eds.), *Psychology and early childhood education* (pp. 17–36). Toronto, Ontario, Canada: Ontario Institute for Studies in Education.

This article discusses Bereiter and Engelmann's first two years working with disadvantaged preschool students to teach them language, arithmetic, and reading skills using the principles of Direct Instruction teaching. Their experiment was based on the assumption that disadvantaged children did not have the same level of educational preparation as their more affluent peers and therefore required an academic program, which would begin at a lower level of presumed knowledge and then would progress at an accelerated rate to allow them to catch up with their peers. The children were told the instructional sessions would represent work rather than play and they would be required to participate and try hard. Positive behavior would be reinforced and inappropriate behavior would be reprimanded. Additionally the article details the content and structure of the academic programs used. Test results indicated disadvantaged students could acquire within two years: (1) the necessary language skills to advance from a year or more below grade average performance up to grade average performance; (2) the equivalent of two and a half years-worth of arithmetic skills for primary school children; (3) over one and a half years-worth of reading and spelling skills for primary school children.

Priorities in Preschool Education

Engelmann, S. (1968a). Priorities in preschool education. In D. W. Brison & J. Hill (Eds.), *Psychology and early childhood education* (pp. 51–60). Toronto, Ontario, Canada: Ontario Institute for Studies in Education.

In response to perceived problems in preschool education Engelmann discusses his suggestions for preschool goals and guidelines in order to fulfill their promises to the fields of education and psychology. The goal of the guidelines is to make preschools more efficient and thus accomplish their goals at a significantly faster rate. Key topics discussed include the status of the preschool, the potential of the preschool, teacher training, development of curriculum, evaluating the worth of a preschool, and basic approaches to restructuring preschool education.

Relating Operant Techniques to Programming and Teaching

Engelmann, S. (1968b). Relating operant techniques to programming and teaching. *Journal of School Psychology, 6*(2), 89–96.

In this article Engelmann examines the relationship between operant techniques and programming and teaching. He argues there are significant differences between operant techniques and instructional planning, which can be seen in almost any teaching situation. Engelmann provides numerous examples of the difference between the two. Additionally he describes how to combine operant techniques and instructional planning. He continues on to discuss the differences between fixed response and variable response learning, and how to develop adequate curricula.

Conceptual Learning

Engelmann, S. (1969a). *Conceptual learning.* San Rafael, CA: Dimensions Publishing.

In this monograph Engelmann outlines his approach to teaching concepts to children and explains the reasoning behind it. He describes the principles behind the process of conceptual learning, showing how a teacher demonstrates the characteristics of a concept by presenting both instances and non-instances, and developing an appropriate test/task the student must perform to demonstrate an understanding of the concept.

Preventing Failure in the Primary Grades

Engelmann, S. (1969b). *Preventing failure in the primary grades.* Chicago: Science Research Associates. (Reprinted in 1997 by ADI Press.)

In response to the failure of schools to educate all children in the primary grades Engelmann sought to identify the reasons why. He determined all children can learn if instructed properly with highly efficient teaching methods. If students failed it was because the teachers failed to teach appropriately. Engelmann discusses how and why these schools have failed in the past using specific examples and then describes what is necessary for all students to succeed. Main topics discussed include causes of failure and their solutions, teaching techniques, instructional design, classroom management, reading for beginning and advanced students, and arithmetic for beginning and advanced students.

1970s

The Effectiveness of Direct Instruction on IQ Performance and Achievement in Reading and Arithmetic

Engelmann, S. (1970a). The effectiveness of Direct Instruction on IQ performance and achievement in reading and arithmetic. In J. Hellmuth (Ed.), *Disadvantaged child, vol. 3. Compensatory education: A national debate* (pp. 339–361). New York: Brunner/Mazel.

In this publication Engelmann examines the relationship between learning and teaching. He asserts that if there is a failure to learn it is due to inadequate teaching procedures. Engelmann analyzes a two-year study that tested the effect of Direct Instruction on the rapid attainment of basic academic concepts in reading and arithmetic by culturally disadvantaged children. He hypothesized that an increase in instruction over the same amount of time would increase productivity.

How to Construct Effective Language Programs for the Poverty Child

Engelmann, S. (1970b). How to construct effective language programs for the poverty child. In F. Williams (Ed.), *Language and poverty: Perspectives on a theme* (pp. 102–122). Chicago: Markham Publishing.

In this chapter Engelmann addresses the issue of disadvantaged children having insufficient language skills to compete on the same academic level as their more affluent peers. He discusses a plan designed by himself and Carl Bereiter for developing language programs to give these children the necessary language skills to succeed and progress in school. Engelmann outlines the construction of the program in five steps: objectives, analysis, tryout, programming, and evaluation. Additionally Engelmann discusses the issue of abuses in program construction, specifically examining developmental approaches, linguistic and psycholinguistic approaches, the verbal and nonverbal dichotomy, and the case history approach.

Does the Piagetian Approach Imply Instruction?

Engelmann, S. E. (1971a). Does the Piagetian approach imply instruction? In D. R. Green, M. P. Ford, & G. B. Flamer (Eds.), *Measurement and Piaget* (pp. 118–126). New York: McGraw-Hill.

In this article Engelmann addresses Piaget's theory of development and education and its relationship to instruction. Piaget's theory refers to the mechanism by which children progress from one stage of development to the next and how this limits their ability to learn concepts until developmentally ready. Engelmann questions the validity of this theory in terms of instruction. Engelmann argues Piaget's theory is more of an account of normative data than a universal theory of how and why children develop. He provides examples of flaws in Piaget's theory by showing how learning is not subordinated to development as Piaget claims. Additionally Engelmann references his own experiments with young children in which he disproved key components of Piaget's theory. Engelmann concludes that Piaget's theory is nothing more than a series of accurate descriptions about the performance of children at different ages, not a theory that clearly implies instruction, lack of instruction, or evaluation of instruction.

Failure Prevention: A Programming Necessity

Engelmann, S. (1971b). Failure prevention: A programming necessity. In J. G. Morrey (Ed.), *Learning and behavior management in teacher training: A BECRA symposium on essential components* (pp. 140–174). Pocatello, ID: Idaho State University.

Engelmann's article addresses the issue of at-risk children failing in schools and how to prevent it. He describes his early career in education and his experiences in Project Follow Through. Engelmann uses specific examples of working with children to discuss the design of effective instruction for at-risk children and the difficulties involved in teaching them.

The Inadequacies of the Linguistic Approach in Teaching Situations

Engelmann, S. (1971c). The inadequacies of the linguistic approach in teaching situations. In Center for Applied Linguistics (Ed.), *Sociolinguistics: A crossdisciplinary perspective* (pp. 141–151). Washington, DC: Center for Applied Linguistics.

In this article Engelmann responds to criticisms from linguists on structured language programs such as the Bereiter-Engelmann program. He analyzes their interpretations and conclusions about these language programs. Engelmann critiques these linguists' claims, labeling them as absurd because of their lack of evidence and a theory that would support their position. He examines the linguistic approach, showing how its position does not imply any kind of instruction. Therefore he believes linguists should not be qualified to recommend teaching programs and labels them as dangerous. Engelmann provides examples of the problems in applying linguistic theories to instruction. Furthermore he directly challenges specific linguists' interpretations and conclusions about the Bereiter-Engelmann program.

Program Description and 1973 Outcome Data: Engelmann-Becker Follow Through Model

Becker, W. C., & Engelmann, S. (1973a). *Program description and 1973 outcome data: Engelmann-Becker Follow Through model.* Washington, DC: Bureau of Elementary and Secondary Education, Div. of Compensatory Education. ERIC Documentation Reproduction Service No. ED096780.

Becker and Engelmann describe their academic program used in Project Follow Through. This program was based on their DISTAR instructional materials. They state the objectives for the students enrolled in their programs and detail the role of teaching procedures, program objectives, class schedules, staffing requirements, class management, parental involvement, teacher training, progress tests, and monitoring procedures. An overview of the DISTAR reading, arithmetic, and language programs is provided. Additionally, results of the programs' use over four years with 9,152 elementary school children are presented and discussed. Of the students, 78% were classified as economically disadvantaged and the discussion of the results focuses on these students. Results from the Wide Range Achievement Test (WRAT), Metropolitan Achievement Test (MAT), and Slosson Intelligence Test are discussed. Results indicated that students who began the program in Kindergarten demonstrated an accelerated gain in reading and arithmetic skills.

Summary Analysis of Five-Year Data on Achievement and Teaching Progress with 14,000 Children in 20 Projects

Becker, W. C., & Engelmann, S. (1973b). *Summary analysis of five-year data on achievement and teaching progress with 14,000 children in 20 projects*, Technical report 73-2, Preliminary Report. Washington, DC: Bureau of Elementary and Secondary Education, Div. of Compensatory Education. ERIC Documentation Reproduction Service No. ED096781.

Becker and Engelmann provide a preliminary analysis of the academic achievement of 9,000 Follow Through students from Kindergarten through third grade who participated in an academic program based on Engelmann and Becker's DISTAR program. Of these students, 78% were classified as economically disadvantaged and were the focus of their analysis. The report features statistical analysis and graphs showing student progress. Results from the Wide Range Achievement Test showed that the students who began the program in Kindergarten finished the third grade with average grade level scores of 5.21 in reading, 3.86 in arithmetic, and 3.74 in spelling. Students who began the program in first grade performed above norms, but not as high as students who began in Kindergarten. Students in the third grade scored at or above grade level on most subtests of the Metropolitan Achievement Test. Students beginning the program in Kindergarten had a projected IQ gain of 9.1 points, which was maintained through the third grade. Students who began in first grade had a projected IQ gain of 8.55 points over the same time span.

Accountability

Engelmann, S. (1974a). Accountability. In M. Csapo & B. Poutt (Eds.), *Education for all children* (pp. 106–120). Vancouver, British Columbia, Canada: British Columbia Federation of the Council for Exceptional Children.

In this article Engelmann argues the central focus of accountability should be for teachers to sit down with students to try to change their behaviors. The process of changing the behavior of children in specified ways demonstrates teaching has occurred. Engelmann discusses the difficulty in defining what teaching is, as well as the influences and restraints of administrative and political bodies in creating a definition. He argues the central focus of teaching must be changing behaviors in specified ways because then it becomes meaningful to specify programs and to determine what the objectives are for changing behavior. At that point it would become logical to create a system of advocacy for the children to ensure quality education. To ensure a system of accountability Engelmann argues there must be a philosophy of education, which clarifies the role of schools, teachers, administrators, programs, and tests.

Low Performer's Manual

Engelmann, S. (1974b). *Low performer's manual.* (Revised in 2005, available from: http://zigsite.com/PDFs/LowPerfManual.pdf)

In response to difficulties teachers faced in teaching low-performing students Engelmann designed this manual to provide instructions and guidelines on how to best teach these students, effectively and efficiently. He discusses the necessity for specific teaching strategies and how low-performing students differ from average students in terms of how they learn. The manual is divided into four sections: traditional issues (behavioral objectives, educational diagnosis, and what to teach), basic teaching techniques, procedures for diagnosing the learner and accompanying programs, and teaching new motor responses. Engelmann concludes that to teach low-performing students effectively, teachers must have far more skills and knowledge about teaching than teachers of higher-performing students because low-performing students make a much larger range of errors and thus teaching must be more carefully administered.

A Video-Tape Format for Greatest Control

Engelmann, S. (1974c). A video-tape format for greatest control. *Instructional efficiency: A means for reducing formal classroom time* (pp. 13–17). Saigon, Vientam: SEAMEO Regional Center for Educational Innovation and Technology.

In this article Engelmann discusses the necessities for effective instruction and the benefits of using videotape-based instruction in underdeveloped countries. He proposes using videotapes in underdeveloped countries to teach reading, language, and arithmetic. Engelmann explains how the use of videotape instruction would be more effective than other instructional techniques in these countries. The implementation of videotape instruction would require the development of a supervising center to manage the dissemination of tapes, the monitoring of progress of every classroom, and the training of supervisors and teachers. Engelmann concludes that the plan may be impractical, but it is offset by its potential and ability for quick implementation.

Tactual Hearing Experiment with Deaf and Hearing Subjects

Engelmann, S., & Rosov, R. J. (1974d). *ORI Research Bulletin, 14*(5), 1-43. ERIC Documentation Reproduction Service No. ED098770.

In response to the theory that deaf children suffer from feedback deprivation, due to their difficulty or inability to hear, which could cause problems with cognitive operations and communication, Engelmann and Rosov sought to develop and test a device that could function as an ear to help the individuals learn about pitch, loudness, and characteristics of each phoneme. For this study they used tactual vocoders with four hearing and four deaf students to determine if each group could recognize words transmitted through the vocoder. The four hearing participants ranged from 20 to 30 year olds and the deaf participants ranged from 8 to 14 year olds. During the training the hearing participants wore headphones playing white noise to provide artificial deafening. They practiced recognizing isolated words presented randomly, words in connected sentences, inflection copying, and rhyming. This training was primarily done without face-to-face contact with the speaker. Training for the deaf students was similar with few exceptions such as the use of a reinforcement system and additional training in articulation. Results indicated that individuals who are deaf could be taught to hear fine speech discriminations using the tactual vocoder, hundreds of corrected repetitions are required for both hearing and deaf individuals to learn simple tactual discriminations, and that individuals' memory and ability to discriminate increases as the number of words they have mastered increases.

Your Child Can Succeed: How to Get the Most Out of School for Your Child

Engelmann, S. (1975). *Your child can succeed: How to get the most out of school for your child.* New York: Simon & Schuster.

In response to the academic failure of students as well as the connected issues with teachers and school systems, Engelmann offers his opinions on how best to rectify these problems. He argues that children can be taught successfully if the appropriate technology is used, children are properly motivated through behavioral modification techniques, and if we have a strong moral and economic commitment to the success of children. Engelmann discusses common problems in schools and why students from various backgrounds and abilities continue to fail. Despite the differences in these students, Engelmann believes all have the ability to succeed if careful instructional procedures are followed. Engelmann analyzes the roles of the schools, teachers, and students and how they must work together to succeed, providing multiple examples to illustrate his points. Other areas of discussion include preparing the teacher, the role of instructional programs, achievement tests, students' legal rights, and how to work with schools.

Tactual Hearing Experiment with Deaf and Hearing Subjects

Engelmann, S., & Rosov, R. (1975). Tactual hearing experiment with deaf and hearing subjects. *Exceptional Children, 41*(4), 243–253.

This article summarizes a study published in 1974 in the ORI Research Bulletin and summarized above. In this experiment Siegfried Engelmann and Robert Rosov used tactual vocoders with four hearing and four deaf students to determine if they could recognize words transmitted through the vocoder. The experiment was designed to find an alternative form of instruction for deaf children apart from a visual approach using an oscilloscope. Subjects were given words through a tactual vocoder and then attempted to identify the words without looking at the trainer. Results of the hearing and deaf students were similar, however the deaf students' performance was slightly slower during the first stages of training. Results indicated deaf students could be taught to hear fine speech discriminations through the tactual vocoder, performance was positively correlated with practice as a function of training, and hundreds of corrected repetitions were required for both subjects to learn simple tactual discriminations.

Analysis of Achievement Data on Six Cohorts of Low-Income Children From 20 School Districts in the University of Oregon Direct Instruction Follow Through Model

Becker, W. C., & Engelmann, S. (1976). *Analysis of achievement data on six cohorts of low-income children from 20 school districts in the University of Oregon Direct Instruction Follow Through model.* Technical report 76-1. Washington, DC: U.S. Office of Education, Bureau of School Systems, Division of Follow Through. ERIC Documentation Reproduction Service No. ED145922.

Becker and Engelmann present their analysis on the effectiveness of the Engelmann-Becker Direct Instruction model, which was designed to develop basic academic skills for disadvantaged primary-grade children in order for them to be at grade level by the conclusion of third grade. The program's principles and objectives are described and the rationale behind them is explained in detail. Becker and Engelmann analyzed data from 12,000 disadvantaged students in 20 regions across the U.S. Fifty percent of the students began the program in Kindergarten while the remainder began in first grade. The students were instructed using the DISTAR program, which utilized small-group face to face instruction by a teacher using carefully sequenced daily lessons in reading, arithmetic, and language. The Wide Range Achievement Test, the Metropolitan Achievement Test and the Slosson Intelligence Test were used to measure the students' achievement. Results showed the students were at or near national norms by the conclusion of third grade. Additional follow up testing in fifth and sixth grade showed the continued effectiveness of the DISTAR program, even though there were losses against the norms, which were attributed to the change in the format of instruction following third grade.

Becker and Engelmann conclude that their program is clearly effective with low IQ students and that entry IQ is not a major determinant of academic gains. They argue for an early start to basic skill instruction, a systematic expansion of basic vocabulary, and the extension of the use of the program until minimal adult competencies are met.

A Structured Program's Effect on the Attitudes and Achievement of Average and Above Average Second Graders

Engelmann, S., & Carnine, D. W. (1976). A structured program's effect on the attitudes and achievement of average and above average second graders. In W. C. Becker & S. Engelmann (Eds.), *Analysis of achievement data on six cohorts of low-income children from 20 school districts in the University of Oregon Direct Instruction Follow Through model: Technical report 76-1 Appendix B: Formative research studies* (pp. 102-117). Eugene, OR: University of Oregon, College of Education, Follow Through Project. ERIC Documentation Reproduction Service No. ED145922.

In this article Engelmann and Carnine discuss the effect of the DISTAR instructional program on the achievement of both average and above average second grade students. Their analysis was done in part to respond to educators who believed the DISTAR programs were only designed for low-performing students and would not be appropriate for students of average or above average performance. To determine the effect of the DISTAR reading and arithmetic programs a study was conducted, consisting of 30 middle-class second grade students. The students' performance was tested using the second-grade Stanford Achievement Test (Primary Battery 2) for reading, arithmetic, and science, the Wide-Range Achievement Test for oral reading, and the Gates-McGinitie test of Speed and Accuracy (for fourth through sixth graders). The students were also given an attitude questionnaire developed by the investigators to determine the students' feelings toward the reading program, their teacher, and themselves. Results indicated that the performance of the students was significantly above the norms by the end of the second grade. Student opinions about the program indicated they generally liked the program, felt confident about their performance, and recognized their teacher required them to work "a lot." The students in this class completed class lessons at an average rate of 2.56 per day, while low-performing students in the Engelmann-Becker Follow Through Program averaged 1.75 lessons per day. Additionally the authors directly confront prominent negative statements about highly structured programs such as the DISTAR programs.

Sequencing Cognitive and Academic Tasks

Engelmann, S. (1977). Sequencing cognitive and academic tasks. In R. D. Kneedler & S. G. Tarver (Eds.), *Changing perspectives in special education* (pp. 46–61). Columbus, OH: Charles E. Merrill Publishing.

In addressing the problems of misinterpretation in cognitive and academic tasks and the problems that result from them, Engelmann provides guidelines to sequencing successful and efficient cognitive and academic tasks. He argues learning disabilities are made not born. He estimates 90% of students are labeled "learning disabled" not because of any problems with their perception, synapses, or memory, but because they have been taught with ineffective methods. To avoid this mislabeling adequate and efficient teaching must be utilized. Engelmann provides an overview of the principles for constructing appropriate sequences for cognitive and academic tasks. The key principles for effective teaching include carefully designed instruction, demonstrations consistent with only one interpretation, operations that are initially overt and perfectly clear, and teaching and identifying the essential pre-skills. Additionally he provides an array of examples to illustrate these principles.

Engelmann, S., & Granzin, A. (1977). Principles of Unfamiliar Learning. *Proceedings from the Conference on Speech-Analyzing Aids for the Deaf.* Washington, DC: Gallaudet College.*

Developing a Tactual Hearing Program for Deaf Children

Engelmann, S., & Skillman, L. (1977). Developing a tactual hearing program for deaf children. *Proceedings from the Conference on Speech-Analyzing Aids for the Deaf.* Washington, DC: Gallaudet College.

In this article Engelmann and Skillman discuss the Oregon Research Institute's development and use of a tactual hearing program for deaf children. They review the development of tactual vocoders and research studies conducted with hearing and deaf participants. The use of production, perception, and language activities is analyzed and examples of these procedures are provided. Additionally the difficulty of teacher training is discussed.

Systems for Basic Instruction : Theory and Applications

Becker, W. C., & Engelmann, S. (1978). Systems for basic instruction: Theory and applications. In A. C. Catania & T. A. Brigham (Eds.), *Handbook of applied behavior analysis: Social and instructional processes* (pp. 325–377). New York: Irvington.

In the first part of this chapter Becker and Engelmann describe and explain the rationale behind the key principles for developing instructional programs. These principles are the basis for designing, selecting, and sequencing tasks for instructional programs. In the second part of the chapter, Direct Instruction programs using these principles are examined and explained in great detail, showing how they have succeeded and the problems encountered. The authors review the key goals of the instructional programs and how the principles and the procedures developed from them aid the achievement of the program goals. Other topics covered include teaching

---

* A copy of this publication was not located.

a general case, concept learning, discrimination learning, cumulative programming, and teaching to mastery.

Diagnosing Instruction

Engelmann, S., Granzin, A., & Severson, H. (1979). Diagnosing instruction. *The Journal of Special Education, 13*(4), 355–363.

This article addresses the issue of diagnostic approaches towards teaching while emphasizing the importance of evaluating the instructional context and not just the student. The authors argue teachers are aware of the students who are having problems so they need to know how to adjust instructional strategies to teach more effectively. Traditional diagnostic approaches have informed teachers that if the students fail, it was the result of some basic flaw in the learner. However these diagnoses do not specify the extent to which the learner's problems are related to poor instruction and precisely what the teachers could do to remedy an observed problem. The teacher can only achieve behavioral change by manipulating environmental events. Teachers need to be clearly informed of how to manipulate the environment to resolve the issues through teacher behaviors. Effective diagnosis must focus both on the learner and the teacher in order to determine the solution to the problem. Examples are made to discuss procedures and assumptions critical to an adequate diagnosis of the instruction. The importance of instructional diagnosis is to understand which aspects of instruction are inadequate, how they are inadequate, and to determine how to correct the inadequacies. By not examining the role of instruction the implications for teaching methods are limited.

Teaching Language to the Truly Naive Learner: An Analog Study Using a Tactual Vocoder

Williams, P., Granzin, A., Engelmann, S., & Becker, W. C. (1979). Teaching language to the truly naive learner: An analog study using a tactual vocoder. *Journal of Special Education Technology, 2,* 5–15.

This article discusses an experiment on teaching highly unfamiliar word discriminations to a group of 20 college students or college graduates using a tactual vocoder. The subjects were randomly assigned to one of four treatment groups: easy sequence–low criterion, hard sequence–low criterion, easy sequence–high criterion, and hard sequence–high criterion. Each group was tactually presented a set of 12 words using two orders of introduction: one that juxtaposed minimally different words (hard sequence), and one that juxtaposed grossly different words (easy sequence). Results indicated that most subjects could learn difficult tactual discriminations in the time limit provided. Subjects in the hard sequence–easy criterion group demonstrated the greatest progress, which was attributed to the hypothesis that the hard sequence would lead to faster learning because it required a greater focus on critical discriminations early in the training process, and that the lower criterion likely facilitated a faster introduction of the larger set and avoided overlearning of false discriminations. Results suggested that unfamiliar learning is even difficult for college level adults. Additionally theoretical considerations and other research on unfamiliar learning are discussed.

1980s

Direct Instruction Technology: Recent Developments and Research Findings

Becker, W. C., Engelmann, S., & Carnine, D. W. (1980). Direct Instruction technology: Recent developments and research findings. In J. Ward & S. Bochner (Eds.), *Recent developments in special education*. Proceedings of the Professional Seminar in Special Education Held at Macquarie University in 1979 to Commemorate the International Year of the Child (pp. 4–91). Sydney, Australia: Macquarie University.

This article was presented at a lecture series about recent developments in special education. The authors provide a comprehensive review of Direct Instruction programs and technology along with the results of research on the effectiveness of Direct Instruction with learners of varying skills. Main areas of focus about Direct Instruction include the origins of Direct Instruction, assumptions and principles, and basic features. Research projects on Direct Instruction discussed include the National Follow Through Project for the disadvantaged and studies on "severely disabled" and "severely retarded" students in Australia. The authors conclude that Direct Instruction is an effective approach to the alleviation of skill deficiencies and Direct Instruction programs have been shown to be consistently effective in a wide range of settings, with students of varying abilities.

Direct Instruction

Engelmann, S. (1980a). *The instructional design library series (Vol. 22): Direct Instruction.* Englewood Cliffs, NJ: Educational Technology Publications.

In this book Engelmann describes in detail the Direct Instruction model he created. Designed to teach effectively in the most efficient manner the Direct Instruction model is a highly structured program, which can be applied to most instructional problems with students of different abilities. Engelmann describes the theories behind the Direct Instruction model, how they are used effectively, and the results of successful application of the theories. Additionally he provides examples of the teaching programs and procedures used. The book is divided into seven sections; use, operational description, design format, outcomes, developmental guide, resources, and appendix. The Appendix lists the facts and principles discussed in the book as well as summaries of studies that examined these facts and principles.

Toward the Design of Faultless Instruction: The Theoretical Basis of Concept Analysis

Engelmann, S. (1980b). Toward the design of faultless instruction: The theoretical basis of concept analysis. *Educational Technology, 20*(2), 28-36.

In this article Engelmann discusses the design of instruction and how to make it flawless. He explores the process of learning and why information is learned or not learned, whether there was a problem with the learner, the teacher, or a combination. Engelmann organizes his discussion of instructional design by examining the basic differences between cognitive and behavioral approaches. Through this discussion Engelmann analyzes the problems with each model and provides rules for constructing faultless instruction. Additionally he examines the role of concept analysis in the process of designing instruction.

Assessing Labor Cost of Objectives

Engelmann, S., & Granzin, A. (1980). Assessing labor cost of objectives. *Directions, 1*(4), 54–62.

In this article Engelmann and Granzin examine the procedures for assessing the potential labor cost of changing speech and language behavior of profoundly deaf children. The assessment was based on the performance of children on a series of tasks. The assessment determined whether the labor cost would be very low or high. Major topics discussed include patterns of responses, inferences on pattern distortion, and characteristics of difficult learning. The authors provide examples of the procedures used and how they help to determine the children's skills and the labor cost involved in changing behavior. Additionally they discuss a case study using a tactual vocoder with a profoundly deaf child, detailing the stages of learning and the problems encountered.

Implementation of Basal Reading in Grades 4–6: Final Report

Engelmann, S., & Steely, D. (1980). *Implementation of basal reading in grades 4–6: Final report.* Chicago: Science Research Associates.

This research project was designed to report relevant information on typical reading instruction in Grades 4–6 in order to provide a knowledge base for a marketing strategy. The research consisted of three phases: an intensive analysis of teaching techniques; the relationships between teacher behavior, programs, and student performance; and determining to what extent a larger population of teachers produces the pattern of verbal responses produced by the smaller group of intensively observed teachers and what kinds of responses may serve as key predictors of particular behavior patterns. The four major topic areas are teacher's verbal reports, program specifications, teaching behavior, and student mastery. The report includes a description of the research design, the procedures for obtaining data (audio interviews, video-taping, program analysis, and student performance), and a discussion of the results.

Direct Instruction Model

Becker, W. C., Engelmann, S., Carnine, D. W., & Rhine, W. R. (1981). Direct Instruction model. In W. R. Rhine (Ed.), *Making schools more effective: New directions from Follow Through* (pp. 95–154). New York: Academic Press.

This publication provides a detailed outline and analysis of the Direct Instruction model and examines research on its effect. The development of Direct Instruction and the DISTAR models is discussed as well as the foundations for their theory of instruction and the principles of the programs. Components of the models covered include the role of teachers, use of time, training, supervision, and the role of parents. Additionally the sponsor's evaluation of the Direct Instruction model and the national longitudinal evaluation of Project Follow Through are discussed. Areas of focus include the success of Direct Instruction students in comparison to national norms, whether more exposure to the model results in larger gains, if students maintain gains after leaving the program, and the achievement of low-performing students in the program. Additionally the authors provide a guideline for changing school systems to become effective for all students.

Direct Instruction Technology: Making Learning Happen

Becker, W. C., Engelmann, S., Carnine, D. W., & Maggs, A. (1982). Direct Instruction technology: Making learning happen. In P. Karoly & J. J. Steffen (Eds.), *Improving children's competence: Advances in child behavioral analysis and therapy*, (Vol. 1, pp. 151–206). Lexington, MA: D. C. Heath & Company.

This article examines the issue of skill deficiencies in education, specifically examining Direct Instruction in terms of assumptions, underlying principles, methods, and research on using Direct Instruction to prevent and remedy these deficiencies. A comprehensive overview of Direct Instruction's origins, principles, techniques, and programs is provided. Examples of teaching strategies are included. Additionally, evaluation studies of Direct Instruction programs are examined, specifically looking at the results from the national Follow Through Project for the disadvantaged and studies of learning disabled and "severely retarded" children in Australia. The authors conclude that Direct Instruction is an effective approach to the alleviation of skill deficiencies and Direct Instruction programs have been shown to be consistently effective in a wide range of settings, with students of varying abilities.

Advocacy for Children

Engelmann, S. (1982a). *Advocacy for children*. (Available from: http://zigsite.com/AdvocacyChildren.html)

This article was written in 1982, but it was not published until 2012 when Engelmann put it on his website, zigsite.com. In this article Engelmann addresses the problem in education of a lack of advocacy for children. He argues there is a very strong non-advocacy system, which is backed by the entire educational system. The educational system described includes the law, colleges of education, local school districts, educational publishers, federal and state grant supporters, and teacher unions. Engelmann summarizes the various ways each of these entities support this non-advocacy system. He describes this system as a crisis that requires immediate action, specifically showing how these entities are responsible for the creation and continuation of this crisis. Engelmann believes the solution lies with the involvement of businesses, whether they are ready for the challenge or not.

On Observing Learning: An Essay for the DI Teacher

Engelmann, Z. (1982b). On observing learning: An essay for the DI teacher. *ADI News, 1*(2), 1, 16. (Reprinted in 1988 in *ADI News, 7*(4), 3–5.)

In this article Engelmann discusses his views on effective teaching and the environment of learning, while drawing comparisons to the Direct Instruction models. He explains how one needs to understand what children know and how they will respond to the outputs one provides. Then you will see children's minds growing and developing new pathways of understanding. Engelmann stresses understanding all the variables of how children can interpret information presented to them and how, like an experiment, it is necessary to control the variables. He focuses on these key aspects of successful instruction: show great interest in the material presented, reinforce effectively, and ensure the material is appropriate to the child's ability. Additionally he emphasizes that a teacher must challenge the student, stressing the importance of the material while still showing empathy to the difficulty of the task. Another key aspect of learning discussed is practice of the skills developed in order to establish mastery of the subject and to signify their importance to the child.

Piaget and Instruction

Engelmann, S. (1982c). Piaget and instruction. *ADI News, 2*(1), 1, 6-7.

In this article Engelmann discusses the problems with Piaget's theory of instruction. Engelmann argues Piaget's theory is basically irrelevant to instruction because it is not a theory. Rather it is a normative model that is possible, but has not been shown to be consistent with the observed behavior of children. Engelmann uses examples to demonstrate the problems with Piaget's theory in relation to instruction. He argues the major problem with Piaget's tests is not that they show the things children can't typically do at a certain age, but rather the interpretation of what the failure means.

Additionally he provides an example of his own experiment showing some of the faults of Piaget's reasoning. Engelmann concludes that it is misguided to assume that failure in Piaget's tests indicates a generic mental operational deficiency in the learner. It is more practical to view the failure as revealing things the child has not learned.

A Study of 4th–6th Grade Basal Reading Series: How Much Do They Teach?

Engelmann, Z. (1982d). A study of 4th–6th grade basal reading series: How much do they teach? *ADI News, 1*(3), 1, 4–5, 19. (Reprinted in 1989 in *ADI News, 8*(4), 17–23.)

This article reports findings of a study of teacher behavior in Grades 4, 5, and 6 as well as an analysis of the major basal reading programs used in these grades. The programs analyzed included Ginn, Scott Foresman, Houghton Mifflin, and Holt. Seventeen teachers from across the country were included in the study. The analysis focused on the clarity of communication, the adequacy of the practice, and other aspects expected to be controlled by an effective program. The major objectives of the study were to determine how well each program would teach the average student, how much teachers deviated from the guidelines of the programs, how well students responded to the instruction, how accurate and knowledgeable teachers were about their program, and what types of problems the students had. Results indicated that if a teacher followed the average program precisely, the programs would be incapable of teaching the average student because the student would be exposed to too many spurious prompts, could be confused by distractors and variation in teacher wording, would be misled by the set of examples, would receive poorly designed practice, and would experience ambiguous and confusing instructions from the teacher. The design of the programs creates the inability to teach the average student, but good teachers are able to adapt the programs in order to teach effectively to the average student. Teacher interviews revealed teachers would deviate from the program about 20% of the time. Engelmann concludes teachers are aware of the students' problems, but are not trained to effectively fix the problems.

Why Attend the Eighth Annual DI Conference?

Engelmann, Z. (1982e). Why attend the eighth annual DI conference? *ADI News, 1*(3), 1, 20.

In this article Engelmann describes the Eighth Annual DI Conference in Eugene, Oregon and the benefits of attending. Such benefits included additional training in Direct Instruction programs with some of the best trainers in the world, sessions on a variety of Direct Instruction topics, experiencing the beautiful city of Eugene and the surrounding areas filled with outdoor activities, a closing day picnic, and a tax deductible business expense. He also describes previous DI conferences and their successes and failures. Additionally Engelmann states that attendees will work hard at the conference, but will leave as better teachers.

Direct Instruction Outcomes with Middle-Class Second Graders

Engelmann, S., & Carnine, D. (1982a). Direct Instruction outcomes with middle-class second graders. *ADI News, 1*(2), 4–5. (Reprinted in 1989 in *ADI News, 8*(2), 2–5.)

This article examines a study of the effectiveness of the DISTAR instructional program on 30 middle-class second grade students. The students were tested on their academic achievement and attitude towards the Direct Instruction program. On average the students performed better than the publishers' norm score for the Stanford Achievement Test and the Wide-Range Achievement Test. Ten students were administered the Gates-McGinitie Test of Speed and Accuracy (for fourth through sixth graders) and performed above the publisher's norm. When surveyed on their attitude towards the curriculum the majority of the students enjoyed the stories, workbook, and materials either some or a lot. The authors suggest this study provides good support for the implementation of Direct Instruction programs with all students, not just children who are difficult to teach.

Theory of Instruction: Principles and Applications

Engelmann, S., & Carnine, D. (1982b). *Theory of instruction: Principles and applications.* New York: Irvington Publishing. (Reprinted in 1991 as *Theory of instruction: Principles and applications* (Rev. ed.). Eugene, OR: ADI Press.)

Engelmann and Carnine developed their theory of instruction through the application of logical analysis to existing empirical observation, following the principles of natural science theories. Their theory is based on two assumptions: learners perceive qualities, and they generalize upon the foundation of the sameness of qualities. Engelmann and Carnine provide guidelines to effective instruction to ensure all children can learn. This comprehensive coverage of their theory is divided into 9 sections: overview of strategies, basic forms, joining forms, programs, complete teaching, constructing cognitive routines, response-locus analysis, diagnosis and corrections, and research and philosophical issues. Each section further explains the principles behind their theory, while providing examples of efficient and effective instruction.

Engelmann Compares Traditional Basals with SRA's New *Reading Mastery* 3 & 4

Engelmann, S. (1983). Engelmann compares traditional basals with SRA's new *Reading Mastery* 3 & 4. *ADI News, 2*(3), 28–31.

In this article Engelmann compares the Direct Instruction program *Reading Mastery* with traditional basal programs. He explains how *Reading Mastery* was designed to solve the typical problems students encountered in traditional basal reading programs. The major problems with basal programs are outlined, and how they are accounted for within the *Reading Mastery* program is explained. These problems include developing decoding and comprehension skills, the lack of integration of skills, and the use of less-effective literature. The article provides examples of literature used by *Reading Mastery* and basal programs, highlighting how the *Reading Mastery* literature is more effective. Engelmann describes how appropriate literature selection aids the development of vocabulary, comprehension, inductions, and perspectives.

Teach Your Child to Read in 100 Easy Lessons

Engelmann, S., Haddox, P., & Bruner, E. (1983). *Teach your child to read in 100 easy lessons.* New York: Simon & Schuster.

This book consists of 100 short step-by-step lessons for beginning readers. The program was originally designed for parents to help their children become good readers. The program is an abbreviated version of *Reading Mastery* Levels I and II, using the same orthography and sequence of introduction for letter-sound correspondences.

Generalized Compliance Training: A Direct-Instruction Program For Managing Severe Behavior Problems

Engelmann, S., & Colvin, G. (1983). *Generalized compliance training: A Direct-Instruction program for managing severe behavior problems.* Austin, TX: Pro-Ed Publishing.

This book discusses a Direct Instruction program for managing severe behavior problems in children. This program, *Generalized Compliance Training,* is designed for students with severe behavior problems, which cannot be treated using sensible instruction, appropriate reinforcement, pacing, and other generally effective teaching techniques. The program has the ability to dramatically change behavior after a few weeks of implementation, leading to greater compliance with teacher requests. The program's main goals are eliminating the child's noncompliant and inappropriate behaviors, and teaching compliant behaviors. The book is divided into sections covering the major topics of program design and objectives, generalizations, administering the program on a case by case basis, working with parents, and research on generalized-compliance training.

DI for Severely Handicapped Learners

Singer, G., Close, D., Colvin, G., & Engelmann, S. (1983). DI for severely handicapped learners. *ADI News*, 2(4), 3–4.

This article discusses the difficulties of teaching students with severe handicaps and how the authors have used aspects of the Direct Instruction model to more effectively teach these student new skills and prevent their social failure. Multiple examples of applying Direct Instruction principles to teaching severely handicapped learners with various conditions are provided. Results of a norm-referenced measure of adaptive and maladaptive behavior indicated the instruction had a statistically significant effect on gains in adaptive behavior and significant reductions in maladaptive behaviors. Additionally some of the students described were able to return home from the state hospitals they resided in following treatment.

The Direct Instruction Model

Carnine, D., & Engelmann, S. (1984). The Direct Instruction model. In S. C. Paine, G. T. Bellamy, & B. Wilcox (Eds.), *Human services that work: From innovation to standard practice* (pp. 133–148). Baltimore, MD: Brookes Publishing.

Carnine and Engelmann provide an overview of the Direct Instruction model, detailing its structure, goals, rationale and history. The major assumptions behind the Direct Instruction model are listed. The key components of the Direct Instruction model are thoroughly detailed, explaining their rationale in terms of the programs' goals. The components of Direct Instruction covered include specialized staff roles, Direct Instruction materials, staff training, time use, an implementation plan, a supervision and management system, data collection and monitoring procedures, and active parent involvement. Carnine and Engelmann also describe the current use of the Direct Instruction model as well as its involvement and success in Project Follow Through. Additionally the authors discuss how to build a successful model and the difficulties doing so.

Reading Comprehension Instruction in Grades 4, 5, and 6: Program Characteristics; Teacher Perceptions; Teacher Behaviors; And Student Performance.

Engelmann, S., & Meyer, L. A. (1984). *Reading comprehension instruction in grades 4, 5, and 6: Program characteristics; teacher perceptions; teacher behaviors; and student performance.* Paper presented at the 68th Annual Meeting of the American Educational Research Association (New Orleans, LA, April 23–27, 1984). Chicago: Science Research Associates.

This paper discusses a three-part study designed to examine reading comprehension in Grades 4, 5, and 6 to determine the effectiveness of instructional materials, the adequacy of teacher presentation, and the student outcomes they achieve. In the first part of the study four basal reading programs were analyzed in terms of clarity of communication, adequacy of skill practice provided, and other components related to comprehension. The second part involved videotaping 17 teachers as they taught two comprehension topics. The teachers were subsequently interviewed to determine their opinions on the programs used and their students' level of mastery of the content.

Their responses were compared to a larger study of teachers who had filled out a questionnaire. The third part examined the performance of the students of the observed teachers on criterion-referenced tests, developed to cover the content taught. Results indicated the programs' text presentations were inadequate in terms of their instructional design. Additionally teachers did not alter the text to improve the instruction and their perceptions on their teaching skills and student achievement were inaccurate. Engelmann and Meyer conclude basal reading programs must be revised to include more direct teaching and practice in reading comprehension.

Hanner, S., & Engelmann, S. (1984). Learner Verification for *Corrective Reading* Program. *Australian Association for Direct Instruction Newsletter,* May, 3–5.*

Video Disk Instruction

Carnine, D., Engelmann, S., & Hofmeister, A. (1984–1985). Video disk instruction. *ADI News, 4*(2), 3, 5, 2.

This article describes the effectiveness of video disk instruction and the issues of its implementation in schools. The authors describe the video disk as "one of the most potent technologies available to educators," because of its ability to store and present tens of thousands of images as well as easy navigation. Video disks are able to provide tutorials, as well as simulations and drill and practice sessions, while still allowing the teacher to maintain a central role in the instruction process by determining areas of focus and review. The use of video disks has been shown to simplify the instruction of scientific concepts, because of the ability to utilize slow motion and freeze frames. A video disk program titled *Core Concepts* is discussed in terms of effectiveness, specifically its focus on teaching to mastery and teacher feedback.

Designing Videodisc-Based Courseware for the High School

Hofmeister, A. M., Engelmann, S., & Carnine, D. (1985a). *Designing videodisc-based courseware for the high school.* Paper presented at the Annual Meeting of the American Educational Research Association (Chicago, IL, March 31–April 4, 1985).

This article discusses the development of a videodisc instructional program for high school math and science classes, *Core Concepts in Math and Science,* and the issues with designing a videodisc program for the needs of a public high school. The paper is divided into two sections: a rationale for interactive videodisc instruction and an overview of a videodisc program (*Core Concepts in Math and Science*). The first section classifies the different types of videodisc instruction and discusses staff development and student achievement. The second section provides an overview of the program,

---

*   A copy of this publication was not located.

explaining the instructional format, development and validation procedures, and observations from field testing. The authors conclude that properly implemented videodisc technology along with mastery learning procedures can provide a teacher with a flexible and powerful resource.

Videodisc-Based Courseware for the High School Mainstream

Hofmeister, A. M., Engelmann, S., & Carnine, D. (1985b). *Videodisc-based courseware for the high school mainstream.* Paper presented at the Third Annual Conference on Interactive Instruction Delivery in Education, Training, and Job Performance (February 13–15, 1985, Orlando, FL). Warrenton, VA: Society for Applied Learning Technology.

This paper discusses the use and development of videodisc instruction technology, and presents the results of field testing on a videodisc instructional program designed specifically for the needs and characteristics of public high schools. Key areas of focus for the program include an emphasis on core concepts common to most courses of study, the use of a direct mastery-oriented approach to instructional presentations, associated classroom management procedures, a videodisc design, which allows the disc to be used at both Level 1 and Level 3 modes, and an emphasis on dynamic presentations of effective instructors instead of a "programmed learning" format. Additionally the math and science programs were designed to aid staff development in addition to student learning.

The Development and Validation of an Instructional Videodisc Program

Hofmeister, A. M., Engelmann, S., & Carnine, D. (1986a). The development and validation of an instructional videodisc program. In W. Sybouts & D. J. Stevens (Eds.), *National videodisc symposium for education: A national agenda* (pp. 25–33). Lincoln, NE: University of Nebraska–Lincoln.

This article discusses the development and validation of the Direct Instruction videodisc program *Mastering Fractions*. The discussion is divided into three sections: formative development, stress testing with younger students and remedial students, and independent regional implementations and evaluation. Additionally observations from field testing are included.

Observations from the Development and Field Testing of an Instructional Videodisc Program

Hofmeister, A. M., Engelmann, S., & Carnine, D. (1986b). Observations from the development and field testing of an instructional videodisc program. *Journal of Special Education Technology*, 7(3), 42–46.

This article discusses the development and validation of a videodisc program *Core Concepts in Math and Science*, which was designed to fit the needs of students of varying skill levels. Main topics discussed include instructional format, development and validation procedures, and observations from field testing. Results from field testing showed that interactive videodisc technology in combination with well researched instructional design and mastery learning procedures provided the teacher with a powerful and elastic teaching tool.

Videodisc Technology: Providing Instructional Alternatives

Hofmeister, A. M., Engelmann, S., & Carnine, D. (1986c). Videodisc technology: Providing instructional alternatives. *Journal of Special Education Technology, 7*(3), 35–41.

This article discusses the use of videodisc instruction in public schools as well as the various models of videodisc instruction and the technology involved. The different models are described in detail and are discussed in terms of student achievement goals, staff development, and school resources. Particular attention is given to the application of videodisc instruction to special education students as an effective alternative approach to traditional instruction. The authors speculate on the effectiveness of implementing the various videodisc instruction models. They conclude that videodisc instruction is one of the best technological alternatives for modeling effective teaching presentations and increasing student achievement. Additionally, they argue that interactive videodisc technology has the ability to let teachers adapt the instruction for students of various skills.

Videodisc Technology: Providing the Teacher with Alternatives

Hofmeister, A. M., Engelmann, S., & Carnine, D. (1986d). Videodisc technology: Providing the teacher with alternatives. In W. Sybouts & D. J. Stevens (Eds.), *National videodisc symposium for education: A national agenda* (pp. 34–39). Lincoln, NE: University of Nebraska–Lincoln.

This article discusses the use of videodisc technology in education, specifically the rationale used to develop videodisc based instruction for high school mathematics. Videodisc instruction would be designed for a variety of learners and settings, including group and individual instruction. Main topics discussed include videodisc hardware, instructional potential, clarifying types of instructional videodisc configurations, educational implications, staff development and student achievement, and effective instruction and the high-school learner.

Videodisc Instruction in Fractions

Carnine, D., Engelmann, S., Hofmeister, A., & Kelly, B. (1987). Videodisc instruction in fractions. *Focus on Learning Problems in Mathematics, 9*(1), 31–52.

In response to major problems in teaching fractions in the U.S. this article discusses the applicability of laser videodisc technology to teaching fractions more efficiently and effectively. The authors promote videodisc technology as a potential solution because of its effective teacher presentation techniques, which involve clear explanations of key concepts, and the ability to provide effective remediation for both groups and individuals. Main topics discussed include the development and instructional design features of the *Mastering Fractions* program, a review of relevant research on mathematics instruction, an overview of the use of videodisc technology, how videodisc curriculum was field tested to increase efficiency, and results from an experimental study.

Educational Guidelines: Who is Kidding Whom?

Engelmann, Z. (1987). Educational guidelines: Who is kidding whom? *ADI News, 6*(4), 2–3.

In this article Engelmann describes the problems he has encountered with school policies and guidelines. He asserts that the current practices and guidelines are outdated and hinder the ability to promote students' academic success. Engelmann states schools are failing by not following intelligent techniques for solving their problems. He provides multiple examples to illustrate his argument. Engelmann explains how schools are aware of their failure to teach students necessary skills for their grades and are not reacting in a way to rectify the problem effectively. Schools create guidelines, which Engelmann argues function as self-fulfilling prophecies that will result in skills not being taught effectively. He believes that one of the major issues with the guidelines is that they are created by people who have most likely not been in classes where these guidelines and practices are used to teach students. Therefore, they do not have the first-hand experience to understand what works in classrooms. To solve this problem, Engelmann believes guidelines should be based on data. Programs should only be adopted if they have been proven to be successful for all students within the predicted time frame. Additionally it must be determined if all teachers can be successfully trained to teach the program and if the school district can provide monitoring to insure proper implementation.

Graduate Training in Special Education: A Focus on Instructional Leadership

Woodward, J., Carnine, D., Gersten, R., Engelmann, S., & Gleason, M. (1987). Graduate training in special education: A focus on instructional leadership. *ADI News, 7*(1), 10–11.

This article describes a Special Education doctoral program at the University of Oregon. The program focuses on the details of instruction, such as the amount of practice it takes for a teacher to teach effectively and the amount of practice for children to learn a skill. The program focuses on the details of instruction, basing its design on the theory that a strong understanding of the details of instruction is critical to making administrative decisions. The design of this program is the result of research that found that instructional supervisors were not properly trained enough to provide adequate systematic teacher feedback to instructors with difficult-to-teach students. Three key areas of training are supervision, in-service training and college teaching, and research and evaluation. The program was designed for graduates to develop a firm understanding of the relationship between the supervisor's decisions, teacher instruction, and the performance of the special education students.

The Logic and Facts of Effective Supervision

Engelmann, S. (1988a). The logic and facts of effective supervision. *Education and Treatment of Children,* *11*(4), 328–340.

In this article Engelmann analyzes what he determined to be the six key components to effective supervision: going beyond teachers' verbal report to direct observation in analyzing problems, timely identification of problems before they become chronic, careful analysis of programs being used for their design adequacies and correcting inadequacies when required, providing for extensive teacher practice in structured settings, providing additional supervised practice in the classroom, and recognizing that the supervisor must be well trained in the specific skills needed to be effective. He provides a series of facts about teaching and supervision, and a conclusion about each problem or assessment presented. Engelmann argues controlling teacher behavior in the classroom is essential for managing what students learn, how they learn, and how their attitudes are changed. Additionally Engelmann reviews research on the impact of supervision in education.

Theories, Theories, Theories: A Critique of Logic of Whole Language Arguments

Engelmann, S. (1988b). Theories, theories, theories: A critique of logic of whole language arguments. *ADI News, 7*(3), 5–6.

In this article Engelmann thoroughly critiques the theories behind Whole Language reading instruction. Engelmann believes the Whole Language approach lacks scientific data of its success and its theories are logically unsound. The rationale behind the Whole Language approach is that written language should be learned incidentally because oral language is learned incidentally. However Engelmann argues oral and written language are quite different and thus require more specifically tailored instruction. He provides counter arguments to the premises of the Whole Language theories, demonstrating the irrationality of its assumptions. Engelmann concludes that even though the Whole Language program is a popular means of instruction in multiple states, its argument is a study of fantasy.

The Direct Instruction Follow Through Model: Design and Outcomes

Engelmann, S., Becker, W. C., Carnine, D., & Gersten, R. (1988). The Direct Instruction Follow Through model: Design and outcomes. *Education and Treatment of Children, 11*(4), 303–317.

This article examines the results of the Direct Instruction model from project Follow Through. Research findings are discussed as well as the components of the Direct Instruction model. Key components covered include the curriculum, increasing teaching time, efficiently teaching, implementation, teacher expectations and attitudes, parental involvement, and comprehensive services. Follow Through researchers determined Direct Instruction students were close to or at national norms on all measures of achievement and the Direct Instruction model was the only model to show consistently positive outcomes across all measures. Additionally one researcher reported Direct Instruction parents believed their children received better education in the primary grades than parents of students enrolled in the other programs. Direct Instruction students were reported as developing both basic and cognitive skills. Studies of low-IQ students showed the Direct Instruction program was clearly effective with students who had a higher probability of failure. During the 1980–81 school year the Department of Education's Joint Dissemination Review Panel certified all 12 Direct Instruction Follow Through projects as exemplary in reading and mathematics for the primary grades. The authors conclude the article by providing implications of the findings on the Direct Instruction model.

Supporting Teachers and Students in Math and Science Education Through Videodisc Courses

Engelmann, S., & Carnine, D. (1989). Supporting teachers and students in math and science education through videodisc courses. *Educational Technology, 29*(8), 46–50.

In response to the poor performance of students in mathematics and science nationwide Engelmann and Carnine promote the use of videodisc curriculum in mathematics and science to support student and teacher achievement. The videodisc curriculum they promote would work with virtually all students, provide benefits quickly, and the implementation would be manageable. Research indicates students who used the videodisc programs learned significantly more than students in traditional programs. Furthermore research on students with learning disabilities showed they achieved the same performance as above average students in traditional programs. The authors also discuss the importance of field testing and revisions with the videodisc programs.

Developing and Validating Science Education Videodiscs

Hofmeister, A. M., Engelmann, S., & Carnine, D. (1989). Developing and validating science education videodiscs. *Journal of Research in Science Teaching, 26*(8), 665–677.

This article discusses the conceptualization, development, and formative evaluation of a series of videodiscs entitled *Core Concepts in Math and Science.* The program was designed to be used for both group and individual instruction. Main topic areas covered include hardware, courseware and instructional settings, development and formative evaluation procedures, and field test results. The authors conclude that data implies videodisc programs can enhance the effectiveness of teachers, student achievement and student attitudes.

Teaching Absolute Pitch

Williams, P., & Engelmann, S. (1989). Teaching absolute pitch. *ADI News, 9*(1), 23–26.

This article addresses the issues of trying to teach highly unfamiliar skills and its relation to understanding human growth and development. Williams and Engelmann conducted a study to teach a group of first graders to develop absolute pitch using effective Direct Instruction strategies. The majority of the students could not sing on pitch prior to the study. A control group of high school music students was included in the study. Success was determined by the student's ability to discriminate notes and produce notes. Results indicated the experimental students outperformed the control group in overall ability to estimate the notes. The authors concluded that the process of learning absolute pitch follows the same pattern of learning other highly unfamiliar content. Furthermore the use of reinforcement, models, and basic instructional techniques were shown to be effective in teaching new skills.

1990s

Making Connections in Third Grade Mathematics: *Connecting Math Concepts*

Carnine, D., & Engelmann, S. (1990). Making connections in third grade mathematics: *Connecting Math Concepts. ADI News, 10*(1), 17–27.

In this article Carnine and Engelmann discuss how their mathematics program *Connecting Math Concepts* helps to instill an integrated schema for mathematics in third grade students. They assert that once students understand the key relationships in mathematics they will make important connections that are critical to developing computational proficiency. Carnine and Engelmann provide a series of examples showcasing their strategies to instructing students and how these strategies help students understand important math concepts. The program helps students develop strategies for solving addition, subtraction, multiplication, division, fraction, and word problems that were considered the most prevalent and frustrating math application in primary grade mathematics programs. The program was designed to develop understanding and proficiency in mathematics as well as preparing students for more complicated problem solving, which they will encounter in later grades. Early evaluations of the program showed that the *Connecting Math Concepts* students outperformed students in traditional basal programs.

Teachers, Schema, and Instruction

Engelmann, S. (1990). Teachers, schema, and instruction. *ADI News, 9*(3), 27–35. (Reprinted in 1991 as Teachers, schemata, and instruction. In M. Kennedy (Ed.), *Teaching academic subjects to diverse learners* (Rev. ed., pp. 218-233). New York: Teachers College Press.)

In this article Engelmann critiques Robert E. Floden's "What Teachers Need to Know about Learning." He begins by providing his own answers to Floden's question of what teachers need to know about learning and then concludes by explaining why he would not follow any of Floden's recommendations. Engelmann promotes some of the principles of Direct Instruction such as appropriate pacing, appropriate inflection and stress, appropriate responses to students who perform well, and appropriate responses to students who make errors. He believes teachers need to act like technicians, identifying problems with the instruction and reacting effectively and efficiently. Furthermore they need to fully understand the relationship between teaching and student performance. Engelmann thoroughly refutes Floden's answers for what teachers need to know about learning by explaining why they won't work or won't work as efficiently as his ideas. He uses multiple models to show the problems in Floden's theories and how his own are more effective and efficient. Engelmann concludes that even if programs are well designed to teach all students, the program only has potential. The potential can only be achieved if a teacher has the necessary skills to effectively communicate with the students.

Teaching Problem Solving in Mathematics

Steely, D., Carnine, D., & Engelmann, S. (1990). Teaching problem solving in mathematics. *ADI News*, *10*(1), 28–39.

This article describes Engelmann and Carnine's sameness analysis and how it is used to develop an understanding of mathematical relationships in order to solve mathematics problems. The authors begin by investigating the definition of problem solving and then analyze the issues of teaching it. They go on to show how the sameness analysis works by using a series of examples applied to a variety of problem types for students in Grades 1 through 7. The sameness analysis is based on strategies that can be applied to a variety of problem types. Relevant background knowledge is essential to utilizing strategies effectively and efficiently. Mastery of background strategies is essential to learning new strategies. Otherwise background knowledge must be learned simultaneously, which may cause confusion for the student.

Change Schools Through Revolution, Not Evolution

Engelmann, S. (1991a). Change schools through revolution, not evolution. *Journal of Behavioral Education*, *1*(3), 295–304.

In this article Engelmann aggressively advocates for comprehensive school reform in order to overcome the history of failure in public schools. He argues an extreme approach is needed to overcome the indoctrinated practices currently present in school systems and to achieve success for all students. Engelmann asserts school systems reject practices that are not in line with their guidelines and objectives even if these guidelines and objectives have led to very poor implementation and underwhelming results. He provides examples of this level of failure in school systems and then continues on to provide solutions for the success of all students. In order to achieve success the foundation of these schools must be changed and become data-oriented, focused on what has been proven to be successful in the past. Additionally administrators must have technical understanding and both administrators and teachers must be viewed as causes of failure for students. Engelmann provides guidelines to establish change in school systems. A key concept of his guidelines is to fire administrators who fail to meet attainable student achievement goals thus providing positive reinforcement to administrators when students achieve. Administrators would be held accountable for student success, ensuring teachers are properly instructing students with the best methods, and the students are in the best environment to achieve.

Engelmann, S. (1991b). How Sensible is Your Reading Program? A Closer Look at Learner Verification. *California Journal for Supervision and Curriculum Improvement, 4(1), 16–22.*

Why I Sued California

Engelmann, S. (1991c). Why I sued California. *ADI News, 10*(2), 4–8.

This article examines Siegfried Engelmann's lawsuit against the California State Board, Department of Education and Curriculum Commission. Engelmann's lawsuit was intended to reverse the education practices of the state of California, which were theoretically based and supported by peripheral data or anecdotal information, instead of field data. Engelmann argues that no one in the decision making hierarchy had an expert understanding of teaching or management and they were not willing to adjust teaching practices to create equity. Additionally Engelmann critiques the current teaching practices, which promoted whole language instruction as well as the justifications for their implementation. He also addresses the issues of legal compliance, content evaluation for the current teaching practices, and discusses the *DISTAR Reading Mastery* program.

Making Connections in Mathematics

Engelmann, S., Carnine, D., & Steely, D. G. (1991). Making connections in mathematics. *Journal of Learning Disabilities, 24*(5), 292–303. (Reprinted in 1992 in D. Carnine & E. J. Kame'enui (Eds.), *Higher order thinking: Designing curriculum for mainstreamed students* (Rev. ed., pp. 75–106). Austin, TX: PRO-ED.)

In response to the perceived link between math textbooks and poor math performance by U.S. students, this article describes the problems of current math textbooks used in the U.S. and then provides an alternative perspective on mathematics instruction, Engelmann and Carnine's sameness analysis. The sameness analysis is explained in depth, describing how it teaches the addition-subtraction and multiplication-division relationships, as well as their interrelationships in order to solve word problems. In support of the sameness analysis, the authors cite research conducted with at-risk students and students with learning disabilities, and provide examples and diagrams to explain how the sameness analysis is applied and mathematical relationships and interrelationships are developed.

Technology and Teacher Enhancement: A Videodisc Alternative

Hofmeister, A. M., Engelmann, S., & Carnine, D. (1991). Technology and teacher enhancement: A videodisc alternative. *Technology in Education*. Alexandria, VA: Association for Supervision and Curriculum Development.

---

* A copy of this publication was not located.

In response to the concern of technology-based products stressing instructor replacement in schools and the effectiveness of these programs this article discusses the design and validation of a series of math and science videodisc programs. These programs were designed to enhance the instructional effectiveness of teachers and use effective methods, which would apply to both individual and group instruction. The authors examine the problems involved with implementing videodisc programs. Major topics discussed include hardware and courseware, capturing characteristics of effective instruction, initial development, validation results, and enhancing teacher effectiveness. Additionally an independent study on the use of the *Core Concepts* programs is discussed.

War Against the Schools' Academic Child Abuse

Engelmann, S. (1992). *War against the schools' academic child abuse.* Portland, OR: Halcyon House.

In this book Engelmann examines the major problems in the U.S. educational system. He describes the problems with the various instructional programs and theories, the schools that adopt them, and the teachers who utilize them. Engelmann attributes the problems in schools to the ignorance of what can be done with kids versus what is currently being done. He goes on to describe rules that education publishers, boards of education, teacher training institutions, school administrators, funding agencies, and the educational press need to follow in order for the active academic child abuse and unnecessary failure to be resolved in three to four years. Major topics covered include the reform cycle, basal programs, academic child abuse, effective teaching, theories of instruction, the roots of failure, and the path to success.

The Curriculum as the Cause of Failure

Engelmann, S. (1993). The curriculum as the cause of failure. *The Oregon Conference Monograph, 5*, 3–8. (Also available from http://zigsite.com/PDFs/Curriculumascauseoffailurepdffinal.pdf)

In this monograph Engelmann discusses why students fail to learn, specifically looking at the role of curriculum. He explains why curriculum is responsible for the failure of some students and not the students' abilities. Engelmann describes the importance of communication in curriculum and avoiding mis-learning. Examples of problems resulting from poor communication and poorly designed programs are discussed and analyzed. Additionally Engelmann describes how to develop successful curriculum programs that avoid the problems described and commonly found in popular curriculum.

Research on Direct Instruction: 25 Years Beyond DISTAR

Adams, G. L., & Engelmann, S. (1996). *Research on Direct Instruction: 25 years beyond DISTAR.* Seattle, WA: Educational Achievement Systems.

This book was written in response to the unfounded negative views of Direct Instruction and a lack of a thorough scientific review of the effectiveness of Direct Instruction. It is designed to show what Direct Instruction is and is not while also providing a comprehensive meta-analysis consisting of 37 research articles. Results of the meta-analysis showed a large effect size, rarely produced in academic achievement. Engelmann begins the book by providing a history of Direct Instruction, an overview of its principles, and a discussion of common misconceptions about its programs. Adams provides his rationale for the meta-analysis, the procedures used for the meta-analysis, and the results of the meta-analysis. He goes on to review Project Follow Through as well as subsequent follow up studies on the success of the Direct Instruction students. Additional studies and technical reports, which did not meet criteria for inclusion in the meta-analysis are listed. Even though they were not included in the meta-analysis they also showed the positive effects of Direct Instruction programs and its principles.

Sponsor Findings from Project Follow Through

Becker, W., & Engelmann, S. (1996). Sponsor findings from Project Follow Through. *Effective School Practices, 15*(1), 33–42.

In this article Becker and Engelmann report their findings from the results of the National Evaluation of Project Follow Through. They describe the structure of Project Follow Through, the groups included in the study, the tests used to determine success, the final report's findings, teacher opinions, and implications of the findings on Direct Instruction. Results indicate the Direct Instruction model was by far the most effective program of all the programs tested. Additionally results showed the Direct Instruction model was almost as effective with low-IQ students as with high-IQ students. Follow up studies showed Direct Instruction students continued to outperform the comparison students in high school. The Department of Education's Joint Dissemination Review Panel reviewed the remaining Direct Instruction Follow Through projects and certified them all as exemplary in reading and mathematics for the primary grades.

Direct Instruction

Engelmann, S. (1997a). Direct Instruction. In C. R. Dills & A. J. Romiszowski (Eds.), *Instructional development paradigms* (pp. 371-389). Englewood Cliffs, NJ: Educational Technology Publications.

Engelmann thoroughly examines and explains what defines Direct Instruction (upper-case DI) and what makes it different from other terms and processes known as direct instruction (lower-case di). The major difference between the two is that Direct Instruction is much more specific in terms of details about teacher presentations and curricular details. The main topics covered include the need for logical analysis, instructional programs, logical hierarchies, generalizations and limitations, familiarity vs. logic, and efficiency. Additionally Engelmann describes the theories behind Direct Instruction and its various applications with students of different ages and skill levels.

Theory of Mastery and Acceleration

Engelmann, S. (1997b). Theory of mastery and acceleration. In J. W. Lloyd, E. J. Kame'enui, & D. Chard (Eds.), *Issues in educating students with disabilities* (pp. 177–195). Mahwah, NJ: Lawrence Erlbaum.

In this article Engelmann explains and discusses the use of the theory of mastery and acceleration. His discussion of the theory builds on his previous work with Douglas Carnine on how children learn in the book *Theory of Instruction*. Engelmann discusses the importance of teaching to mastery and the difficulties in doing so, especially with low performing students. He demonstrates how learning to mastery enhances the child's ability to learn how to learn, which leads to an acceleration of intellectual performance in any field of study. Key topic areas discussed include appropriate materials, appropriate placement of children in programs, operating plan and structure, evidence of effectiveness, and implications. Additionally Engelmann discusses the success of multiple Direct Instruction sites that followed the plan outlined.

The Benefits of Direct Instruction: Affirmative Action for At-Risk Students

Engelmann, S. (1999a). The benefits of Direct Instruction: Affirmative action for at-risk students. *Educational Leadership, 57*(1), 77, 79.

In this article Engelmann examines the problem of at-risk students not achieving the same level of success as their more affluent peers. He provides an explanation for why at-risk students do not exhibit the same levels of academic success as their peers and how the use of Direct Instruction programs could reduce the achievement gap. Engelmann believes the optimum time to reduce the achievement gap is between preschool and first grade because at-risk students typically come into first grade substantially behind their peers in pre-reading, language, and number skills. To solve this achievement gap Engelmann proposes a well-designed highly structured preschool-Kindergarten, which allows teachers to provide more practice in less time than traditional schools. The structure helps push the at-risk students academically ahead of their more affluent peers. If the at-risk students are academically ahead when leaving Kindergarten they are more likely to remain competitive despite the competition favoring the more affluent students.

Phonemic Awareness in *Reading Mastery*

Engelmann, S. (1999b). Phonemic awareness in *Reading Mastery*. *Effective School Practices, 17*(3), 43–49.

In this article Engelmann explains the use of phonemic awareness in teaching children to read, specifically how it is used in the instructional program *Reading Mastery*. He discusses the history of the use of phonemic awareness and how it is used to identify metacognitive underpinnings that enable children to relate sounds to the symbols that compose words. Additionally he describes the various practices to develop phonemic awareness, such as word segmentation, word blending, rhyming, and alliteration. Other topics covered include the relation between phonemic awareness, the DISTAR reading programs, and effective instructional design for teaching reading skills. Engelmann provides examples and models from *Reading Mastery* to demonstrate how phonemic awareness is developed.

A Response: How Sound is High/Scope Research?

Engelmann, S. (1999c). A response: How sound is High/Scope research? *Educational Leadership, 56*(6), 83–84.

In this article Engelmann critiques the research of J. Schweinhart and David P. Weikart in their paper "Why Curriculum Matters in Early Childhood Education." Schweinhart and Weikart argued that students who had attended a Direct Instruction preschool had a higher rate of felony arrests than students who attended the High/Scope or the Nursery School preschools, claiming the results were based on what they labeled as rigorous research. Engelmann thoroughly examines and critiques their research, highlighting potential areas of manufactured statistics and arguing that there was no strong evidence linking felony arrest records solely to preschool instruction. The main topics discussed include mathematical inconsistencies, variations in student experiences, errors and discrepancies, arrests versus conviction data, and the effect of the duration of the preschool experience. Engelmann concludes that the study provides no statistically significant data linking felony arrest records with the experience of attending a Direct Instruction preschool and that the authors' arguments liberally break the rules of logic and common sense.

Response to "The High/Scope Preschool Curriculum Comparison Study Through Age 23."

Engelmann, S. (1999d). Response to "The High/Scope preschool curriculum comparison study through age 23." *Effective School Practices, 17*(3), 18–23.

In this article Engelmann responds to the Schweinhart and Weikart study entitled "The High/Scope Preschool Curriculum Comparison Study Through Age 23." He thoroughly challenges their statistical findings as well as their assertion that a Direct Instruction preschool was directly related to antisocial behavior. Engelmann determined there were many areas of concern over the design of the study and the interpretation of the data. Besides having the majority of the data being non-significant, the authors use percentages rather than actual numbers when discussing the data, giving the impression that the study included a large student population when it did not. Engelmann shows discrepancies in the data analysis, specifically when percentages listed are mathematically impossible due to the number of students in the study and the reported interviews with those students. Additionally the data, which was used to suggest that Direct Instruction directly relates to antisocial behavior, is based on arrest records not whether the individuals were found guilty of the crimes they were arrested for. Engelmann concludes that Weikart and Schweinhart's conclusions are unscientific and illogical.

Student-Program Alignment and Teaching to Mastery

Engelmann, S. (1999e). Student-program alignment and teaching to mastery. Paper presented at the 25th National Direct Instruction Conference, Eugene, OR. (Reprinted in 2007 in the *Journal of Direct Instruction, 7*(1), 45–66.)

In this article Engelmann explains the importance of teaching to mastery and the necessity of having a curriculum program that does so. He describes the features of a Direct Instruction program, which teaches to mastery. The main features covered include properties of mastery, criteria and procedures for measuring mastery, procedures for teaching to mastery, procedures for aligning student skills with appropriate programs, and the benefits of learning to mastery. Engelmann concludes that teaching to mastery is the most effective use of instructional time and results in students learning how to learn.

2000s

About Reading: A Comparison of *Reading Mastery* and *Horizons*

Engelmann, S. (2000). About reading: A comparison of *Reading Mastery* and *Horizons*. *Effective School Practices, 18*(3), 15–26.

In this article Engelmann compares and contrasts two reading programs he developed; *Reading Mastery* and *Horizons*. Each program has been shown to be effective in teaching reading skills to any child with an IQ of 70 or above in a similar time period. Engelmann lists the features the programs have in common and then goes on to explain how they differ. He provides an overview of each program, highlighting the goals for the program, assumptions about the students, and strategies used. *Horizons* was created in part to resolve criticisms of the *Reading Mastery* program. Engelmann uses various examples to show how the different techniques are used for each model.

Wesley Becker, the Man

Engelmann, S. (2001). Wesley Becker, the man. *Journal of Direct Instruction, 1*(1), 27–29.

Following the death of Wesley Becker, Engelmann reflects on Becker's career and his relationship with him. Engelmann covers his early professional relationship with Becker beginning in the 1960s at the University of Illinois. He praises Becker's disciplined work habits, determination to succeed in the face of adversity, passion for educating children, and many professional accomplishments.

Models and Expectations

Engelmann, S. (2002a). *Models and expectations.* Eugene, OR: National Institute for Direct Instruction, 1–22.

In this article Engelmann discusses the process of how people learn roles and develop positive self-images. Both of these are important aspects in learning. If students play the role of good students and have positive and confident self-images their ability to succeed in school is heightened, because they are more likely to work hard and learn faster. Additionally students with positive attitudes are easier to teach in terms of their willingness to learn and ability to receive and learn new information. Engelmann details the components to developing positive roles and self-images in students and describes a program that dictates the appropriate steps to accomplish this.

Hirsch's Cargo Cults Revisited

Engelmann, S. (2002b). *Prologue to Hirsch's cargo cults revisited.* Available from http://zigsite.com/HirschPro.htm; *Hirsch's cargo cults revisited.* Available from http://zigsite.com/Hirsch.htm

In this article Engelmann responds to E. D. Hirsch's "Classroom Research and Cargo Cults." He speculates the article was intended to discredit research on Hirsch's teaching approach *Core Knowledge*, which did not show significant achievement gains with at-risk students. Engelmann thoroughly criticizes *Core Knowledge* for its overly broad application target and the design of its cultural-literacy scheme. Engelmann's responses are based in part from his experience with the academic programs in Baltimore schools. He believes Hirsch's work is well intended, but Hirsch does not know what works in schools and why programs would work.

Response to Allington: Allington Leveled Serious Allegations Against Direct Instruction

Engelmann, S. (2002c). Response to Allington: Allington leveled serious allegations against Direct Instruction. *ADI News, 2*(2), 28–31.

In this article Engelmann responds to Richard Allington's criticisms of Direct Instruction in his paper "What do we know about the effects of Direct Instruction on student reading achievement?" Engelmann thoroughly refutes Allington's criticisms of Direct Instruction. Allington argued research on Direct Instruction is tainted and the effectiveness of it is misrepresented, including the results of project Follow Through. Engelmann asserts Allington misinterprets quotes about project Follow Through. Furthermore he challenges his interpretation of data and describes Allington as needing help in basic logic regarding some of his conclusions.

Summary of Presentation to Council of Scientific Society Presidents

Engelmann, S. (2002d). *Summary of presentation to Council of Scientific Society Presidents, December 8, 2002.* (22 pp.). Available from http://zigsite.com/PDFs/CSSP_Acceptance.pdf

In this article Engelmann summarizes the effectiveness of Direct Instruction and discusses the importance of supporting basic research with detailed evaluations and studies of effective programs and interventions. He uses statistical data with accompanying charts and graphs from Project Follow Through and more current programs to show the effectiveness of Direct Instruction. Engelmann also discusses in detail Direct Instruction programs and their controllable variables.

Science Versus Basic Educational Research

Engelmann, S. (2003). *Science versus basic educational research.* (19 pp.). Available from http://zigsite.com/PDFs/ScienceVersus.pdf. (Reprinted in 2008 in *Australasian Journal of Special Education, 32*(1), 139-157.)

In this article Engelmann discusses two methods for identifying the variables for effective instruction: scientific research and basic educational research. He identifies four different approaches to determining the variables and debates the pros and cons of each. Following this assessment Engelmann examines the Commission on Reading's research methods and interpretations. He analyzes their reviews on the data of the Direct Instruction model from Project Follow Through and more recent studies. He determined the Commission's recommendations were based on opinion, hypotheses, statements of conventional wisdom, suppositions, and not facts. Engelmann analyzes the effect of their non-scientific approach on the selection of educational programs and thus the education of children.

About *Inferred Functions of Performance and Learning*

Engelmann, S. (2004a). About *Inferred functions of performance and learning*. Available from http://zigsite.com/InferredFunctions.htm

This article discusses Engelmann and Donald Steely's book *Inferred Functions of Performance and Learning* and its importance to understanding how learning happens. He believes the book has received little attention from the field of education, specifically professionals who study theories of instruction. Engelmann details the design of the book, its key principles, and the theories behind them. He explains the inferred function analyses, while providing details about its design along with examples to illustrate the principles behind it.

At-Risk Reading Naiveté

Engelmann, S. (2004b). *At-risk reading naiveté*. Available from http://zigsite.com/EdWeekResponse.htm

In this article Engelmann responds to Dennis Baron's criticism of Direct Instruction in his article "The President's Reading Lesson." Engelmann thoroughly critiques Baron's assessments and arguments, citing the author's naiveté of at-risk students and the paper's lack of educational literacy. He provides numerous examples of the flaws in Baron's article and explains the multiple issues with them.

Chapter One, *Data Be Damned*

Engelmann, S. (2004c). Chapter one, *Data be damned*. Unpublished book. Available from http://zigsite.com/AtRisk.htm

In this article Engelmann addresses the issue of educational policy makers not making decisions based on data, but rather personal beliefs and prejudices. He argues the decision to ignore data led to the implementation of less effective educational programs and the failure of some students in school and later as adults. Engelmann begins the article by discussing the problem of teaching at-risk students and how educational policy makers attempted to solve the issue through circuitous ways. Other topics examined include the use of Direct Instruction, Project Follow Through, current education programs and trends, and scientific reasoning. Engelmann concludes that the educational system fails because it disregards data and in order to prevent this failure it is necessary is to insert people who respect and understand data into positions of power.

Comparative Preschool Study: High and Low Socioeconomic Preschoolers Learning Advanced Cognitive Skills

Engelmann, S. (2004d). Prologue Comparative preschool study: High and low socioeconomic preschoolers learning advanced cognitive skills. Available from http://zigsite.com/CompPreschPro.htm; Comparative preschool study: High and low socioeconomic preschoolers learning advanced cognitive skills. (95 pp.). Available from http://zigsite.com/PDFs/CompPreschool.pdf.

In these articles Engelmann describes his 1964 study, in which he worked with two groups of preschool students to teach them highly unfamiliar content. The first group consisted of African American students of a low socioeconomic status (SES). The second group consisted of Caucasian students from a higher SES. Engelmann's goals for the study were to teach formal operations described by Jean Piaget. He intended to teach these students formal operations, determine if the two groups displayed different patterns of learning, and to determine the types of mistakes students would make while learning the content. Engelmann provides his daily log from the experiment, which contains his predictions of which students he believed would pass the post-test after each group had completed four sessions. Additionally he provides summaries of each day he worked with the students. In conclusion Engelmann determined language skills were critical to understanding instructions, proper placement in the experiment according to skill level greatly affected student performance, students' self-image was greatly influenced by their performance, and effective instruction will strongly affect students' developmental patterns of cognitive growth. Engelmann's experience conducting this study greatly influenced the creation of the Bereiter-Engelmann preschool, the development of Direct Instruction programs and practices, his understanding of the importance of language skills in learning new content, and led to the development of the Basic Language Test. In the prologue he reflects on the experiment, what he learned from the children in the study, and the process of conducting the experiment. Additionally Engelmann describes the significant influence the experiment had on the remainder of his career.

The Dalmatian and Its Spots: Why Research-Based Recommendations Fail Logic 101

Engelmann, S. (2004e). The dalmatian and its spots: Why research-based recommendations fail logic 101. *Education Week, 23*(20), 34-35, 48. (Reprint available at http://zigsite.com/Dalmatian.htm)

In this article Engelmann addresses the illogical reasoning of researchers for establishing effective instruction. He provides examples of the flaws in logic of these researchers and the effects they have in the selection of educational programs. He goes on to explain how these flaws in reasoning occur. Engelmann concludes by providing a solution to overcoming these flaws in logic and enhancing research procedures.

District-Based Teacher Certification Model

Engelmann, S. (2004f). Prologue District-based teacher certification model. Available from http://zigsite.com/DistrictBasPro.htm; District-based teacher certification model. Available from http://zigsite.com/PDFs/DistBaseModel.pdf

In this article Engelmann discusses the need for highly trained teachers, specifically for at-risk students. He analyzes current colleges of education in terms of perceived problems with their ideology and practices. Engelmann believes colleges are not teaching the most effective approaches to teaching at-risk students. Furthermore he argues it is unlikely to convince these colleges to change their practices. Engelmann proposes a plan for district based licensure to properly train teachers in the most efficient and effective practices. He provides a detailed outline of the procedures for teacher training. Additionally he gives suggestions for issues relating to the implementation of the proposed district based model, such as licensing issues, cooperation with colleges of education, recognition of certification by other districts, and union requirements. In the prologue he describes his reasoning for writing the article as well as his experience in training teachers, supervisors, trainers, teacher aides, and high school students. Additionally Engelmann discusses how his plan is radically different from current procedures because those procedures are the cause of the problem in teacher training. In order for at-risk students to learn from the most sophisticated teachers Engelmann argues there must be meaningful changes in the regulations, policies, traditions, and laws of education.

Professional Standards in Education

Engelmann, S. (2004g). Professional standards in education. Available from http://zigsite.com/Standards.htm

In this article Engelmann discusses professional standards in education by comparing the research protocol required for graduate students and the professional standards for state and school districts. He argues that both the state and graduate students experiment on students and thus should be held to the same standards and legal requirements. Engelmann discusses specific examples of failed experimentation by the state in education reform and its consequences. He explains how if the state used the same ethical standards required by graduate students, education reform would have been more careful and strategically implemented, which would have led to the greater success of all children. Engelmann reviews specific standards required of graduate student research and demonstrates how and why they should be applied to education standards. Engelmann concludes with a discussion of the various flaws in the education system and what it takes for a real educational reform to occur.

Impediments to Scaling Up Effective Comprehensive School Reform Models

Engelmann, S. E., & Engelmann, K. E. (2004). Impediments to scaling up effective comprehensive school reform models. In T. K. Glennan Jr., S. J. Bodilly, J. R. Galegher, & K. A. Kerr (Eds.), *Expanding the reach of education reforms: Perspectives from leaders in the scale-up of educational interventions* (pp. 107-133). Santa Monica, CA: The RAND Corporation.

In this article Engelmann and Engelmann discuss the various problems involved with scaling up comprehensive school reform models in order to reverse the failure of schools to educate all students. Their identification of problems and solutions are based on their experiences implementing the Direct Instruction model of comprehensive school reform. The authors focus on three main issues: the relationship between the characteristics of a design and the ease of scaling up the design, patterns of scaling up those designs, and common obstacles to reform found in school districts. Additionally the design and theories behind the Direct Instruction model are discussed as well as experiences in implementing the model. The authors determined the most serious impediment to scaling up effective reform models is school districts' structures and practices. They argue the process would be simplified if school districts were organized well enough to allow for the implementation of models with fidelity.

Inferred Functions of Performance and Learning

Engelmann, S., & Steely, D. (2004). *Inferred functions of performance and learning.* Mahwah, NJ: Lawrence Erlbaum.

In this highly theoretical book Engelmann and Steely break down the critical elements necessary for learning new actions and concepts. They diagram the necessary functions and systems for any organism or machine to perform an unlearned task. By analyzing the key components for the simplest organisms or machines to learn Engelmann and Steely are able to construct meta blueprints to better understand the simplest and most efficient way for humans to learn. The authors determined that once the foundation for unlearned responses is established, learning mechanisms can be attached to the foundation, thus allowing for the demonstration of new, learned acts. The accumulation of new, learned acts will lead to higher order demonstrations involving concepts and language. The book is divided into four parts: performance of non-learning systems, basic learning, extended learning, and human learning and instruction. Additionally the authors assess the implications of their model in relation to artificial intelligence entities.

Litmus Test for Urban School Districts

Engelmann, S. (2005a). Litmus test for urban school districts. Available from http://zigsite.com/LitmusTest.htm

In this article Engelmann discusses the success of students in terms of two key factors, the instructional approach and the implementation. He argues the success of the program depends on the proper implementation by the school district of the program according to the developer's guidelines. Engelmann examines the problems of implementing Direct Instruction in the Chicago public schools and City Springs school in Baltimore. He concludes the paper by discussing the benefits of using a litmus test to attempt to solve the issues of implementation in large and small schools.

Reading First = Kids First

Engelmann, S. (2005b). Reading first = kids first. *Oregon's Future, 6*(1). (Reprint available from http://zigsite.com/OregonsFuture.htm)

In this article Engelmann addresses the issue of early child learning and the belief that children develop the ability to learn new concepts and skills in progressive steps and certain age ranges. Engelmann writes about the early education of an imaginary at-risk student who experiences typical problems of at-risk students in public education. The student's experiences are based on Engelmann's firsthand observations in classrooms. He demonstrates how poorly designed teaching techniques and strategies in early education not only have an immediate effect on students, but long lasting effects as well. Engelmann discusses the problems with state reading tests and how this often involves teaching children to pass the test, not teaching them to read at grade level. He concludes by discussing the effectiveness of the Direct Instruction model, its minimal use and familiarity in the education system, and the *Reading First* program, which is designed to help at-risk students succeed in school.

Zig's Commentary on Bersin's Article "Making Schools Productive."

Engelmann, S. (2005c). Zig's commentary on Bersin's article "Making schools productive." Available from http://zigsite.com/bersinsArticle.htm

In this article Engelmann responds to Alan Bersin's article "Making Schools Productive." He believes Bersin's assessment does a good job of covering some of the problems in education at a political level, but by not addressing the smaller more detailed problems found in schools and school districts any substantive school reform proves to be far more difficult. Furthermore Bersin identifies important problems in education, but seems to lack the knowledge of how to rectify these issues. Engelmann applies Bersin's logic and assessment of reform to the San Diego school district in order to create a school reform plan. If Bersin executed this relatively affordable plan he would have discovered the impressive success schools achieved with the Direct Instruction model. Engelmann concludes the article by questioning why Bersin would not administer such a plan to solve the problems he described.

Rubric for Identifying Authentic Direct Instruction Programs

Engelmann, S., & Colvin, G. (2006). *Rubric for identifying authentic Direct Instruction programs.* Eugene, OR: Engelmann Foundation.

This book was intended to articulate and illustrate most of the major principles followed in the design of Direct Instruction programs. By understanding these principles a critic will be able to determine if a program is truly a Direct Instruction program or a program based on the Direct Instruction model, following some, but not all of its principles. Furthermore Engelmann and Colvin demonstrate the high level of detail involved with what students are told, how they are tested, and how the material is practiced, reviewed and expanded in Direct Instruction programs. The book is divided into six sections: empirical features of DI, axioms of Direct Instruction, applications of DI axioms, reorganization of content, strategies for applying the DI rubric, and conclusion.

Improving Reading Rate of Low Performers

Engelmann, S. (2007a). Improving reading rate of low performers (27 pp.). Available from http://zigsite. com/PDFs/readingrate.pdf

In this article Engelmann discusses the difficulties for both students and teachers in improving the reading rate of low performers. He describes common problems encountered in teaching a faster reading rate and offers solutions to these problems. Key problems discussed include how to measure progress, how to set goals, and how to determine average, below-average and above-average performance. Additionally Engelmann provides examples of successful techniques and activities to increase reading rates.

Teaching Needy Kids in Our Backward System: 42 Years of Trying

Engelmann, S. (2007b). *Teaching needy kids in our backward system: 42 years of trying.* Eugene, OR: ADI Press.

Engelmann documents his expansive career in education and his role in developing Direct Instruction education programs designed for disadvantaged children. Engelmann and his colleagues developed the programs to aid disadvantaged children so they could be as successful as affluent children. He details the history of Project Follow Through and his experience in it, working with schools to implement Direct Instruction curriculum. Engelmann critiques the effectiveness of Project Follow Through and the bureaucracy involved. He also describes his work following the conclusion of Project Follow Through as well as the efforts of his colleagues and other education professionals in implementing and promoting Direct Instruction programs.

Direct Instruction

Crawford, D., Engelmann, K. E., & Engelmann, S. (2008). Direct Instruction. In E. M. Anderman & L. H. Anderman (Eds.), *Psychology of classroom learning: An encyclopedia* (pp. 326-330). New York: Macmillan.

This article discusses the key components of the Direct Instruction model and the philosophy behind it. The design of the Direct Instruction model is discussed as well as its history. Various Direct Instruction programs are examined and compared to other instructional programs in terms of structure and effectiveness.

Achieving a Full-School, Full-Immersion Implementation of Direct Instruction:

Engelmann, Z. (2008a). Achieving a full-school, full-immersion implementation of Direct Instruction (10 pp.). Available from http://www.nifdi.org/pdfs/Dev_Guide.pdf

In this article Engelmann discusses the challenges of and necessary procedures for achieving a full-implementation of Direct Instruction in schools. Engelmann developed a formula to accomplish this goal based on the essential principle of doing what it takes to be accountable for maximum acceleration in the performance of all students. The process takes a significant restructuring of the school's priorities, practices, classroom interactions, and infrastructure. Engelmann examines the critical roles of acceleration and accountability in the implementation process.

Machinations of What Works Clearinghouse

Engelmann, S. (2008b). Prologue Machinations of What Works Clearinghouse. Available from http://zig-site.com/prologue-wwc-10-7-08.htm; Machinations of What Works Clearinghouse (33 pp.). Available from http://www.zigsite.com/PDFs/MachinationsWWC%28V4%29.pdf

In this article Engelmann critiques the What Works Clearinghouse, basing the majority of the assessment on a letter from *Mathematica* to the National Institute for Direct Instruction's Director of Research, dated September 8, 2008. He claims the What Works Clearinghouse is irreparably biased and would require a total restructuring of its practices and management to truly determine what works in education. Engelmann's accusations are based on the What Works Clearinghouse's determination that no studies on *Reading Mastery* and its predecessor *DISTAR Reading* met their evidence standards despite there being over 90 studies regarding their effectiveness. Engelmann believes there is a critical difference between the What Works Clearinghouse's standards, procedures, and evaluation criteria and those of the researchers of the *Reading Mastery* and *DISTAR Reading* studies. He thoroughly examines what he views as problems in their standards, procedures, and evaluation criteria, which led to the dismissal of so many studies. Engelmann believes the rejection of so many studies is highly improbable and likely the result of intent and possibly ineptitude as well. He specifically analyzes the legitimate studies the What Works Clearinghouse found and the distortion techniques used. In conclusion Engelmann calls for action, specifically a full-fledged assault on the What Works Clearinghouse's framework and practices with the help of the scientific community.

Socrates and Education: Bussing

Engelmann, S. (2008c). Socrates and education: Bussing. Available from http://zigsite.com/PDFs/SocratesAndBussing.pdf

In this article Engelmann presents a dialogue between Socrates and the fictional character Dr. Gibbs, a prominent professor of education, in which they discuss learning at a coffee shop. They debate how children learn and if it is dependent upon age as Piaget's theories state. Additionally they discuss the issue of bussing and its role in aiding learning. Socrates and Gibbs debate the legitimacy of bussing and the justification for its application.

Prologue to *Low-Performer's Manual*

Engelmann, S. (2009a). Prologue to *Low-performer's manual*. Available from http://zigsite.com/LowPerformersPro.htm

This article is a response to recurring questions regarding what to do with children whose language skills are too low for the beginning language program *Language for Learning*. Engelmann published the *Low Performer's Manual* in the 1970s (Engelmann, 1974b) for children with low language skills, and this article is a continuation of his original suggestions and guidelines. Engelmann explains the difficulty in teaching these lower performers and the procedures necessary to teach students the skills required to start beginning language programs. Additionally Engelmann summarizes the *Low Performer's Manual* and its guidelines and suggestions.

Socrates on Teacher Training

Engelmann, S. (2009b). Socrates on teacher training. Available from http://zigsite.com/PDFs/SocratesTeacherTraining.pdf

In this article Engelmann presents a dialogue between Socrates and the fictional character Donald Dickerman, an executive of an organization that accredits teacher-training institutions. Situated on the deck of a cruise ship heading to the Mediterranean, the two discuss teacher training programs, specifically examining their structure, goals, and accreditation. Dickerman explains how only five states require teacher-training institutions to be accredited by an agency recognized by the U.S. Department of Education and how there are over a hundred accreditation agencies that are not recognized. The two continue their discussion focusing on the goals and structure of an accreditation program and how to determine and teach the most necessary teaching skills. Furthermore Socrates questions the validity of the accreditation agencies and the proof that they are indeed teaching the necessary skills.

2010s

The Dreaded Standards

Engelmann, S. (2010a). The dreaded standards. Available from http://zigsite.com/PDFs/TheDreadedStandards.pdf

In this article Engelmann responds to the new Common Core Standards in education, describing them as distasteful, vague, and lacking understanding of how to teach young children. He reviews the seven mandates of mathematical practices for Kindergarten and the first grade, which were devised by the committee who created the Common Core standards. Engelmann addresses the flaws in each of these mandates, specifically in relation to their use with at-risk students. He determined these mandates are the result of the committee's reliance on the Piagetian model of how children learn. Engelmann concludes by asserting that the fundamental problem with these standards and others is that they are not based on empirical evidence of what children learn and the technical details of how they learn.

Thank You, Josh Baker

Engelmann, S. (2010b). Thank you, Josh Baker. Available from http://www.zigsite.com/PDFs/ThankYouJoshBaker.pdf

In this article Engelmann discusses his first job and the influence of a co-worker named Josh Baker on his life and professional career. At age 15 Engelmann worked a summer job at Ingersoll Steel Company on the south side of Chicago. The work proved to be very physically demanding, forcing Engelmann to consider quitting after the first day. Baker convinced Engelmann he should not quit because he would learn how to perform the job properly and become efficient. He taught Engelmann the importance of understanding all aspects of the job, specifically the technical details, in order to think straight and solve difficult problems as efficiently and effectively as possible. Engelmann was not only influenced by Baker's philosophy about work, but his attitude as well. Baker taught Engelmann that understanding all of the technical details of the job allows you to control them to work harmoniously and that having control and confidence over a job can make it an enjoyable experience.

Could John Stuart Mill Have Saved Our Schools?

Engelmann, S., & Carnine, D. (2011). *Could John Stuart Mill have saved our schools?* Verona, WI: Full Court Press.

Engelmann and Carnine examine British Philosopher John Stuart Mill's 1843 publication "A System of Logic" in terms of education. Mill described four major templates for organizing examples so they only support one interpretation. Mill did not apply his logic to education, viewing it as an art rather than a science. Engelmann and Carnine hypothesize the effects of Mill's methods on teaching if applied beginning in the 19th century. The authors believe that if Mill's theories on instruction were implemented in the early 19th century the way children were taught would have changed dramatically. By approaching instruction as a scientific practice the development of misguided instructional theories and failed expectations, which have been prevalent in the past 200 years, would have likely been avoided. Engelmann and Carnine also explore how John Dewey would have been affected if Mill's logic was applied to education. Additionally the authors demonstrate the similarities between Mill's logic and the principles behind Direct Instruction programs.

Critique and Erasure: Responding to Eppley's "*Reading Mastery* as Pedagogy of Erasure"

Engelmann. S. (2011a). Critique and erasure: Responding to Eppley's "*Reading Mastery* as pedagogy of erasure." *Journal of Research in Rural Education, 26*(15), 1–4.

In this article Engelmann responds to Karen Eppley's critique of Dr. Jean Stockard's article "Increasing Reading Skills in Rural Areas: An Analysis of Three Rural School Districts." He argues Eppley's assessments and conclusions are critically flawed, not being supported by fact and reporting the opposite of what the facts show. Engelmann combats Eppley's core arguments by pointing out the flaws in her statements, faulty associations, and her misinterpretations of data. Additionally Engelmann discusses the design and intent of Direct Instruction, its proven effectiveness over four decades, and popular reviews by its users.

Socrates on AYP and Social Justice

Engelmann, S. (2011b). Socrates on AYP and social justice. Available from http://zigsite.com/PDFs/Socrates-on-AYP.pdf

In this article Engelmann presents a dialogue between Socrates and the fictional character Dwayne Washburn, an educational policy management expert, in a coffee shop at a convention center. They discuss important issues in education such as the Common Core Standards and No Child Left Behind with its regulations on adequate yearly progress (AYP) for schools. They debate the justifications for these initiatives and their effects on students, teachers, and the school system. Socrates explains a system of instruction and implementation that would allow for at-risk students to meet the requirements of No Child Left Behind and become competitive with their more affluent peers.

Socrates on *Reading Mastery*

Engelmann, S. (2011c). Socrates on *Reading Mastery*. Available from http://zigsite.com/PDFs/SocratesOn-ReadingMastery.pdf

In this article Engelmann presents a dialogue between Socrates and the fictional character Dr. Baram Rosenthal, an educational guru, in a campus coffee shop. Socrates and Rosenthal discuss the structure of an effective beginning reading program and debate the essential components to guarantee success. Socrates questions Rosenthal's conclusions about program design, which are based on correlations, rather than causation. They discuss the design of *Reading Mastery*, its key principles, and guidelines. Additionally they debate the role of the teacher's instruction and designed lesson plans in the success of a program.

Homework is Cruel in the Primary Grades

Engelmann, S. (2012a). Homework is cruel in the primary grades. Available from http://zigsite.com/PDFs/HomeworkisCruelPrimaryGrades.pdf

In this article Engelmann examines the effectiveness of homework on children in the primary grades. He argues against the use of homework in academic programs for at-risk children, because their home environments typically differ in significant ways from their more affluent peers. At-risk children do not always have the same helpful resources, such as knowledgeable parents and/or siblings who can assist them with their assignments. Additionally Engelmann discusses the effectiveness of homework in the primary grades in comparison to middle and high school, and the role of teachers and parents in students' education. Engelmann provides a guideline to the use of homework in the primary grades to enhance the success of all children.

Middle-Class Follow Through Students

Engelmann, S. (2012b). Middle-class Follow Through students. Available from http://zigsite.com/PDFs/FTMiddleClass3.pdf

In this article Engelmann discusses the performance of middle-class students in Project Follow Through. The majority of students in Project Follow Through were labeled at-risk. The program was designed to include about a 10–15% population of middle-class students, but this was not always possible in some sites. Engelmann examines the performance of the middle-class students, which had previously been ignored by nearly all significant discussions of Project Follow Through and the Direct Instruction model. The middle-class students showed a similar growth in learning rate as their less affluent peers. Studies by Wes Becker showed similar learning patterns for students in Grades 1–3 with the Direct Instruction model, regardless of IQ level. Engelmann concludes with a discussion of the importance of well-designed instruction for all students and the potential success of its use in all grades.

Socrates on Chicago's Failure

Engelmann, S. (2012c). Socrates on Chicago's failure. Available from http://zigsite.com/PDFs/SocratesOnChicagoFailurev2.pdf

In this article Engelmann presents a dialogue between Socrates and the fictional character Dr. Sidney Williams, an influential education policy and management entrepreneur. Socrates and Williams discuss the effort of Chicago Public Schools to improve the performance of struggling readers during a five year study. Socrates questions Williams about the study's goals, design, implementation, and scope. They continue on to discuss the results of the study year by year, its effectiveness, and the varying interpretations of the data.

Socrates on Program Adoptions

Engelmann, S. (2012d). Socrates on program adoptions. Available from http://zigsite.com/PDFs/SocratesOnProgramAdoption.pdf

In this article Engelmann presents a dialogue between Socrates and the fictional character Henry Baxter, a marketing director of a leading educational publishing company. As they are flying from New York to Los Angeles, the two discuss the publisher's role in the adoption of educational programs. Socrates questions the motives and possible ethical dilemmas of publishers who sell multiple programs, when some have been proven to be more effective than others. Baxter explains each step of the adoption process for the programs, and the rationale behind it. Socrates and Baxter debate the role of programs and instruction in a child's learning process.

Socrates on Gold Standard Experiments

Engelmann, S. (2013). Socrates on gold standard experiments. Available from http://zigsite.com/PDFs/SocratesOnGoldStandards.pdf

In this article Engelmann presents a dialogue between Socrates and the fictional character Dr. Eugene Emery, an expert on experimental design of studies, inside Dr. Emery's office. Socrates and Emery debate the effect of gold standards on experimentation and its subsequent effect on conducting research. They discuss the importance of randomization in experiments to allow for a comparison and control group. Socrates attempts to convince Emery of the validity of including older studies in research today, if each study is reviewed on a case by case basis. Additionally, Socrates discusses the What Works Clearinghouse and their conclusion that Direct Instruction has virtually no evidence of effectiveness in teaching beginning reading, despite the existence of over 100 studies demonstrating Direct Instruction's effectiveness in doing so.

APPENDIX C
A CHRONOLOGY OF ENGELMANN'S CAREER HIGHLIGHTS

1950s

1955: B.A. Philosophy with Class Honors, University of Illinois, Urbana.

1960s

1960–1964: Worked in different advertising agencies and began analyzing techniques for marketing to children in order to determine what type of input was necessary to induce retention.

1963: Filmed his teaching sessions with his twin sons in order to demonstrate the effectiveness of his techniques and theories of instruction to education departments in various universities.

1964–1966: Worked with Carl Bereiter as a research associate for the Institute for Research on Exceptional Children, University of Illinois, Champaign, Illinois.

1964: Creation of the Bereiter-Engelmann preschool.

1966: *Give Your Child a Superior Mind* is published.

1966: Visiting Professor, Ontario Institute for Studies in Education, Toronto, Canada.

1966: First criticisms of Jean Piaget are published.

1966–1968: Senior education specialist, Downs Syndrome Project, Children's Research Center, University of Illinois.

1966–1970: Senior educational specialist, Institute on Exceptional Children and Bureau of Education Research, University of Illinois.

1968: Project Follow Through begins.

1968–present: President of Engelmann-Becker Corp., Eugene, Oregon.

1969: First *DISTAR* instructional programs are released. Initially *DISTAR Reading* and *Language.*

1970s

1970–1974: Associate Professor of Education, University of Oregon, Eugene, Oregon.

1970: *DISTAR Arithmetic I* instructional program is published.

1972–1975: Visiting Research Associate, Oregon Research Institute, Eugene, Oregon.

1974: Engelmann's first study using tactual vocoders with deaf subjects is published.

1974–2003: Professor of Special Education, University of Oregon, Eugene, Oregon.

1975–1981: Research Associate, Oregon Research Institute, Eugene, Oregon.

1975: *Your Child Can Succeed: How to Get the Most Out of School for Your Child* is published.

1975: *Corrective Reading* instructional program is published.

1975: First DI Conference is held, Eugene, Oregon.

1976: *Spelling Through Morphographs* instructional program is published.

1980s

1980: *Spelling Mastery* instructional program series is published.

1980: *The Instructional Design Library Series, vol.22: Direct Instruction* is published.

1981: *Corrective Mathematics* instructional program is published.

1982: *Theory of Instruction* is published.

1983: *Generalized Compliance Training: A Direct-Instruction Program for Managing Severe Behavior Problems* is published.

1983: *Reading Mastery* instructional program is published.

1983: *Teach Your Child to Read in 100 Easy Lessons* is published.

1984: Honorary doctorate degree, Western Michigan University.

1985: *Mastering Fractions* instructional program is published, the first in a series of videodisc programs.

1985: *Expressive Writing* instructional program is published.

1987: *Understanding Chemistry and Energy* instructional videodisc program is published.

1988: *Earth Science* instructional videodisc program is published.

1990s

1991: *Reasoning & Writing* instructional program is published.

1991: Engelmann sues the California State Board, Department of Education and Curriculum Commission.

1991: *Theory of Instruction* is revised and republished.

1992: *Connecting Math Concepts* instructional program is published.

1992: *War Against the Schools' Academic Child Abuse* is published.

1994: Engelmann receives American Psychological Association Fred Keller Award of Excellence.

1996: *Sponsor Findings from Project Follow Through* is published.

1996: *Research on Direct Instruction: 25 Years Beyond DISTAR* is published.

1997: National Institute for Direct Instruction (NIFDI) is established with Engelmann as the director.

1997: *Horizons Learning to Read* instructional program is published.

2000s

2000: Zigsite.com is launched.

2000: Engelmann is named one of the 54 "most influential people" in the history of special education by *Remedial and Special Education.*

2000: *Journeys Direct Instruction Reading* program is published.

2001: *Funnix Beginning Reading* instructional program is published.

2001: *Español to English (Language for Learning)* instructional program is published.

2002: Engelmann receives the Council of Scientific Society Presidents 2002 Educational Research Award (Award of Achievement in Education Research).

2002: *Funnix Reading 2* instructional program is published.

2003-present: Professor Emeritus of Special Education, University of Oregon, Eugene, Oregon.

2004: *Inferred Functions of Performance and Learning* is published.

2007: *Teaching Needy Kids in Our Backward System: 42 Years of Trying* is published.

2008: *Socrates and Education: Bussing* is published on zigsite.com (first in Socrates series).

2010s

2010: *Direct Instruction Spoken English (DISE)* instructional program is published.

2010: *Could John Stuart Mill Have Saved Our Schools?* is published.

2011: *Funnix Beginning Math* instructional program is published.

AUTHOR BIOGRAPHIES

Editor

Jean Stockard is professor emerita at the University of Oregon and director of research and evaluation for the National Institute for Direct Instruction. She has BA degrees in mathematics and sociology and an MA and PhD in sociology. Recent and on-going work includes studying influences on student achievement, including the impact of curricular change and teacher training; exploring the role of leisure in the lives of middle-aged adults; analyzing cohort variations in life expectancy and violent behavior; exploring the influence of the built environment and other environmental characteristics on health and subjective well-being; analyzing the impact of gender and minority status on career advancement, especially in the physical sciences; and examining variables that affect attitudes and behavioral responses to climate change.

Chapter Contributors

Shepard Barbash is a graduate of Harvard University in the field of history and science. His writings span more than three decades and have appeared in *The New York Times, Wall Street Journal, Washington Post, Smithsonian Magazine, City Journal, Education Next* and other publications. He is former bureau chief of the *Houston Chronicle* in Mexico City and is the author of several books, including *Clear Teaching*, published in 2012 by the Education Consumers Foundation. He and his wife, photographer Vicki Ragan, have published an alphabet book of limericks and three illustrated books (including one for children) on the folk art wood carvers of Oaxaca, Mexico. As a volunteer he has advised the Georgia Governor's Office and the Atlanta Public Schools (APS) on curricular issues and has organized teacher training programs and written grants for APS. He has also worked for E. D. Hirsch at the Core Knowledge Foundation.

Cristy Coughlin holds a PhD in school psychology from the University of Oregon and an undergraduate degree in psychology from Western Michigan University. Coughlin has been involved in the Direct Instruction community as a researcher, school-based consultant, and program evaluator in DI implementations in the U.S. and Australia. Her major areas of interest are oriented around data-based decision making, multi-tiered systems of academic and behavior support, and linking educational research to practice.

Kurt E. Engelmann, PhD, is the administrative director and president of the National Institute for Direct Instruction (NIFDI), a position he began in July 2000. Before becoming president of NIFDI, Dr. Engelmann served as an outreach coordinator in the Jackson School of International Studies at the University of Washington. As administrative director and president of NIFDI, he is responsible for organizing administrative support for Direct Instruction (DI) implementations, serving as the liaison between school district administrators and NIFDI, and coordinating medium and long-term planning of NIFDI implementation efforts. Under his direction, NIFDI has implemented the DI model in 19 states, the territory of Guam and Australia.

Siegfried "Zig" Engelmann is professor emeritus of education at the University of Oregon and the primary architect of the Direct Instruction (DI) approach, an approach based on the principles originated in the Bereiter-Engelmann Preschool in the late 1960s. Engelmann is the senior author of more than 100 curricula using DI principles and numerous other articles and books. He has a bachelor's degree in philosophy from the University of Illinois and an honorary doctorate from the Psychology Department of Western Michigan University. He is the 1994 recipient of the Fred S. Keller Award from the American Psychological Association's Division of Experimental Analysis of Behavior. In 2000 the journal *Remedial and Special Education* named him as one of the 54 most influential people in the history of special education, and in 2002 the Council of Scientific Society Presidents awarded him the 2002 Award of Achievement in Education Research.

Caitlin Rasplica is a doctoral student in the school psychology program at the University of Oregon. Rasplica has worked at the National Institute for Direct Instruction (NIFDI) as the assistant director of research where she has been involved in several projects involving the application of Direct Instruction research. Her major research interests are in school readiness and Kindergarten transition, systems-level change, and the integration of academic and behavioral support systems.

Timothy W. Wood is a researcher for the National Institute for Direct Instruction. He received his BA in History from Lewis & Clark College with a focus on twentieth century U.S. history in 2009. In 2012 he graduated from Northwestern University's Museum Studies program. He currently works as a docent at the Driehaus Museum in Chicago, while pursuing his ambitions as an artist, musician, and outdoor enthusiast.

Acknowledgments

I would like to thank the following people: Tom Torkelson, JoAnn Gama, and Wyatt Truscheit at IDEA Public Schools, Lyndsay Root at McGraw-Hill Education, and Carrie Beck, Ben Scafidi, and Angela Arismendi.

–S. Barbash

I'd like to acknowledge Jean Stockard for her contributions to this project and to the Direct Instruction research community at large, and express my utmost gratitude for the endless support and stellar advice that she consistently offers to my research, writing, and professional pursuits. I'd also like to personally thank Zig Engelmann for his life-long dedication to developing and disseminating Direct Instruction programs. Your lasting impact on the field of education directly impacts the lives of children every day.

–C. Coughlin

To my father, Siegfried, for his tireless efforts to provide teachers with the means of helping all students reach their potential.

–K. E. Engelmann

I would like to thank Geoff Colvin, Rob Horner, Kent McIntosh and Stan Paine for taking the time to discuss the chapter with me during the conceptualization phase.

–C. Rasplica

Many people contributed to the completion of this book and I wish to thank all of them for their dedication and hard work. The publication production team – Christina Cox, Courtney Burkholder, Tina Wells, and Beth Wood; NIFDI staff members – Ashly Cupit, Margie Mayo, Toni Reeves, Piper VanNortwick, and Christine Wlaschin; each of the authors; and, most especially, Zig Engelmann, who is an inspiration for all of us.

–J. Stockard

This publication could not have been accomplished without the great input and efforts of my colleagues. First and foremost I must thank Zig Engelmann for allowing me to interview him in order to better understand the depth and intricacies of his career. Second Jerry Silbert must be acknowledged for his exceptional effort in working with me to understand the development and evolution of Direct Instruction programs. Jean Stockard proved to be an excellent resource for discussing the format and flow of the chapter to best portray Engelmann's illustrious career. Additionally Sarah Beecroft-Haffner, Alexa Engelmann, and Toni Reeves should be noted for their excellent work in tracking down the numerous books, articles, and programs needed for my analysis.

–T. W. Wood

SUBJECT INDEX

McGraw Hill Education, 144, 155-156, 158

Metis Associates, 58, 60, 76

misbehavior, 124-126, see also behavior management, behavior problem(s)

misrule(s), 129, 134-137; see also error(s)

model-lead-test, 132

N-O

National Assessment of Educational Progress (NAEP), 59, 77, 142, 144

National Council of Teachers of Mathematics (NCTM), 47, 53

National Institute for Direct Instruction (NIFDI), 77, 101, 111, 121, 149, 156, 244, see also external support, technical support

National Mathematics Advisory Panel (NMAP), 28, 47, 53

National Reading Panel (NRP), 12, 24, 28, 45, 47, 53

No Child Left Behind (NCLB), 27, 53, 77, 92, 237

norms of science, 63, 65, 67, 68, 72, 74

normative science, see norms of science

optimism, 142, 154

oscilloscope, 197

P

pessimism

philanthropist(s), 151, 156, 160

philanthropy, 147, 160

phonemic awareness, 12, 45, 164, 222-223

phonics, 12, 45, 71, 164

policy, policies, 25-28, 51-52, 64, 70, 77, 125 138, 142-145, 158, 161, 213, 227, 229, 237, 239

policymakers, 27, 44, 47, 51, 59

policymaking, 141

premature elucidation, 154

preventative strategy(ies), 118-119

principal(s), 22, 101, 114-117, 139, 153, 158

problem behavior, see behavior problem(s)

Project Follow Through, see Follow Through

program development, 3-5, 16-18, 26, 63

program-referenced testing, 15-18, 20, 22, 103

Project STAR, 57, 59, 61, 76

punitive system(s), 125

R

Race to the Top, 148

randomization, 6-7, 28, 51, 56-62, 66, 69-70, 73, 76, 122, 139239

random assignment, see randomization

randomized study, see randomization

randomized selection, see randomization 59, 76

reading, 4-5, 12, 24, 28, 33, 35-38, 45-47, 51-53, 70-72, 77, 86, 117, 122, 144, 149, 163-165, 167, 171-175, 181, 184-185, 207-209, 219, 222-223, 225, 227, 231, 233, 237-238, 241-243, 245

Reading Mastery, 4-5, 28, 37, 45-46, 53, 70-71, 77, 86, 117, 118, 122, 144, 163-167, 171-174, 181, 207-208, 219, 222-223, 225, 233, 237-238, 243

Reading Recovery, 71-72

Reasoning and Writing, 4, 52, 167, 169, 171, 179, 180

reform, 91

remedial strategies 118

research synthesis(es), 27-28, 30, 32-39, 42, 45, 47, 49-52, 78

response to intervention (RTI), 119, 159

Rodeo Institute for Teacher Excellence (RITE) , 52, 57-58, 61, 70, 75

Rubric for Identifying Authentic DI Programs, 18, 23, 100, 122, 232

S

school board(s), 150, 153

school choice, 146, 154, 158

school-wide positive behavior support (SWPBS), 128, 138, 139-140

sociolinguistics, 92, 193

special education, 26, 29, 33, 35, 38-42, 44-49, 52-53, 89, 93, 127, 138-139, 166, 198, 200, 202, 211-214, 226, 242, 245

spelling, 4, 33, 37-38, 50, 168-169, 179, 242-243

Spelling Mastery, 4, 38, 50, 168-169, 179, 243

state tests, state testing, 154, 161

Striving Reader Initiative, 58-62, 76

student-teacher ratio(s), 100, 110

superintendent(s), 149-150, 153, 158

support personnel, 110

systematic review(s), 28-30, 32-33, 35-37, 41, 44-46, 48-50

T

tactual vocoder, 89-90, 196-197, 199-200, 203, 242

Teach Your Child to Read in 100 Easy Lessons, 5, 24, 149, 181, 208, 243

technical support, 122, see also external support, NIFDI,

technology(ies), 89-90, 167 195-196, 200, 202-204, 210-212, 215, 219-220, 221

Tennessee, 57-58, 61, 76, 78, 142, 144-145, 152, 154, 156, 158, 160

Texas, 142, 146, 148-150, 159, 167

Teach for America (TFA), 146, 149, 159

test prep, 20, 170

theory(ies), 4, 18, 23 26, 48, 64-66, 76, 81-83, 84-90, 92-94, 100, 126, 128, 131, 139, 146, 153, 184, 186-189, 192-193, 196, 199, 202, 204-205, 207, 213-214, 217, 220, 222, 227, 230, 234, 237, 241, 243-244

Theory of Instruction, 18, 23, 66, 76, 81-83, 87, 100, 121, 131, 139, 153, 204-205, 207, 222, 243

training(s), 10, 17-18, 31, 53, 70-71, 92, 105, 108, 110-113, 115, 127, 149, 155-156, 158, 171, 180, 187-190, 193-197, 199, 201, 204, 206, 208-209, 211, 213, 220, 229, 234, 243

U-W

U.S. Department of Education, 52-53, 69, 77-78, 148, 215, 221, 234

U.S. Government Accountability Office, see Government Accountability Office (GAO)

War Against the Schools' Academic Child Abuse, 91, 220, 244

What Works Clearinghouse (WWC), 58, 62, 69-73, 77-78, 93, 233-234, 239

Y-Z

Your Child Can Succeed, 5, 24, 196, 242

zero tolerance policy(ies), 125, 138, 140

zone of proximal learning (ZPL), 101-103

NAME INDEX

ABOUT NIFDI PRESS

The National Institute for Direct Instruction (NIFDI) is a non-profit organization focused on supporting Direct Instruction implementations with schools around the world. NIFDI also maintains a publication arm to the organization: NIFDI Press. Dedicated to publishing high quality works that support the development of effective implementations of Direct Instruction programs, the press publishes manuals and books designed to help a variety of audience purposes:

- teachers, coaches, and administrators implementing DI programs in their schools;

- parents preparing or supporting their children in academic success;

- researchers in search of theoretical and empirical studies regarding the development, efficacy and implementation of DI.

The Press also distributes other Direct Instruction and education-related titles, including:

- *Teach Your Child to Read in 100 Easy Lessons*
- *Teaching Needy Kids*
- *Theory of Instruction*
- And more!

You can order through our website at http://nifdi.org/resources/store or by calling toll-free 877.485.1973.